Om Shantih Shantih Shantih

The Soundless Sound: Peace Peace Peace

Extemporaneous talks given by Osho at OSHO International Meditation Resort, Pune, India

OSHO

Om Shantih Shantih Shantih

The Soundless Sound: Peace Peace Peace

MACMILLAN

First published in 2016 by Macmillan
This edition published in India 2024 by Macmillan
an imprint of Pan Macmillan Publishing India Private Limited
707 Kailash Building
26 K. G. Marg, New Delhi 110001
www.panmacmillan.co.in

Pan Macmillan, The Smithson, 6 Briset Street, Farringdon, London EC1M 5NR
Associated companies throughout the world
www.panmacmillan.com

ISBN 978-93-82616-83-2

The material in this book is a transcript of a series of original OSHO Talks, *Om Shantih Shantih Shantih – The Soundless Sound: Peace Peace Peace*, given to a live audience. All of Osho's talks have been published in full as books, and are also available as original audio recordings. Audio recordings and the complete text archive can be found at www.osho.com

1 3 5 7 9 8 6 4 2

Typeset in Adobe Garamond Pro by R. Ajith Kumar, New Delhi
Printed and bound in India by Gopsons Papers Pvt. Ltd., Noida

Contents

Preface

I have talked to you about *satyam-shivam-sundaram*, *sat-chit-anand*, *hari-om- tat-sat*, *om-mani-padme-hum*, *om-shantih-shantih-shantih*. These five I have chosen as the most significant, as the most deep-going. I will try to give you the meaning also, because that meaning will help the significance to become deeper. That meaning will not only touch your heart, it will also touch your intelligence – and you have to be touched in your totality to be transformed.

I will begin with the last one. That is the sound every Eastern scripture ends with: *om-shantih-shantih-shantih*. It means 'The soundless sound, or the sound of silence, peace, peace, peace' – just giving you the sense of the whole scripture in these few telegraphic words. Every scripture in the East ends the same. It may be Hindu, it may be Buddhist, it may be Jaina – it doesn't matter. They are all different in their philosophies. They are all different in their theologies. They are different religions, continuously in controversy for at least ten thousand years. But strangely, they all end their scriptures with 'the sound of silence: peace, peace, peace.' It seems they are all different roots of this experience.

They may differ about their roots, about the description of their roots. They may quarrel, they may contradict each other, but as far as the end is concerned, when they reach the highest peak of consciousness, all that is found is the sound of silence and utter peace, so deep that they have to repeat it three times: peace, peace, peace.

Osho
Sat Chit Anand

A Note about Language

Spoken Words: Osho's books are not "written" but rather are transcribed from recordings of his talks. These talks are extemporaneous, without reference to notes other than copies of questions, stories or scriptures he has been asked to comment upon, or jokes he might use to drive home a particular point. He has asked his editors to preserve that quality of the spoken word in his printed books.

Pronouns: When hearing him speak, it is quite clear to the listener that generally when Osho talks about "man" he is referring to "human beings." His use of "he" as a default pronoun simply serves an ease and flow of speaking – in no way does it imply that "she" (or "they") is being dismissed or disregarded.

Osho's unique vantage point is good to keep in mind:

A meditator is neither a man nor a woman,
because meditation has nothing to do with your body;
neither does it have anything to do with your mind.
In meditation you are simply and purely consciousness.
And consciousness is neither male nor female.

-Osho

1

Om: The Music at the Heart of the Universe

Osho,
I am always intrigued by Eastern scriptures that begin with *om shantih shantih shantih* and end with *om shantih shantih shantih.* Would you please talk about this?

The East has approached reality in an almost diametrically opposite way to the West. First, the simple meaning of the word should be understood, and then all the implications. All Eastern scriptures begin with *om shantih shantih shantih* and they also end with the same.

Om is the symbol of the universal heartbeat; it is not a word. And as you come closer and closer to the universal heartbeat, the by-product is a deepening silence. *Shantih* means silence and it is always repeated three times because by the time you reach the fourth, you are no more – just the silence has remained. You have disappeared as an entity separate from the universe.

The West has not been able to begin even a single scripture with this intention. It is understandable. They never went into the deeper communion between your heart and the bigger heart of the universe. They have taken a wrong route: that of fighting, of conquering, of being victorious. They have chosen to be extroverts. Their world is true, but they don't know anything about themselves. The outside is true and the inside has not been explored.

The Bible says, "In the beginning was the word." Now, this can be said only by someone who is absolutely ignorant, because a word means a sound with a meaning. These sounds made by the words are just sounds; you cannot call them words. The moment you say, "In the beginning was the word," unknowingly you have accepted that there is someone who gives meaning to it, but then the word is not in the beginning.

In the beginning is one who gives meaning to the word. And the Bible says, "God was with the word." Anyone who wrote it must have felt uneasy that the world should begin only with a word. Immediately, he needed someone to give meaning to it; hence the second statement that God was with the word. If you look into things very impartially, deeply, you will be amazed how much they can reveal. Then he must have become aware of, "Who is first? God or the word?"

The third sentence then tries to make a compromise. It says, "God and the word were one." No one in the whole Eastern search will agree with it. The East has not experienced the beginning because naturally you cannot see the beginning: you are already there, the beginning has happened. In your being you have preceded the beginning, so there is no possibility of any witness of the beginning. But there is a possibility to be a witness of the end.

The Eastern meditators found as they entered their inner being that first they are surrounded with a tremendously beautiful and musical sound. It is not the sound of any music being played, it is simply the heartbeat of the universe. And once they come in tune with the heartbeat of the universe, silence descends. They would like to dance and declare to the world about silence, but they can only say three times, "Silence, silence, silence" – and they are melting and merging.

Rather than their declaration of silence becoming louder, it is becoming more and more like a whisper and finally, they are not. But they have witnessed the end. Now it is a logical conclusion that the end and the beginning cannot be different.

The seed grows into a tree, blossoms, brings fruits and again seeds. Just as in existence everything moves in a circle, the earth, the moon, the sun, the faraway millions of stars; they all move in a circle that meets at a point. The end and the beginning are the same. That's why the Eastern scriptures begin with the declaration, om: the sound of the soundless, the very music of the heart of the universe. And as they go deeper, silence becomes the only reality. They want to declare silence to the world, but no one has been able to go beyond the third because each time they say "Silence," it becomes more of a whisper.

I am reminded…

I had a doctor friend who was perhaps the most famous doctor in those parts. I said to him, "I would like to experience something for which there is no reason. You can help me. I want to go slowly and deeply into the unconscious."

He said, "This is against medical practice. You don't have any reason, and I cannot use something without reason and make you unconscious."

But I persuaded him. I said, "Find any reason, I am not going to tell anyone." Although, I have told it to the whole world.

He put me on his table, sent all the servants and nurses away because he was doing something against the medical code. While he was covering my face so that I could only breathe the anesthetic, he said to me, "Do one thing. While you are going into the unconscious, go on saying one, two, three, four, five…as long as you can."

Strangely, I could not go beyond three. I tried hard. I was aware of the fact that I had only come up to three, and the four would not come. Later on I told him, "This was my reason to be put into the unconscious state. I wanted to see why every scripture stops at three."

I asked him to tell me how I was saying one, two, three. He said, "One was clear, two was not so clear, three was almost a whisper, and beyond that you never uttered anything."

This was my way through a scientific experiment to see why all the scriptures stop with three. They begin with the same and they end with the same. The beginning we cannot know; we are already here. The beginning has happened, but the end we can know – the disappearance into absolute silence. But if we know the end, we can conclude with absolute certainty that this is how the beginning must have started: from silence, not from words. Silence is the beginning and silence is the end, and if you are a meditator, silence is the middle. Silence is the whole fabric of existence.

This is not a hypothesis, nor is it a philosophical idea. It is the experience of thousands of mystics who have entered their own being. First they have heard om, and as the om becomes overwhelming, silence follows. We are made of sound and silence. Sound is our mind and silence is our being. Sound is our trouble and silence is our liberation. It has been discovered by some unknown explorer of the inner, it has been followed by thousands of people – but you are not to repeat it. That's where the masses have got lost. They think that by repeating *om shantih shantih shantih* they are doing some spiritual meditative act.

In each temple in the East you will find a metal disc and everyone who enters the temple hits the disc with a steel rod. The whole temple becomes full of sound and then slowly, slowly the sound also disappears. In Tibet, they have even made a very special thing: a small pot of metal with a rod; it has been made with great calculation. When I first saw it, I could not believe that it was possible, but the thing was in front of me.

One of my friends in Patna was a great collector of all kinds of things...

He was continually telling me whenever I was in Patna, "Come to my museum." Even the prime minister, the president and everyone had visited. He was a very rich man and had gathered things from other lands – strange things. But when he told me that he had recently received a metal pot which repeated *om shantih shantih shantih.* I could not resist.

Patna is a strange city. It is not spread out in all directions, it has only one main street running by the Ganges – because the Ganges is so beautiful everyone wants to be around it. So Patna is a very long city, perhaps twenty miles. And my friend used to live thirteen miles away from my place. But I went to see the pot; it was a really great experience.

The pot is made of many metals and you move the rod in the pot round and round for a certain number of times. Then you stop. And suddenly, the sound comes from the pot, *om shantih shantih shantih.* These things may be beautiful, creative, but they are not in any way religious. Every Hindu temple is resounding with the sound, everyone is praying, but they have misunderstood the whole thing. It is not your repeating om that is going to lead you to the reality; it is your becoming utterly quiet, and then from your very being arises the sound om.

You are just a witness, you are not a doer. And as the sound settles, you feel silence, silence, silence… Then everything disappears and there remains only a universal reality of which you are just a part. Just as a dewdrop disappears in the ocean, you disappear in the ocean of existence.

The East has found this to be the only spiritual experience, not God, not holy scriptures, not prophets; they are all creating fictions. Not even your prayers because they are nothing but your desires. The only thing that is really significant is to be quiet, centered, grounded, in the very life source, in your very being. This sutra of *om shantih shantih shantih* is heard when you are at your very center. It is not by your repeating it that you will reach it. It is not exactly the same either. We have invented it, approximately, just to communicate what has happened: something similar, but far deeper; something similar, but far more delicate; something similar, but not the same.

The mystics' writings start exactly the way the universe has started, and they end exactly as the universe finally goes to rest. There is a statement relevant to this sutra by Gautam Buddha. It is very significant. He says that it is absolutely foolish to think the way all the theologians of the world think about the beginning – how the world began. I can see the significance of a statement that you can never come to a conclusion about how the world began because you were not there. How can you be before the world began? You are part of the world. So all that you say about the beginning is just imagination, hypothesis, guesswork.

Buddha says that the mystic is not interested in how the world began, his interest is in how it ends. Because in that very ending you will find the beginning too. But without finding the ending, you can only guess, argue, fight about the beginning. And it is all futile. The philosopher's work is absolute nonsense. The mystic is very earthbound, very pragmatic, very realistic. Buddha says, "First find how it ends" – and it is to be found within you.

You cannot wait for the whole world to end. That way it never ends. It is always there – beginningless, endless. But how did the world begin within you? And how does the world end within you? Those who remain clinging to the world are the materialists. Those who start looking inside and try to find how everything ends and still you *are* – but just a pure consciousness, just a pure awareness – the flower disappears; only the fragrance remains.

I agree with Gautam Buddha that if you have found the fragrance within you, you know the whole secret of existence because every individual is a miniature universe. What is happening on a vast scale in the universe is happening on a very small scale within you. If you have tasted a simple dewdrop, you have tasted all the rivers and all the oceans and all possibilities of water anywhere.

And you *are* the dewdrop. Rather than running here and there, just taste yourself.

The East has approached reality in a very different way. And certainly because it has reached in a different way, it has produced a different kind of enlightened people. The West has produced popes – the worst is the Polack pope. And now the Nobel Prize committee is nominating him for a Nobel Prize! A Polack and a Nobel Prize? In this way, the Polack is not given respect; in this way, the Nobel Prize loses all nobility, all grace.

And what experience does the Pope have? What is his authority? He represents Jesus Christ. Jesus Christ himself does not seem to be enlightened. An enlightened person does not bother about saying, "God is my father. I am the only begotten son of God." Who cares? We have seen thousands of enlightened people in the East. None of them has claimed that he is the only begotten son of God. That would be laughed at for centuries: "That man has gone mad!"

So in the first place he represents Jesus Christ – who seems to be a lunatic. Either his nuts and bolts are loose, or too tight. He does not show the grace of a Gautam Buddha. Neither does he show the dance of a Meera nor the grace of a Mahavira. Because he is uneducated, what he goes on talking about he has gathered from the society. And popes, hundreds of popes in these two thousand years have represented him. It is a hierarchy: the pope, Jesus, God… You cannot go unless you follow the proper channel! I have always wondered that even the intelligent people in the West never think about what the contribution of these popes is. A man who is a representative of God must show something: some sensitivity, some grace, some blissfulness; some fragrance should surround him. But the pope is elected!

It is so hilarious that people elect someone as enlightened. Enlightenment is not an election campaign. Then many candidates can stand up and say, "I am enlightened." Enlightenment is an inner opening of the rose. Those who are in search of the truth of their being will be immediately pulled toward the man of enlightenment.

It is not dependent on anyone's election or nomination. It does not even represent God or anyone. It simply declares its own heart and invites and welcomes anyone – any wayfarer who wants to share this juice, this music of the eternal om; one who is in search of finding a living silence and a dancing silence.

This sutra contains the whole; the beginning and the end. But it starts from the end and reaches the beginning. The statement of Gautam Buddha is: "Ignorance has no beginning and enlightenment has no end, and both make a circle." Because you know you have been utterly ignorant of yourself and now you are so alert, so full of joy, so much is dancing in your every cell, every fiber. This is an experience; it is not a hypothesis, and it has never been argued about.

There have been Hindu mystics, there have been Buddhist mystics, there have been Jaina mystics… But as far as this sutra is concerned they have never quarreled about it, they have never argued. This is simply accepted because it is the experience, it is not theoretical guesswork. It is not philosophy. It is *philosia*, it is darshan.

They have seen it within their own being and there is no way not to agree with others who have also seen it. But by repeating it one is simply being stupid. One has to come to an inner space where it explodes on its own and you are just a witness. Then it transforms your being, gives it beauty and grace, gives it sincerity and truth.

Osho,

The words *resistance* and *surrender*, extremely common in the early days of your first ashram in Pune, are no longer being used to punish, judge, and reject. The experiences in your commune in America helped. Now the ashram is less fear-orientated.

But how to distinguish between resistance and healthy rebellion, between surrender and resignation, in private life? The pitfalls of my habitual unconscious stubbornness make me suspicious of my imperceptibly false yes and no.

Is there any simple test? Is it authentic when it just feels good?

When you feel something authentic, you can stand against the whole world. But the authenticity should not be another name of your ego. No one else can make it clear, you know it. When it is the ego, you know perfectly well that your desire is to be someone special. And when it is an authentic truth, you also know that it has nothing to do with your personality, with your ego. You are not going to gain anything out of it except a tremendous joy. Let joy be the criterion.

As far as I am concerned, neither your yes means anything to me nor your no means anything to me. You are so asleep that whether you say yes or no in your sleep does not matter. Whatever you say, I am going to pour a bucket of cold water on your head. Your yes and no are not important. Your awakening is important. And out of your awakening whatever happens is right. The moment you are alert, awake, conscious, your revolt and your surrender are not two different things.

It is the unconscious mind which either wants to surrender to avoid the unnecessary trouble of revolting – cheap surrender – or it wants to revolt because it does not want to lose its ego. Those are by-products. My insistence is not on by-products. My insistence is on a single thing: I call it witnessing. Be aware, and if your awareness leads you to surrender, it is perfectly beautiful. And if your awareness leads you to revolt, that's how it should be. It will be difficult for you to understand that surrender is the greatest revolt. Revolt against the ego, revolt against your conditioning. But it should not be imposed on you that you surrender.

Here, no one is interested in your surrender. What will we do with your surrender? I don't see any use of it. And no one is interested in your revolt. The only difference will be, if you really want to revolt, go to M.G. Road. What the hell are you doing here? This is a gathering of people who are searching for the real life, who are trying to awaken themselves. Neither revolt nor surrender is of any importance.

The only important thing is to become absolutely alert and aware, and then whatever you do is right. All the religions have labeled things: this is right, this is wrong; this is good, this is bad; this is virtue, this is sin. Things are fixed. My whole approach is that things are constantly changing, nothing is fixed. So I cannot say to you that this particular thing is right, and that particular thing is wrong. In a different context, things will be different. So it is better to give you an awareness which will decide spontaneously, moment to moment, what is right and what is wrong.

You should not be dependent on dead and old scriptures, and you should not be dependent on either dead or alive saints! You should be simply free in your awareness and let your own awareness respond to reality as it comes. And reality is continuously changing.

Sometimes surrender may be perfectly right: if you meet a buddha, how are you going to revolt? He will enjoy all your jogging and jumping, but what revolt… And it is not his problem, it is your problem. By your revolt are you creating more peace, more silence for yourself, or more anxiety, more anguish, more tension, more trouble?

If you meet Ronald Reagan, then surrender is not the thing. One should have a certain dignity, a certain self-respect. Surrendering to criminals – they may be powerful – cannot be said to be right because it is surrender. Surrender is good only to a source of humbleness, light, freedom; a surrender which will make you more free than you have ever been; a surrender which will not cut your wings and destroy your joy of flying across the sky. A surrender to the man who is alert, aware and has a deep respect is beautiful.

I have told you a small anecdote many times…

In his past life, Gautam Buddha heard about another man who had become enlightened. He was not much interested, but curious to see what kind of phenomenon enlightenment was and what it did to the man. He went and as he came close to the man something started melting in his heart; something that was hard and arrogant was disappearing. And as he came very close, he witnessed himself touching the feet of the man. He was not touching, he had not even the idea of touching the feet of the man, but he saw that he was touching his feet. The man had such a beauty and such a grace that it was such a joy even to touch his feet.

But the most miraculous thing happened as he stood up: the man also touched Gautam Buddha's feet. Gautam Buddha said, "What are you doing? You are enlightened. I can feel the peace that surrounds you. I can feel the light and the fragrance that you have become. It is absolutely right for me to touch your feet and surrender myself, but what are you doing? I am an ignorant man, very stubborn, very egoistic and you are touching my feet."

The enlightened man said to Gautam Buddha, "Today you are asleep; tomorrow you will be awake. Today you are not enlightened, but enlightenment is your very nature. I don't care about your arrogance and your ego and stubbornness; they are not your self-nature. I am touching your feet to remind you that you are not what you are thinking, and also to remind you that when in your next life you become enlightened, be respectful of those who are still groping in the dark."

Now, to touch the feet of such a man is a beauty, a grace, a blissfulness.

Germany seems to be my land. I own it because for two years in the German parliament they have been continually discussing me. Our sannyasins have won cases in two German courts. Their parliament calls Christianity a religion and my movement a cult. And in Germany, the word *cult* is condemnatory. Two courts have given their verdicts against the parliament, and the parliament is still continuing to call my people a cult.

Just the other day I received news from one of my sannyasins who is also a member of the parliament that they are very stubborn and they go on changing. First they said, "You are not a religion because you don't believe in the fiction of God." I am going to reply to the parliament, "Then that means you should not call

Buddhism or Jainism a religion because they do not have any God." Now they have changed the argument because I have been jailed in America and my attorneys have been blackmailed to accept that I have committed two crimes.

Sometimes I look at this world – it is so hilarious. The government attorney in America placed thirty-four crimes that they said I have committed, and they asked my attorneys to negotiate and not to go for a trial. And the negotiation was: "If you accept any two crimes, then Osho can be released from the jail. If you don't accept then you are putting his life in danger because the case could go on for twenty years, thirty years..."

This is sheer blackmail. My attorneys were at a loss what to do because I have not committed those crimes. But to save me they accepted the two crimes, such petty crimes that generally in America the punishment would be twenty-five dollars or fifty dollars at the most. And that's what my attorneys were thinking: get it finished with fifty dollars.

But when those two crimes were accepted, the punishment was four hundred thousand dollars, nearabout six million rupees. And now there was no way for my attorneys to do anything; they had accepted and the judge had given the judgment.

So now in the German parliament, they have changed their whole idea. Now they say they will not allow me to enter Germany because I am a criminal; a confirmed criminal convicted of the maximum punishment. Four hundred thousand dollars is the maximum fine; no one has been punished that much. You can murder – still you will not get that much punishment. You can rape... All that I had done, that they had accepted, was so tiny, so meaningless.

First, they said that I had the intention of staying in America and I had deceived the immigration department. For "the intention," the simple way is not to give me residence. Secondly, they said that I had arranged a marriage for the purpose of getting residence. That is sheer stupidity. If I had wanted to be a resident, rather than persuading others to get married, I myself should have married – as many American women as they required.

But because I have been punished and deported, they are using the argument in the German parliament that my followers are a cult and I am a criminal. I have to inform my attorney there that, if I am a criminal, what about Jesus Christ whose punishment was certainly more than mine? Deport *him*. Make a law that Jesus Christ cannot enter Germany – because after resurrection... No one knows where he has gone. And secondly, those who follow Jesus Christ should not call their religion a religion. Call it a cult; it is very simple.

The parliamentary secretary said that *cult* is not derogatory. I am informing my attorney: "Ask that if *cult* is not derogatory, then why make any distinction? Christianity is a cult just as any group of people is a cult." But strange people and criminal minds...

You are saying to me that before, the ashram was "fear-oriented." You should not have been in the ashram. The whole world is outside the ashram. If you wanted to be in the ashram, that shows more about you than about the ashram. You wanted to be in some place where you are dominated. Always remember, problems are yours. It is *your* problem. If the ashram is fear-orientated, then can you name any religion which is not fear-oriented? Then what is the purpose of hell?

In fact, this is the only place where no one cares about hell. In fact, if I am going to hell, all my people are ready to go, dancing and singing. No one is fear-oriented here. We are not afraid to deny God. People are always afraid, "Who knows, perhaps he may be there and after death, how will you face him?" I am preparing my people so that God will be afraid of *them*. Just do Dynamic Meditation the moment you see God!

I used to live in a place near a Mohammedan cemetery. The caretaker called me saying, "You are going to create a riot in the city."

I said, "What happened? I have not said anything against anyone."

He said, "That is not the question. A deputation of Mohammedans has come to me and they say, 'The people who are around Osho… Early each morning they start "Hoo! Hoo! Hoo!" That disturbs the people who are lying in their graves. So many of them have come out – and we are afraid of ghosts. If this man is allowed… The whole city will be full of ghosts. No one can rest – Hoo!…'" So he said, "Tell your people to do some silent meditation; they are disturbing the ghosts."

I said, "It is strange, for the first time I have come to know that ghosts are afraid of 'Hoo!'"

The caretaker said, "Personally, my opinion is that anyone will be afraid if so many people come just shouting "Hoo! Hoo!" It hurts deeply."

So, my people are not fear-oriented. Now you think that the ashram is less fear-oriented? The ashram is the same. It is the same river: water flows; people come and go. It is the same caravan: someone joins, someone departs; someone takes his own route, someone comes from some other route. It is your mind. The mind is always fear-oriented.

All the societies have tried to make your mind fear-oriented because that is a simple strategy to rule over you – and man is so fear-oriented. He does not show it; he hides it inside. But on a dark night, alone, he starts running. There is no one, and when he starts running, his own steps make a sound and he looks back to see if someone is following.

You can create fear in any person for any absurd reason…

In my village there was a grocer. I always loved to find people's actions and reactions. So whenever I passed – and I had to pass at least four times as it was exactly in the middle between my house and the school – I would just keep one of my eyes closed.

At first the grocer said, "Strange, why should he do it?" But when I did it again, he called me, "What is the matter?"

I said, "I don't know. The moment I see you, my whole being… I feel to do it. And it is not only me, many others are feeling…"

He said, "My God!"

And it spread – one thousand students passing by the grocer's with one eye closed. Now, it was nothing to do… Absolutely irrelevant, but he became so afraid that he would hide whenever it was the time for going to school and coming from the school. He would hide inside; he would close the shop. But I was not going to be satisfied so soon. We would knock on his doors shouting, "What has happened? I am a customer."

Hearing that a customer was knocking, he would open a window and he would see me. He reported to the police, "This boy is torturing me; I cannot sleep. One thousand people are passing four times a day and the whole neighborhood is laughing. They are all telling me, 'Don't be worried, they are doing you no harm. It is *their* eyes; if they want to pass with one eye closed…'"

He said, "But it creates great fear."

I was called to the police station. I went with one eye closed. They said, "What is the matter? Why do you keep one of your eyes closed?"

I said, "I am a very spontaneous person. If I feel to do… It is my eye. Seeing you, I felt the same."

The police officer said, "Just stop it here. I will never interfere in your affairs, but don't start telling all the school because those idiots will start passing in front of the police station with one eye closed. That will damage our power and people will laugh." And he said, "It is not gentlemanly, it is not nice to harass people."

I said, "I will stop."

I stopped – but the neighbors got it! They started moving… Anyone who came to his shop would come with one eye closed.

He called me one day. He said, "You are very nice because you have stopped. But you have spread the disease so much that now it is uncontrollable. Last night my wife faced me with one eye closed. It creates much fear."

I said, "But why should you fear anything? It has nothing to do… They are not closing your eye. If you want, I can tell people that they should start closing one eye – your eye."

He said, "Don't do that; that is too much. They will kill me."

You say, "Now the ashram is less fear-oriented." You have become more mature. Always think about your own psychology. The world remains the same; only you change. And you are asking, "But how to distinguish between resistance and healthy rebellion in private life?" If you can distinguish between healthy rebellion and unhealthy rebellion, if you are that intelligent, I think you will be able to see whether you are resisting or you are in rebellion. You need to sharpen your intelligence a little.

Resistance is not always bad. If you are facing a fascist regime, resist. But here, there is no fascist regime, no hierarchy. No one is torturing you, no gas chambers – even Jews are not killed. You are perfectly safe.

Just something for your fear to disappear…

Lord and Lady Bating, the English aristocrats, hire a new butler called James. He has not had much experience. So on the first day, he goes up to their room and says, "Frederick and Cynthia, dinner is served."

Lord Bating comes out and says sternly, "No, James. You must not call us by our first names. You must call us Lord and Lady Bating."

James is embarrassed. "Please forgive me," he says, "Lord and Lady Bating, dinner is served."

James then goes along to their daughter's room and says, "Caroline, dinner is served."

She comes to the door and says angrily, "I am to be called Mistress Bating and don't forget it."

James excuses himself and then goes to the son's room. Before speaking, he thinks for a moment and then calls out, "Are you in there Master Bating?"

"Okay, okay," calls the son nervously. "You caught me, but please don't tell my parents."

2

An Open Future with No Reverse Gear

Osho,
I see your enlightenment as a speaking medium between existence and all sannyasins – based on love as the only true way to go. I've heard you say that you are beyond enlightenment. What, theoretically speaking, is the difference between enlightenment and beyond enlightenment?

Life is a continuous change. It knows no stop – not even a semi-colon. Enlightenment is not to get stuck somewhere. No one has talked about beyond enlightenment, because what is the point? People are not even enlightened. But I'm certain *my* people are going to be enlightened, and I have to make them aware not to get stuck. Even enlightenment has to be transcended. Even transcendence has to be transcended. One has just to go on and on.

Existence is infinite, in multidimensions. And there is no end anywhere. You can never say, "I have come." You are always coming closer and closer and closer, but you never come because once you have come what will you do? Then the only way is to return home.

One has to go beyond enlightenment; otherwise you will find yourself in a very difficult situation – stuck in a waiting room of a railway station. No train goes back; all trains go ahead, and all that is left behind, you have experienced. You are tired of it; you don't want to go back. Even if you want to go back nature prohibits it.

Can a young man become a child again? Can a child be in the womb of the mother again? There is no possibility of going back. The young man will become middle aged; the middle aged will become old age. There is an open future, but there is no reverse gear in your lifestyle. Simply nothing can be done about it.

I have heard…

When Henry Ford died he met God, and God asked him, "Are you satisfied with my creation?"

He said, "No, if I had created life, I would have corrected many mistakes. For example, when I created the car there was no reverse gear: if you have gone two blocks ahead of your house, you cannot come back. Now you have to go around the whole town to come home!"

The reverse gear was Henry Ford's invention; you can go back. And he said to God, "In life you have missed many things, but especially a reverse gear."

An old man wants to become young but cannot. If God had placed a reverse gear, you could have just moved back into your youth again – you have to go on. When I say one has to go beyond enlightenment, I am saying that enlightenment is not the end. It is the beginning of a new existence, a new universe, a new world. It is difficult even to conceive what enlightenment is; naturally it is more difficult to conceive the beyond, but "theoretically speaking" it can be understood.

While all the others are hanging around, Silvester Sperm is exercising doing push-ups, swimming laps and lifting weights. One of the other sperms asks him: "Silvester, how come you spend so much time exercising?"

"Well," replies Silvester very seriously, "when the time comes, I want to be the one."

"Ah, really," says the sperm. "Well, your chances are about one in a million."

Just then the time comes and all the sperms start swimming. Silvester is way out in front when all of a sudden he turns around and starts swimming back. "What is the matter?" cries another sperm.

"Get back," cries Silvester, "it's a blow job!"

But you cannot…! That was theoretically speaking. Practically speaking, forget all about the beyond. First become enlightened. It is pointless to think about things which are so far away. Take care of first things first: be enlightened. But you are theoretically interested in the beyond. What are you going to gain? Enlightenment is enough for the time being. Once you are enlightened you will not need any one else to tell you to go beyond. You will go – you will have to go. There is nothing static. No one can stay young and no one can remain just enlightened.

I am the first person to talk about the beyond. All the mystics of the world have stopped at enlightenment for the simple reason that they were not talking theoretically. They were practically concerned that you become unidentified with your body, with your mind; that you become a pure consciousness without jealousy, without anger, without fear. And that you become a love, a flower of eternity, which brings fragrance and blessings not only to you, but even to those who are fast asleep.

Perhaps the noise of the falling flowers of blessing may wake up someone, just to see what is happening. Perhaps the fragrance may wake up someone. Perhaps the light may penetrate someone's darkness. Become enlightened, not theoretically but really, existentially, and the beyond will come on its own. I have talked about it because I want you to be aware of every possibility that is going to happen on the path.

One day Gautam Buddha is passing through the forest…

It is fall time and dry leaves are thick on the ground. Finding him alone, Ananda, his chief disciple, asks, "This question has been arising in me: Have you said everything to us that you know of?"

Buddha bent down, took a fistful of dry leaves, showed those dry leaves to Ananda and said, "I have said only this much. What I have not said is as much as all the dry leaves in this forest."

But I don't want to be so miserly. I want to say to you everything that happens on the path in its minute detail. It is time. Twenty-five centuries have passed since Gautam Buddha. Now man's consciousness is far more mature. It will not be satisfied with a fistful of dry leaves. I offer you the whole garden; hence I talk about many things which you may think are too far away, are perhaps not going to happen to you. But I say unto you, if you listen rightly, everything that I am saying is going to happen. Because it has happened to me, there is no reason why it should not happen to you.

People are very strange. They want great theories, philosophies, but they don't want a great life. They want to be convinced about great philosophical conceptions, but they don't want their hearts to become an open flower dancing in the wind, in the sun, in the rain. Whatever they hear they go on accumulating in their memory. First, they never hear the whole thing. Secondly, they hear something else that has not been said at all. Thirdly, they interpret it according to their own prejudice. Fourthly, they simply go on accumulating it. Just becoming a great encyclopedia is not going to help.

Paddy wins some money at the horse races and treats himself to a meal at a fancy restaurant. While his dinner is being served, he notices that the spoons are made of real silver. So he eats quickly, and putting one of the spoons into his pocket, he gets up to leave. Just as he reaches the door, the waiter rushes after him and calls, "Excuse me sir, what about the bill?"

Paddy turns around and shouts, "What spoon?"

His whole mind is concerned about the spoon that he has stolen. Seeing the servant running he knows that he is coming for the spoon. He does not hear the word *bill*, he hears the word *spoon*. And we can understand; it is natural. You are so filled with stolen spoons, that when a bill is offered, you immediately react: "What spoon?"

Osho,
In my groups, especially the ones without structure, I discover in me a state of alertness, watchfulness about the group and myself; an aliveness and silence that I only experienced after doing a lot of meditations.

Is this "impersonal space" of the group leader comparable to meditation as I feel it, or am I fooling myself because I do not need to look at my own problems while I'm leading a group? Do I love group-leading so much because it gives me the opportunity of meditation or am I just an addict of "group energy"?

Do you want my theoretical or practical comment? Let us start from theoretical. Theoretically you are a great group leader; theoretically in the groups great meditative states arise in you. But you know, I know and everyone else knows that practically the situation is different.

Everyone wants to be a leader, everyone wants to dominate, to direct, to guide; it does not matter whether he knows what he is advising people. What matters is that his advice makes him feel good – that he is a wise man. It makes him feel good that so many people are looking up him to be guided. And naturally, you have understood the point that when you become involved with the problems of other people you forget your own problems.

Forgetting your own problems creates a certain peace. When you are left alone meditating, it is very difficult because how to forget your problems? When you close your eyes they are all standing there in a queue.

One of the Indian Mohammedan emperors was imprisoned by his son because the old man was not dying but was going on and on, and the son was already old. He had waited too long to become the emperor. Finally, he decided, "This old guy may live longer than me." He imprisoned his own father. It was easy because they were in the same palace, and all the armies were under the son – he was the commander in chief. The old man was imprisoned in his own palace.

The next day the emperor sent a message to his son: "I have ruled enough. There was no need to imprison me. You should have simply asked me and I would have given you the empire. Now it does not mean anything to me. I wish you well. Live long and let the empire prosper, but make a little arrangement for me. I want to teach thirty children the holy Koran."

His son, who had now declared himself the emperor, said to the court, "Do you see the psychology? The old man cannot drop the idea of being the guide, the leader, the wise man. Even if it is only thirty urchins brought from the streets, it does not matter, but he is the leader and the teacher. Those thirty children will become the substitute for the whole empire."

Sigmund Freud and his company were not born yet, but the son was saying something immensely significant as far as psychology is concerned.

If you cannot meditate alone, your meditation in the group is false. If you cannot be silent alone, then your silence in silencing others is not authentic.

I am reminded of a famous story…

A dog had become enlightened. Now, no one can prevent… Anybody can become enlightened. There is no law that prevents people; it is not a crime to become enlightened. And the dog was very articulate, he went around the capital telling every dog, "Your only problem is that you unnecessarily go on barking. This disease of barking has been preventing your enlightenment. Look at me: I never bark."

From the morning till late in the night he made a round to every dog until they accepted that he was enlightened, and there was no doubt about it. They felt ashamed, but what to do? A dog is a dog! Whenever a dog sees someone in uniform, he cannot resist barking. Dogs are very much against uniforms – postmen, policemen, sannyasins... Just as the dog sees the uniform, he is immediately against the person. He seems to be a great freedom lover; this uniform represents slavery. There must be some philosophy in the minds of the dogs, because they take so much trouble – they get tired from barking.

Because they could not stop barking, they had to accept the non-barking dog as the enlightened one. He is almost the Gautam Buddha of the dogs, his achievement is great: "We are all proud that you are born among us; we will worship you. We will remember you, we will teach our children about the golden days when you were alive. But forgive us, we try hard. The more we try hard not to bark, the more forcibly the barking comes."

One full-moon night... And dogs are also against the moon; no one knows why. In fact, in all the languages there are words for mad people. In English *lunatic* is synonymous with mad people, a mad person. But in its root meaning *lunatic* means moonstruck; *luna* means the moon. The same is the situation in Hindi: the madman is said to be *chandmara*, killed by the moon. The moon drives people mad; it drives even the ocean mad. Poets get affected, painters get affected. Most of the people who commit suicide do it on a full-moon night; more people go insane on a full-moon night.

So if dogs bark the whole night, no one can condemn them – they have something of the poet, something of the madman, some aesthetic sense, some feeling of the ocean. But they cannot tolerate the full moon and because we don't understand their language, we call it *barking*. Who knows, they may be reciting poetries praising the moon. Perhaps their barking is their way of prayer.

One full-moon night all the dogs decided that there is a limit to being continuously condemned: "That enlightened dog is too much. You bark, and suddenly he comes. He goes on hiding here and there, watching dogs. This full-moon night, make a commitment: we may die but we will not bark. And we will not open our eyes so we won't see the moon."

There was such silence as there had never been. The Gautam Buddha went around the town; he did not even meet a dog. All the dogs had disappeared. What happened? And on a full-moon night; this was the greatest time of his preaching. But the dogs had disappeared into dark corners, hiding behind houses. They were afraid that if they saw the moon, then commitment or no commitment, they could not resist. They knew…! They were aware of their weakness and their frailty, so it was better they were lying down quiet behind the houses in the darkness. But Gautam Buddha was very concerned, "What has happened? Has every dog died?"

Then the moon started rising higher. And for the first time – because Gautam Buddha was always concerned with teaching the other dogs, he had no time to see to the sky – he saw the moon. The whole sky fell down. There was such barking, and dogs came out from every corner.

That day he realized that because of his continuous teaching there was no time to bark. And you cannot do both things together: barking and talking. He was badly ashamed – fallen from the heights. All the dogs surrounded him and asked, "What happened?"

The story is very significant. If you cannot be silent alone, then while leading a group your silence is just an avoidance of your inner noise. You are focused on other people's problems, so you yourself become hidden behind. Silence is authentic only when you are alone and no thought arises in you. And in fact, this should be a teaching to you: be more and more meditative because this is the only criterion.

If you have attained silence, you have the right to tell others to be silent. If you have solved your problems, then you are capable of helping those who cannot figure out how to get out of the mess they have made in their lives.

I have heard about a man who came to a master asking to be a disciple…

As masters are very colorful, unpredictable people, the master looked at the disciple and said, "Listen, to be a disciple is very difficult. You will have to meditate, you will have to drop your ego; you will have to do this and that. A long process of discipline."

The man said, "I never thought that to be a disciple is so difficult."

The master said, "I cannot help it; that is the way. From eternity, disciples have followed the path. I have only indicated a few spotlights."

The man thought for a moment, looked at the master who was relaxing, comfortably in his chair and said, "Then what about if I become a master? If to be a disciple is so difficult, let me become a master."

The master said, "To be a master is very easy."

The man was very happy. He said, "That's what I was thinking. Things should be easy."

But the master said, "You will have to manage a few disciples and that is very difficult. They are stubborn, very angry, always ready to fight. Sometimes it can prove dangerous."

He said, "But you were saying that to be a master is very easy?"

He said, "To be a master *is* very easy. Just look at me, I am at ease. But first one has to either lead disciples or to become a disciple."

The man said, "Both seem to be difficult. What is your suggestion?"

The master said, "My suggestion is rather than getting troubled by so many people, it is better just to be a disciple because you will have your own troubles and not burdened by other people's troubles."

Just as I was coming here, Kaveesha came to see me. She is a very understanding woman and has a clarity of seeing through problems and helps many people. Many people depend on her because I am not personally available to anyone. You know I am lazy. I became a master because it is the easiest job. I have never been a disciple – I don't have any problems.

So when someone has problems, I direct them to go to Kaveesha, to go to someone else. Because I have never suffered from any problem and I have never solved any problems. If they were there, I left them there unsolved and they died. How long can they live if you don't pay attention to them?

Kaveesha has a small group of people around her; Avirbhava belongs to her group. You hear her scream every day. She is a beautiful woman. She screams just to announce that I have come. When she is not there even I miss her. And she is not an ordinary woman. Just yesterday she gave Kaveesha all her money with the checkbook – that is three and a half million dollars – and said, "You take it."

Kaveesha is poor. She thought that this was a good chance of a lifetime to have so much money. But she was not aware that Avirbhava is tricky! She accepted the checkbook, then Avirbhava explained to her, "There are the problems attached to the checkbook – you take them too. I am completely free!" So many problems… In America, sales have gone down. Avirbhava has coal mines, and no one is purchasing coal mines. Nothing in cash; all in problems – three and a half million dollars! So Kaveesha became afraid, saying, "I'm perfectly happy as I am. Now this Avirbhava is making me fall into a hell of problems."

And Avirbhava was very happy, "For the first time I'm feeling free – free of problems, free of money, unburdened."

Kaveesha could not reject the offer because that would be insulting; she could not accept the offer because that would be destructive. So she said to Avirbhava, "Wait, first I have to see my master."

Just before I came here she came to me and said, "This Avirbhava has created trouble. First she said to me, 'I'm giving you three and a half million dollars. Take it. I'm burdened, I want to be free of money. Osho has been saying again and again to be free – I have decided.'

"And later on she came back and said, 'But listen, these are the problems attached: there is no cash.'"

Kaveesha came to me to ask what to do. I said, "Do one thing. Rejecting it is not nice; accepting it is dangerous because you have never had to take on such problems as are attached to those three and a half million dollars. Just go to Avirbhava and say, 'I have offered the money and the problems to my master. And he said to appoint you, Avirbhava, as my agent to take care.'" In a simple way no one is harmed. Avirbhava remains with her coal mines and three and a half million dollars. But now she is no longer the owner. Whenever those coal mines are transferred into dollars, I am the owner. So they come to the commune; there is no problem.

You need a clarity. Just something beautiful to make this silence a living, a dancing silence.

Grandma Saperstein and Grandpa Rabinowitz are sitting on the veranda of the old folks home rocking back and forth in their rocking chairs. Grandpa Rabinowitz rocks forward in his chair and says to Grandma, "Fuck you!"

Grandma Saperstein rocks forward in her chair and says to Grandpa, "I fuck you too!"

Grandpa becomes very excited and shouts, "Fuck you!" swinging forward once again.

Grandma remains graceful but leans forward and says, "I fuck you again."

This goes on. Finally Grandpa says, "You know something, Grandma, this sex thing ain't all it is cracked up to be."

It is just oral, theoretical.

Zabriski is hired to wash the windows of an eighteen-story building.

When he arrives at the job, he finds Paddy and Sean there to help him. The three of them climb the scaffolding to the top of the building and start to work. But after an hour passes, suddenly Zabriski climbs over the scaffolding and jumps eighteen stories to the street below.

The police arrive, and one of the officers asks Paddy and Sean what happened.

"I don't know," says Sean.

"Well," says Paddy, "maybe it was because of his deformity."

"What do you mean?" asks the cop.

"Well," says Paddy, "he kept on saying that he couldn't work with two assholes."

3

Love Is the Art of Being One with the Whole

Osho,
Since you are giving daily talks again and showering us with so much love, my sexual feelings toward my boyfriend have disappeared again. It looks like it seems to be related to my dropping of sex. Osho, I love it! But please go on talking to us, so that I can have a stronger taste of enlightenment. Last time it must have been so subtle that I missed it completely. So please give me a chance – I am very slow in these things.

Nandan, love has many layers: the biological, the social, the spiritual. They need not be in conflict, but I can understand your problem. For centuries man has been told that either you love the world or you love the beyond, you can't have both together.

This has been one of the most stupid teachings that has destroyed man's possibility of blissfulness. This world and the beyond are not two; the beyond has roots in this world. Your love for your boyfriend and your love for me are not competitive. On the contrary, the more you love me, the more you will be able to love your boyfriend. Love is a deepening inside, a cleansing, a flowering. Your boyfriend may be just a small rosebush, but that does not mean that that rosebush cannot be a part of a great garden.

There is no necessity to divide them. If you love your boyfriend, you will love the garden. The boyfriend is perhaps your kindergarten where you learn how to love, but love should not be limited, it should spread. Finally, it should spread to the whole universe. Even your love for me should not be a bondage. Because of this fact, Gautam Buddha used to say to his disciples, "If you meet me while going inward on the path of meditation, kill me immediately."

I should not be a hindrance. I am here to help you, not to hinder you. And I will be happy that your love becomes so big that it contains the song of the birds and the trees enjoying the sun in silence. Your love should be your sky. But we have been brought up in such wrong ways that love has become another name of jealousy. It has become another name of competition, another name of domination. That condition has to be erased; it can be erased. That's the whole work of meditation: to erase all conditions so that you are as vast as the whole.

When I first came across the statement of P. D. Ouspensky... He was one of the greatest mathematicians of this age and he wrote one of the most beautiful books ever written. The name of the book is *Tertium Organum*. And in the very beginning he declares that the first book was written by Aristotle: its name is *Organum*. *Organum* means the principle of knowledge. The second book was written by Bacon, *Novum Organum*. On the same lines he goes far beyond Aristotle. *Novum organum* means the new principle of knowledge. Ouspensky said with absolute humbleness and humility, "I am going to call my book *Tertium Organum*, the third canon of thought, the third principle of knowledge."

Up to that point it was okay. Certainly he has much more to offer now than Bacon. But he goes on, saying, "I want to make a statement that the third canon of thought existed even before Aristotle's first canon of thought. It was just not discovered."

All these three books are concerned with mathematics. In *Tertium Organum* is the statement: "What I am going to write is not mathematics but super-mathematics." In mathematics the part can never be equal to the whole – it is obvious. But in super-mathematics, Ouspensky says, "The part can be as big as the whole."

The part can become the whole. When a dewdrop disappears into the ocean, slipping from the lotus leaf, do you think it remains still a dewdrop? Or do you think it is smaller than the ocean? The moment it slips into the ocean, it becomes the ocean. Then the part and the whole are one. Love is the art of being one with the whole.

On the path you will find many lovers. Don't make them hindrances and don't think of them as obstacles. That's what has been taught to you by all the religions of the world: if you love things of the world, your spiritual growth is retarded. You will never go to the beyond; you will never open your wings to the whole sky, just like an eagle flying across the sun. You will be caught somewhere.

Your boyfriend is simply a first taste, a small taste of love. He is not a hindrance. If you love me and the love toward your boyfriend disappears, then that love was not true. And you cannot be certain about your love for me because there are greater realities. If you come across them, your love toward me will disappear. No, you are thinking in a very wrong way.

My love should make your love with your boyfriend more pure, meditative, musical, authentic. I should not be a competitor, I should be a nourishment to your love. You have to learn this new language which the society has prevented. There have been reasons why the societies around the world have been preventing it: jealousies of all kinds, competitions of all kinds, fear of all kinds… That if you even love a newspaper, your wife will take it away and throw it out: "While I am here, how dare you!" And it is true that you were hiding yourself behind the newspaper so as not to see the woman. You were keeping that newspaper upside down, you were not reading it. It was just to keep a coexistence with your wife to whom you say, "I love you."

The American philosopher Dale Carnegie, who is the most stupid philosopher I have come across, suggests in a book *How To Win Friends and Influence People*… But you know in America that *everything* is superficial, a hypocrisy. He is teaching a hypocrisy. He says: "At least three times a day, you should say to your wife, 'I love you darling.'" It does not matter whether you love her or not. It is a question of coexistence; otherwise she is going to create trouble. Bring roses, ice cream, Coca Cola, just as symbols of your love.

In America, data has been collected showing that everything has a life of only three years: marriages last only three years – that is the average; jobs last only three years; people change cities every three years. Every fashion goes out of existence within three years. Strange! The number three seems to be a very Christian number: God, the Holy Ghost and the Son. America seems to be really Christian – follows the ideology. But this is the average. In the name of love, so many other things go on.

I have heard…

In a marriage registrar's office, a couple were signing the forms. The woman signed and then the man signed. The woman said, "That's enough. I want a divorce."

Even the magistrate could not believe – nothing had happened. "Why do you want a divorce?"

The woman said, "You can see my signature and he has written his signature in such big words; it is going to be a conflict of the egos. It is better to stop it from the very beginning. Why unnecessarily torture me? He is not even polite enough to sign just the way I have signed. He has written as if he is teaching school children on a blackboard. Such big words. What is the need? He is filling the whole form with *his* signature. This is the declaration that this is going to be our relationship: 'You are going to be a nonentity.' I don't want to be a nonentity."

In the name of love, people can pretend or can even believe that they love. But it is biology, it is hormones. Just give an injection of different hormones and the love will disappear and you will hate each other. This is not love, this is physiology, biology, chemistry. Have you ever observed married people happily moving together? The honeymoon lasts only one week or at the most two weeks. And every story says, "After the honeymoon they lived in happiness forever." No one describes what happened after the honeymoon. The honeymoon is a fiction created by your biology – a romance. You are not the master of it.

Once those hormones are satisfied – you have known the woman, the woman has known you, and you are acquainted with each other's geography perfectly – then the question arises how to get rid of... And every society helps you to get married and prevents you from divorce. There is a significant psychology behind it: if divorce is as easy as marriage, then there will be a turmoil, chaos. People will go on honeymoon and then go directly to the magistrate for a divorce. They are finished; they cannot tolerate each other's presence. This is not love.

So first you have to understand clearly what love should mean. I have been watching married couples. They look so sad when they are together. And if you see a man with a woman, happy, it is certain the woman is someone else's woman. Happiness is impossible because twenty-four hours together becomes a torture.

The same conflict, "Why are you late? Where have you been?" And every husband on his way home is trying to figure out the answers: where he has been, what he has been doing. And it is not only that the husband is trying to figure it out, his wife knows that all he is going to say is nothing but lies. Even if he tells the truth, the wife is not going to believe it. Nor does the man believe... Husbands and wives become detectives, watching each other out of the corners of their eyes: What is going on?

A woman was a hypochondriac. Every day, she was picking up some new disease from television advertisements about medicines. She enjoyed it because it is a very dominating position: you are sick, you are ill. The husband cannot be hard on you, he has to be sympathetic. He has to say, "Darling, I will take you to the doctor."

But the doctors were saying that she did not have the disease. "What am I going to treat?" So she would force the husband to go to another doctor for another opinion.

But fortunately, she died. She left a will saying, "On my grave nothing else should be written except: Now you know – or do you still think I was a hypochondriac?"

One loves only if one finds a communion of the spirit. It is not against biology or anything. Those are strategies of nature to continue the species. If one loves as a communion of spirit, the indication, the absolute certainty will be that there will not be any jealousy. Because if the wife finds herself happy with someone one day, and you love her, then you should be happy because she is happy. Love wants everyone whom it loves to be happy. If there is a communion of spirit, there will be no secretiveness. The wife can say, "Look at that man, how beautiful he is," and the husband will not be offended. He will appreciate his wife's aesthetic sense. That's what she is saying; she is not saying anything else.

In nature, no animal is happy while making love. Ordinarily, we don't come across other animals, only the stray dogs. But have you seen their faces? They are so sad while they are making love, and people make them even more sad. People start hitting them with stones. Strange people… You want to love and you don't want anyone else to love. The dogs are not doing any harm to anyone, and a crowd follows them and they are dragging each other in agony.

That's why in the animal world there are only seasons when animals make love. For the remaining year they forget about love completely; that one season is enough. It takes at least nine months to forget what happened.

But man is more stupid. He hates thinking every night, "This is the end! Let tomorrow come…" And by the evening he starts thinking again, "Why not take another chance? What is the harm? Then

I can stop." It never stops, and the strangest thing is, your love, your lovemaking is not making your life more joyful, more musical, more poetic, more dancing. On the contrary, it is making it dry, desert-like. You somehow carry… It is a problem rather than a joy. Yes, in the beginning it seems to be a great blessing, but only in the beginning. The more intelligent you are, the sooner you will be finished with the idea of a blessing.

If your love is just of this lower, the lowest kind of biology, then certainly when you love me, your love with your boyfriend will disappear. Before the higher can be, the lower has to disappear. This should give you an indication that you have to raise your love higher so that it does not disappear but is more nourished. My love is not only showering on you, it is showering on your boyfriend too. You both should dance, you both should feel nourished; new flowers should blossom for both of you. I am not antilife as other religions are. I am absolutely for life, and life in its essence means love.

I don't even want your love to be confined to me; there are higher realms. I am only a door. If I can take you to higher realms of love where love is no longer a dialogue between two persons, but transformed into lovingness, then you don't need a lover. You are love and wherever you move, you are surrounded with the aura of love. You will shower your love on the trees, not with effort; you will radiate love even if there is no one, in emptiness. The ultimate love is lovingness; where the other is no longer addressed; where everyone, the whole of existence, becomes your beloved. The master is only the door to infinity, to eternity, to freedom from duality.

The most important French philosopher, Jean-Paul Sartre, has insisted again and again that the other is hell – and in a way, he is right. To be with the other, it is very difficult not to create misery for yourself and for the other. No one is made for you. You have your likings; the other has his own likings. You are not one; the rhythm of your heart is not one. You live together, you have to live together because you are not capable of living alone. To you, aloneness appears as loneliness, despair; as if you are deserted, abandoned.

You don't know that aloneness is not loneliness. Aloneness is the highest peak of consciousness. And when love is alone, unaddressed, or addressed in all directions, then it becomes a paradise.

But we have to learn step-by-step, we have to fall and we have to rise. If your love for your boyfriend deepens only when I am not coming out and talking, I will not come out. Because I will not commit that kind of sin – destroying poor Nandan's love. When I come out she becomes enlightened – and enlightened women don't have boyfriends. It is an idiotic idea. Why? Enlightened women should have enlightened boyfriends, so rather than deserting the poor boy, help him to be enlightened so I can also come out. Because if I don't come out… You see all these people – they will kill you, both you and your boyfriend!

So, change your strategy. I am not against your love, I am absolutely for it. Love deeply, love without jealousy, love blissfully and help each other to be more meditative. Because what else can we do and what can we share? Man is born naked, without anything. Love should be the beginning of sharing something – not all that rubbish that Dale Carnegie is suggesting.

The only sharing is of silence, joy, celebration. Slowly, slowly your hearts start melting and merging into each other. Your love becomes a spiritual phenomenon. And your love helps each of you to come closer to the master because the master is not separating you but joining you.

It is an ugly fact that even people like Gautam Buddha or Mahavira insisted on you renouncing your wives, your husbands, your children. No one even talks about how many people – the number must be millions in twenty-five centuries – have been deserted, and people have become sannyasins for wrong reasons. It was the easiest divorce and very respectable: you don't have to go to the registrar's office and you don't have to be condemned by the society.

On the contrary, are you aware of the implications if you renounce your wife and your children in the name of religion? – millions of women will suffer poverty, will become prostitutes.

Millions of children will become beggars, thieves, criminals. Who is responsible for all this? Your great so-called leaders.

A few years back I read the life story of a Jaina monk…

He was very respected. The respect came because he was not born a Jaina, he was born as a Hindu goldsmith. Whenever people convert to other religions, they are respected greatly in the new religion because they are giving you the confidence that your religion is higher, greater, truer than their religion. They are becoming a certain argument in favor of your philosophy.

There were other Jaina monks, but this man had more respect than anyone else. I was looking at his biography. He renounced his wife and twenty-six years later, the wife died, poor, doing small things in people's houses: cleaning, washing their dishes, their clothes. The conditioning is such that she was still happy that her husband has become a great saint.

The day the saint received the message that his wife had died, his statement remained with me; I cannot forget it because I cannot forgive it. He said, "My last anxiety is finished." After twenty-six years, he left the woman in utter poverty. What was his anxiety? It is easy to renounce a woman, but it is not easy to renounce sex. So although he had renounced – because so much honor and so much respect – deep down the sex must have been fooling him. His statement: "My last anxiety…" means that for twenty-six years he had been carrying the anxiety, he had not really renounced. But this has been happening all over the world.

I want to transform the quality of your love. I don't want you to renounce anything. Renunciation is for the retarded; transformation is for those who are intelligent. I cannot have millions of people around me for the simple reason that millions of intelligent people don't exist. All kinds of retarded people…

For the first time after the First World War, psychological tests were made to calculate the mental age of a man. Up to that point it was never thought that there are two ages: the age of the body and the age of the mind. And it was such a shock to discover that the average state of the mind is very retarded; its average age is fourteen years. The man may be seventy – that is his physical age – but his mind, his psychology is only fourteen years of age. My effort is to bring your mind equal to the age of your body. In fact, it is possible if a man can be seventy and his mind can be only fourteen, that the vice versa is possible.

Someone asked Emerson, "What is your age?"

He said, "Three hundred and sixty years." Emerson was a man of truth and the man could not believe that he could tell such a lie.

Three hundred and sixty? He pretended that he had not heard. He said, "I am a little deaf. Please repeat. What is your age?"

Emerson said, "You have heard it, but I will repeat, three hundred and sixty."

The man said, "I cannot accept this. You don't look more than sixty."

Emerson said, "Yes, that's true. That is the age of my body. I am talking about my age, the age of my psychology. And that is at least six times more than my physical age."

First, I have to cleanse all the garbage that the old generations have poured in your mind. Your intelligence has to be cleansed, your love has to be cleansed. You have to be given maturity, a centering, an individuality, and then there are not two worlds as all the religions say. I emphatically deny that there are two worlds. The other world is simply a fiction, a consolation for the retarded, for the poor, for the miserable to give them a hope; to give them opium so they can somehow manage to drag themselves to their graves.

This is the only world. It does not mean that with your death comes the end. It simply means that with your death, you move into a higher quality of life. It all depends on you. If in this life you can manage to get rid of jealousies, to get rid of biological and physiological attractions; if in this life you can get in tune, in love; if this life can become a celebration, your innermost consciousness will continue celebrating on higher levels. But there are not two worlds, it is one world, one eternity.

The people who divided it into two were very cunning because that gave them the scope: "If you are poor here, don't be worried. Just pray to God and in the next life you will be in paradise with all the pleasures that you are being denied here." That paradise of all the religions is just a consolation for the poor, for the suffering, for the miserable. It does not give you growth, it does not give you more consciousness. On the contrary, it simply gives you a hope which is not going to be fulfilled.

No one has written from the other world. At least they could have sent a Christmas card saying, "We are happy here." No evidence for it exists, no proof and no argument. It is the greatest fiction: God, paradise and all the joys of paradise.

Jesus says, "Blessed are the poor." And everybody knows who is blessed. If the poor are blessed then we should destroy all the riches that exist on the earth. Make everyone a beggar, make everyone blessed – because only the blessed ones, the poor, will enter the kingdom of God. And their different religions for different climates, different geographies, different problems, have managed to give, promised to give… You will find beautiful women there; here you have to renounce a poor woman, and there you will find beautiful women who never age. They always remain young, fixed at sixteen years of age. They can only be made of plastic; they cannot be real.

Those women have been offered to millions of saints who have entered paradise. You can't find a prostitute on the earth comparable to the prostitutes that are offered in paradise. And you can see a strange thing: beautiful women are provided because all religions are man-made. Beautiful boys are not provided – who cares about women?

Yes, only one religion provides beautiful boys – for homosexuality; that is also for men, not for women. Rivers of wine… Here, wine is condemned and in paradise you swim in wine, you drink, you drown.

Whatever you want to do, you can do. And such utterly nonsensical ideas have been prevalent for centuries all over the world.

I have heard…

Swami Muktananda died; in fact, he was never alive, but theoretically he died. One of his chief disciples could not manage to be separated from the master. He committed suicide and rushed as fast as he could to paradise. Poor Muktananda was lying down just under a beautiful tree with thousands of flowers, and on top of him was lying an American actress, Marilyn Monroe.

The disciple said, "My God, this is not right." And Muktananda was always saying to be celibate: What is happening? Then he realized that the values had changed; this was paradise. He fell at the feet of the couple who were making love and said, "Forgive me. For a moment, a doubt has arisen because I forgot that values have changed. This is not the earth; this is paradise. You are well rewarded; the woman is really beautiful."

Before Muktananda could speak, the woman said, "You idiot, you don't understand a thing. This old guy is not rewarded, I have been punished. They could not find an uglier punishment for me."

There is no other world, but consciousness is eternal. Existence has always been here and will always be here. It is up to you – absolutely up to you – to make the best of this great opportunity. Purify your love and it becomes prayer. Purify your intelligence and it becomes your wisdom. Purify yourself completely and you become one with the whole. And to be one with the whole is the ultimate benediction, the blissfulness, the experience for which thousands of people have been searching down the ages on wrong paths.

This world has to be loved, has to be respected, has to be your temple, your mosque, your church. This world has to be your gratefulness, your gratitude. Nandan, enlightenment is not something of another world. Enlightenment happens now and here. And enlightenment is nothing but a purity of everything that you are. It is not renunciation, it is rejoicing.

I am changing the very definition of sannyas. Up to now sannyas has been defined as renouncing the world. That has been a calamity. Millions of people have renounced the world who could have created a better world, more beautiful. I change the definition of sannyas: I say it is not renouncing, it is rejoicing. Rejoice in your love, rejoice in your songs. Rejoice in your music, rejoice in your dance. Rejoice in these beautiful trees – these innocent sounds of the birds. Rejoice in the night full of stars. We have the most perfect world and there is no other world, but we have to get in tune with it. We have to become one with it.

Enlightenment is not something special, it is simply a purified consciousness in which thousands of flowers of love, intelligence, truth, peace, silence, grow on their own accord. Nandan, you created a very serious silence – the trees don't like it. They wait for your laughter; it is their nourishment. When you laugh the birds understand perfectly the language of laughter. They don't understand Arabic or Sanskrit or Hebrew, but they understand laughter.

A few things for the trees and for the birds…

Paddy is explaining to Seamus what happened when he went into the new Zorba the Buddha self-service restaurant.

"I got myself a cup of coffee," he says, "and set it on the table. Then I went back for a piece of pie, but when I came back with the pie, the coffee was gone. So I set down the pie and went back for another cup of coffee, and the pie was gone. So I wrote a card. It read: 'I put my finger in the coffee.' Then I stuck the card alongside the cup. I went for another piece of pie, but when I came back the coffee cup was empty and someone had written on the card, 'I drank your coffee but I could not find your finger.'"

Herschel Goldberg goes up to his father, Hymie, and says, "Dad, I want to marry Suzy."

"Don't marry her, my son," says Hymie. "When I was a young man, I was pretty wild and to put it bluntly, she is your half-sister."

Sometime later, Herschel comes up to Hymie and says, "Dad, I am in love with Mildred and I want to marry her."

"You can't," says Hymie, "she is your half-sister."

"How about Mabel?" asks Herschel, a few weeks later.

"Sorry," says Hymie, "she is your half-sister too."

Herschel is really determined to get married, so he goes to his mother and complains.

"Dad says I can't marry Suzy, Mildred or Mabel because they are all my half-sisters. What can I…?"

"Don't worry," says Becky, "marry any of them you like – he is not your father!"

4

Relax: Life Itself Prepares the Ground

Osho,

When I first sat in front of you, I heard you say to me, "Bring light into the unconscious." Eight years have since passed and I feel more silent and loving than ever before, and yet sense that there is much more.

Does the light which enters the unconscious come through effort and determination, or is it an existential gift, requiring patience, openness and receptivity?

Could you speak on what it means to bring light into the unconscious?

Every step on the path reminds one of the utter poverty of language. I may have said to you, "Bring light into your unconscious," because in that moment you would not have understood what you can understand now. You can only prepare the ground. Light comes on its own accord. And that is happening in these eight years by your becoming more silent and more loving. But you feel a lingering sense that there is something more – there is much more. Now I can say to you: "Relax in your silence so it can become deeper. And relax in your love so it is no longer a solid thing but becomes more liquid, more flowing in all directions."

In short, learn the art of let-go. The light will come not according to your expectations or by any effort. Every effort will be a great hindrance and every expectation will create distance between you and the light. In fact, forget all about light; just listen to the sound of the rain, the sound of the wind, and enjoy it with such intensity that in every enjoyment you disappear. Slowly, slowly one day you will find you are not. That is the greatest moment in a man's life, because the moment you find you are not, light enters you. It waits until you vacate your innermost being. You are too full of yourself; there is no space for the great light to descend in you.

In a certain sense you have to die to be reborn, you have to *be* no longer to be authentically yourself. This is logically a very contradictory language, but I am not responsible for it. The whole responsibility is on the poverty of language. It has not been made to express the richer and higher experiences of consciousness. The descending of light is the ultimate, then the lingering sense that there is more will disappear.

That does not mean that there is not much more – there is – but what you have received is too much even to believe in it. You don't deserve it, you are not worthy of it and it is so vast that it is inconceivable that there can be much more beyond it. But there is no need for you to be worried about it. Just as the light has come, it comes as a ray entering your unconscious darkness and soon it becomes thousands of suns: light exploding all over in all dimensions. Because of this fact, the experience has been called enlightenment.

You are on the right path. Eight years ago if I had said these things to you, you would not have understood. I had to prepare you before I could say things which are unsayable. And there are so many things to be conveyed to you, but they will have to wait until you are prepared. When you are prepared just give me a hint, "I am ready." Then I can forget logic, language. Then I can directly say the essential experience – whether it is grammatical or not, who cares? One thing is certain, it is existential.

So from now onward remember, stop bringing light into the unconscious – please! From now onward wait for the light to come. Wait with a throbbing heart, with a welcome, doors open, because who knows when the light comes, there is no pre-information. It comes so suddenly, you have to be awake all the time, just waiting by the side of the gate, keeping it open, because the host can come any moment.

It is really the relationship between the guest and the host. You have to disappear and just become a waiting, utterly pure and silent, not waiting for something, simply waiting. The moment you can simply wait without demanding anything from existence and without desiring... Because behind every desire and behind every expectation and demand there is a complaint: "Why am I still in darkness? Why have you not come yet?" You may not say it clearly, but deep down you know that your heart cannot be grateful in such a situation.

Forget all about light because it does not come by your remembering it, so what is the point of remembering? It comes by your deep relaxation, silence, peace, love, meditativeness and utter let-go. One day you will suddenly find your whole being full of light, transformed from mortality into immortality, transformed from misery into blissfulness, into a blissfulness that knows no end.

Osho,
You always say that one becomes a sannyasin because one is seeking for truth. When you say that I always feel very guilty because I know I didn't become a sannyasin for that reason. I became a sannyasin because I wanted to be happy, I wanted to get rid of anguish and to live all the joy my heart can contain. Please tell me something about it.

You are guilty! – because what you call happiness is nothing but a by-product of the experience of truth. You may be seeking happiness, you may be seeking the ultimate, you may be seeking yourself. It doesn't matter, you are seeking the same thing. You are seeking to get rid of your ignorance, your misery, your anguish, but that happens only when you come face-to-face with the truth of your being.

You are guilty of misunderstanding. Now feel guilty no longer. The energy that you are putting into feeling guilty, put it into searching for happiness, and you will find that your search for happiness is another name for what I have called the truth.

"Quick," yells little Ernie as he rushes into the drugstore, "my Dad is hanging upside down by his pants leg on a barbed wire fence!"

"What do you need?" asked the druggist. "Help or first aid supplies?"

"Nothing like that," says Ernie breathlessly, "I want another roll of film for my camera!"

Just misunderstanding is not guilt...

Two old black ladies are about to get their picture taken. As the photographer pulls the black cloth over his head and starts to adjust the lens, one lady asks the other, "What is he doing?"

She answers, "He is going to focus!"

The other lady looks at her friend in shock and says, "Both of us?"

> Osho,
> Sex is disappearing, immense creativity is opening up, love is happening. It feels like a cool breeze inside, unexcited and very alone. Then the mind comes in and says, "Your heart is not open," and tries to doubt this space of coolness.
> Could you please talk about this?

Turiya, again a German! It seems I am going to make the whole of Germany enlightened! Knowing perfectly well what happened with Nandan, still you say, "Sex is disappearing, immense creativity is opening up, love is happening." My God! "It feels like a cool breeze inside, unexcited and very alone. Then the mind comes and says, 'Your heart is not open,' and tries to doubt this space of coolness. Could you please talk about this?" How many times have I to remind you that this kind of enlightenment will happen many times. Sex will disappear – and will appear again. The heart will open – and will close again. It is the natural process. Your mind is not creating a doubt. Your mind is simply reminding you not to get caught up in in great words, "...cool breeze inside, unexcited and very alone." Wake up and become unenlightened again!

Many times, enlightenment needs waking up from the dreams. Because you are all continually listening about enlightenment, and everyone is talking about it, naturally you start thinking it is happening to everyone. It has happened to Nandan – and Turiya is a princess! What kind of enlightenment happens to a commoner and the royal blood is still unenlightened? Jump up, you have to be ahead of all!

But then the cool breeze unexpectedly brings with it the boyfriend. You were not hoping that he would come so soon! And then everything becomes hot. The mind reminds you – it will remind you again. But you say, "Wait, this boyfriend is going to go back again in three weeks." It is only a question of three weeks then you can become enlightened again: "Just for three weeks don't be miserly. Open your heart, let love flow."

And these boyfriends are such – and particularly in this temple – if one boyfriend disappears, another appears. We don't make much fuss about asking, "Who are you? What is your name?" When love knocks on the door you open it and receive the guest. Even if he is not German, it will do; at least for the time being until the German returns! And everyone has a spare boyfriend; it is intelligent always to have some spare parts. In this technological age you cannot simply depend without having spares.

So if the real does not appear the spare comes. And this will happen many times until you are really fed up. Then sex does not disappear; then you simply transcend it. It remains where it is. How can it disappear? Everything remains the same. You are just more mature, more centered, more happy for no reason at all. For the first time your happiness is independent. It does not depend on anyone. For the first time aloneness has a beauty, a tremendous beauty; the beauty which only roses know or the stars.

That day will also come, Turiya, but before it comes these kinds of things will happen many times. Just be a watcher; enjoy these too. It is perfectly good to feel once in a while that sex has disappeared; one feels so clean, as if you have just taken a cool shower. It is beautiful to feel a creativity arising in you; nothing is wrong in it. The trouble is that these are only your dreams, not your realizations. So when they surround you they look as if they are real, but when they disappear leaving you in a dark ditch, you understand that your mind has destroyed everything, doubted. If the mind had not doubted, everything was going so well.

The mind is not disturbing; the mind cannot disturb anything real, and the mind cannot doubt anything real. The mind doubts only the unreal, the belief, the imagination, the dream. And it is good, it is helpful, it is healthy that by doubting, the mind prevents you from falling into the trap of the unreal.

Don't be in a hurry; otherwise you will start clinging to any dream. Be relaxed. Life itself prepares the ground. Life's experiences bring the maturity and the moment in which you are transformed. Then there is no mind to doubt, then there is no question about it. The real has never been questioned.

Do you think when Gautam Buddha became enlightened his mind said, "Just think over it; it may be just a dream." Not for a split second can truth be doubted once you encounter it. Your doubt is perfectly healthy and your experience is perfectly normal. But one day the real will arrive because you *are* searching, seeking, honestly and sincerely with your totality. That day you will not find the mind anywhere. But right now it is too early. Listen to the mind; try to understand. You are not yet ripe. Your meditation is not yet deep enough, but it is deepening. So be happy that you are on the right track.

For sixty years Ruthy Finkelstein has lived with her tight-fisted husband Moishe. One fine day Moishe dies and Ruthy has him cremated.

She takes the ashes home with her in a plastic urn. She walks around her home carrying the urn and talking to the dead Moishe. "Moishe," she says, "look at the fridge! All those years you would not give me money for housekeeping. Now look, it is full of champagne and caviar. And Moishe, look at my closet. All the time we were married you never allowed me more than one new dress every two years. Now look, it is full of silk dresses and fur coats and the jewelry box is full of diamonds. And Moishe, all those years you would not let me have anything to do with the business. Well, today I took over as chairman."

Finally, in the bedroom she opens the little plastic urn and shakes his ashes onto the windowsill. "And Moishe," she says, "you remember that blow job you always nagged me for? Well, here it is…pfft!"

Don't take things seriously; life is so hilarious. There is no urgency to be enlightened. It is unfortunate, I became enlightened too early! But now nothing can be done about it – once enlightened, enlightened forever.

Let life and its different dimensions be experienced by you. As you experience life, slowly, slowly you become aware of its emptiness. Slowly, slowly you become aware that this is not your authentic being. In this slow process of experiencing, one day you come home. Then it is not a dream, not an imagination. And the most significant criterion to remember is that you will not find the mind in your authentic enlightenment. The question of doubt does not arise, not even for a moment. You simply know what the case is.

I know the trouble of being enlightened. That's why I make you alert. Don't be in a hurry; otherwise you will blame me. I don't want to take the blame. No one can say to me, "I am grateful to you that you helped me to become enlightened." I help you to learn, love and live as totally as possible. Out of this, enlightenment is bound to happen someday, but there is no hurry for it. It is your birthright, so you cannot avoid it long enough. Sooner or later – and most probably sooner than later – it is going to happen. But I am telling you, I don't want to take any credit for it because then you will see that this whole life is utterly futile, meaningless, that no action is of any worth; then you will search.

That's why I keep myself locked in my room. I don't want people rushing to me saying, "Now it is your fault. You talked about enlightenment and I have become enlightened. Now what do you suppose I should do?" There is nothing to be done, you have become enlightened, close the door and lock yourself inside! Or if you are really angry, try to make others enlightened. Look what life has done to you. Do it to others!

No one can persuade little Ernie's great-aunt Esmeralda that she does not possess extraordinary, supernatural powers. Little Ernie believes her when she tells him about one of her visions: "Keep a close eye on your father tomorrow," she says. "I feel it in my bones that he is going to pop off before nightfall."

Little Ernie never lets his dad out of his sight the next day. They go to the office together in the morning and then to the park in the afternoon. Nothing unusual happens all day, but when they get home in the evening little Ernie's mother greets them at the front door.

"A terrible thing happened here this morning," she sobs, "the milkman dropped dead on the kitchen floor!"

Turiya, you cannot find a more hilarious life than this. To tell you the truth – after enlightenment there is nothing. So manage to do everything before enlightenment strikes! I will try my best to make you enlightened; you try your best not to become enlightened! Don't get caught up in my words.

Just look at Nandan, she became enlightened and became unenlightened quickly – and now she will not become enlightened again so soon! Most probably by the time I answer the question – it takes two or three days – Turiya may have already dropped the idea of enlightenment: "What is the hurry, why not enjoy a few more days of the juicy life?" I can see her sitting just there behind Devageet. And she is enjoying. That means that the dream of enlightenment is finished!

5

Life Is Not Made of Contradictions but of Complementaries

Osho,
I feel so full inside that it overflows, and at the same time, so empty that it scares me. It seems a contradiction. Would you like to say something about it?

Life is not made of contradictions; it is made of complementaries. Only in the mind do things appear to be opposite. Only in the mind you cannot conceive how they both can be one. That's why Euclidean geometry says that parallel lines never meet, but in fact it has been discovered that parallel lines also meet.

This whole existence is a meeting of many dimensions. That is its beauty, its variety, its unending procession of celebration. If you think about emptiness, you cannot think that fullness and emptiness can be the same. But if you experience it you will be amazed that what the mind has been always proposing, and what philosophers have always been supporting, is absolutely absurd. All philosophies are absurd.

Only experience is truth, not theoretical considerations about experience. We teach people's minds contradictions: emptiness and fullness are absolutely contradictory. But when you come to a point of deep meditation, you are suddenly surprised and scared too, scared because of your conditioning – it is not supposed that emptiness and fullness should be one. But existence never bothers what your philosophers say; it goes on its own way.

When you are utterly empty, you are also utterly full, overflowing. In fact, emptiness itself becomes a tremendous fullness. Looked at from onc side, you can call it empty. For example, if you remove all the furniture and all the junk from your house, which people go on collecting... All are great collectors. If you remove the whole junk, then the room, the house is empty of the junk, but in itself, it is full of itself for the first time. All that furniture and all those things were destroying its fullness.

The meditator is bound to come to the point when he has thrown all the junk from the mind, and suddenly he sees that emptiness is there. There is also a fullness of which logically there is no explanation – but it is not a logical process at all. Your experience is tremendously meaningful. It shows that you have touched a deep point where opposites meet and mingle, when enemies become friends, when life and death are one; when emptiness and fullness are not two separate things, but only two separate names given by the mind.

The mind is so small, it cannot conceive such a vast phenomenon: that life and death are one, that emptiness and fullness are one. It can conceive emptiness is emptiness and fullness is fullness. Those are the discriminations of the mind.

Meditation opens the doors of a vast world; existential not theoretical, where suddenly you are shocked that for the first time emptiness and fullness are one, life and death are one, men and women are one. But it is not a question to be or not to be. Both are one: different names of the same reality.

So don't start thinking about it as if it is a contradiction. That is the mind interfering in your meditation. You have to be very alert; the mind is cunning. It tries in every way because it is very well trained by all the educational systems and by all the societies.

The more a man's mind is trained in being logical, the more he is accepted as a great intellectual. In fact, he has gone far away from existence with a very rare possibility of returning.

I make a difference between intellect and intelligence: intellect divides things into opposites; intelligence penetrates into opposites and creates bridges. Intellect makes walls; intelligence makes bridges. Meditation is the highest form of intelligence because it is the highest form of consciousness. You will come to such points more and more. This is just the beginning. Just say to the mind, "This is none of your business."

The mind has to understand that you are no longer in its power and in its grip. Once the mind understands that you have moved into a totally different world of existence – not of mere thoughts which are soap bubbles – it starts interfering less and less. The day the mind stops interfering, and even great contradictions like life and death are accepted totally as one without any doubt, you have arrived home.

This is a great experience on the path of meditation, but the mind will try in every way to create doubt. Listen to existence and never to the mind, because the mind is a creation of the society. You have been trained by the society for years, so it has become very ingrained; it has destroyed your purity, your clarity. Meditation is simply reclaiming your simplicity, your silence, your perceptivity – where all contradictions dissolve into each other, not as enemies but as friends.

I have heard...

A small child saw his father and mother making love – the window was just a little open. He could not believe that the father was torturing the mother. He rushed to his elder brother and said, "What are you doing here? We have to do something, otherwise that brute, our father, is going to kill our mother; he is sitting on her chest."

The elder brother said, "Be quiet. They are not fighting. It is a kind of exercise."

What else to say to the little brother…?

He said, "Exercise? You don't understand the grave situation. I am going to my uncle."

The uncle said, "Calm down. It is not exercise, it is just fooling around."

The child said, "It is very strange. Everyone is giving different answers and no one is doing anything. And that poor woman, my mother, is suffering under the weight of the heavyweight champion my father? Do something!"

The uncle said, "Don't be worried; they are making love."

The mind is a very small thing compared to the vast existence. It cannot understand that contradictions are in deep love with each other – not only in love, they are in fact one. This experience of oneness will give you such blissfulness, such peace, such tensionlessness that you have never experienced before. With these same eyes, you will start looking into the world with a totally different outlook. Meditation simply changes your vision, your way of seeing, your way of understanding. This whole existence is a love affair. No one is doing any exercise and no one is fighting. It is a tremendous balance between the opposites seen by the mind, but it doesn't see the balance: that there is something more than the apparent oppositions.

When one hundred girls are born, there are always one hundred and fifteen boys born at the same time. Fifteen boys more seems to be something of a non-mathematical thing. But existence knows more than you know. Those fifteen boys will have disappeared by the time they are sexually mature. In fact, within the first two years, those fifteen boys will start disappearing, dying. Nature has to create fifteen more boys, so that by the time of marriage, there is at least a similarity: an equality of numbers between men and women. Nature has its own wisdom.

It is very strange… Just at the beginning of this century, in poor countries like India, nine out of ten children would die before they were two years of age; only one would survive. But even at that time, nature was keeping a balance: more boys and less girls would be born. An equilibrium, a balance has to be maintained. With medical developments the situation has changed; just the opposite is happening today. Out of ten babies born, only one dies, nine live.

It is very mysterious how nature comes to know that the situation has changed, and you have to produce according to a new way. But the balance is kept; it has been kept since eternity. Perhaps they are both coming from the same source: two branches of one reality. But man has certainly disturbed the balance.

There are countries and religions which allow a man to marry four women. Now, if a man marries four women, what about the three other men who will remain unnecessarily celibate? – forcibly. But it happened in countries where men were continuously warring with each other, killing each other. They would rape the women of the enemy but they would not kill them; they would kill the men. So naturally, there were few men and four times more women.

Out of such stupid situations, arbitrary moralities are created. Now those communities have spread all over the world. The situation is not the same but they insist that it is their religious right to marry four women. If you marry four women, then you are certainly creating corruption in the society. Those three men will start falling in love with other people's wives – they have to. For those three men, prostitutes will have to be created; otherwise, what is going to happen to their life energy? All kinds of perversions… But these perversions are man-made. If we listen to the wisdom of nature, nothing is perverted. Everything is very simple, very silently merging, melting with each other. There is no conflict in existence.

I say unto you, that there is no God and there is no Devil. The Devil was created by the people who created God because they could not think how God can exist without the polar opposite. Everything exists with the polar opposite.

Even Friedrich Nietzsche missed the point when he said, "God is dead." He forgot about the Devil. The Devil continues to live because no one has declared his death. I declare that they were two sides of the same fiction. When God died there was no need for the Devil.

When there is no other world, a heaven, there is no need for any hell. These are man-made polarities. Seeing that existence always lives with polarities, opposites, contradictions, man feels a little hesitant to accept that there is only heaven. Then what about the sinners? The reality is the saint and the sinner are not opposites; deep down they depend on each other. If there are no sinners, all saints will disappear. If there are no saints, there will be no sinners. They are not contradictions; they are just part of a beautiful polarity and balance.

In a small school, for almost one hour the teacher has been teaching how not to sin, because those who sin will be thrown into hellfire for eternity. And if by mistake you have committed something which is sin, then pray. God is compassionate. He will forgive you and you will enter paradise with all its pleasures. Then she asked the class…

A small boy raised his hand.

She asks, "What is the way to reach paradise?"

The little boy said, "Sin."

She said, "My God, for one whole hour I have been insisting that if you sin you will fall into hell."

He said, "I understand. But unless you sin, you will not be forgiven either. How will you enter paradise? God will ask what sins you have committed. He is compassionate, he will forgive, but first you have to commit a sin."

Sometimes children can see things in a very different perspective. The boy is right. God will be absolutely useless if no one is sinning. What will he do with his compassion? – out of a job, unemployed… Not even the possibility of a retirement pension!

When we create fiction, we have to create the anti-fiction. Christians talk about the coming of the Antichrist. In the first place, Christ was an uneducated, poor fellow, a little whimsical: riding on his donkey, preaching to a few idiots – who are always available. And in his whole life, he could only find twelve followers. But Christians had to create the idea of the Antichrist. Only then does Jesus become a real Christ, a real savior: he will save you from the Antichrist. Two thousand years have passed. No one has encountered any Antichrist. Many have been condemned by Christianity as the Antichrist, but just by your condemnation you are fulfilling your desire to make Christ a reality.

I was amazed to receive a letter from the president of the Nazi Party who believes that Adolf Hitler is the reincarnation of an Old Testament prophet, Elijah. He wrote to me saying, "You have been speaking again and again against Adolf Hitler. Perhaps you don't know that he is a very religious person; he is the reincarnation of the Old Testament prophet Elijah. Please stop speaking against him."

I told my secretary to write to him and say, "I will continue whatever I want to do. No one can dictate to me, but I can see that you are utterly stupid: in the Old Testament Elijah was a Jew, and a Jew and Adolf Hitler… Can you think of how many Jews he killed? – six million. A great reincarnation of Elijah the Jewish prophet killing Jews." Seeing the point, he has not replied to me that it's true.

But you can find idiots who even think that Adolf Hitler is a religious man. And there is nothing in his life to make him religious. You have to go back to the rotten Old Testament to find a figure that no one remembers, Elijah – and he becomes the incarnation. If he had been the incarnation of Elijah then he would have killed all the Germans and not the Jews. And what was his reason for killing the Jews? – that the Jews are the cause of all misery and suffering in the world. A strange cause because here almost half of you are Jews, and I don't think any Jew is creating suffering or misery for anyone. I have found them the nicest people.

I am reminded…

A rabbi was on his morning walk and he came across Adolf Hitler. Adolf Hitler said to him, "Rabbi, do you agree with me or not?"

The rabbi said, "I agree absolutely with you. The world is miserable, in suffering, because people are using bicycles. Just destroy all the bicycles and you will see the whole world becoming a paradise."

It is the same; it is arising again. Anando brought me news from Japan. In Japan there are not many Jews, but two very important books have appeared – and are being sold on a great scale – which say that the world is going toward destruction because of a Jewish conspiracy.

It is strange that man can be convinced by any stupid idea.

An old Jew was dying and his wife said to him, "Pray your last prayer to God."

He said, "Yes, I am praying. I was praying silently, but now I will pray openly so that you can all hear: 'God, you have chosen the Jews as your people. Now it is time you chose someone else; we have suffered enough.'"

And it is true that Moses is in some way responsible for giving this idea to the Jews that they are the chosen people of God. It gave them an idea of superiority. That hurts everyone, particularly those who have similar kinds of ideas. The Hindus think they are the chosen people of God. God gave the Hindus his first book, the Rig Veda – and Hitler felt very inferior: "If the Jews are the chosen people of God, then who are the Germans?"

Somehow, some way had to be found – and Hitler found it. He sent his people to India and to Tibet to find some way so that he could declare it. He found out that Jainism in India is the oldest religion in the whole world; its symbol is the swastika. That symbol was chosen by Adolf Hitler and he claimed that it was given to the Germans first, as an indication that they are the chosen people.

He started calling Germans "Aryans." Hindus and Jainas had been calling themselves Aryans. No one had heard before that Germans were Aryans. But Aryans are the oldest race; perhaps Germans are also a branch of the Aryans. By becoming Aryans and having the symbol of the swastika, he declared his superiority over the Jews. And because he had the power, he killed six million Jews.

Only forty years have passed, and there are idiots who are writing books that there is an international Jewish conspiracy. The Jews are not spread all over the world; they don't have power; they are in trouble in Israel. But rather than looking at reality, people always find excuses: it is a Jewish conspiracy; Jews have to be completely eradicated from the world, then the world will be happy! There is no logic in it. The same logic as bicycles... Destroy all the bicycles and suddenly you will see the world becoming richer, stronger, healthier. Those books are bestsellers; even in Japan, where there are very few Jews. It is dangerous, and when I received the letter from the president – I had never thought that there still existed a Nazi Party, that there are still people who believe in Adolf Hitler as a religious leader.

Six million, that is the number of Jews he killed. The total number of people killed because of him in the Second World War was fifty-two million. These criminals... And then I inquired of my friends about the Party and what their program is. Their program is that they are waiting for the reincarnation of Adolf Hitler.

Rather than collecting your energies and your intelligence to make you a beautiful and graceful being, people go on destroying their very energy which could have been a great transformation and enlightenment to them. So don't for a single moment allow the mind to interfere with your meditation. Meditation is very delicate – and in the beginning very fragile. The mind is almost ten million years old; it is very strong, very stubborn. You have to protect your meditation and you have to be alert that the mind does not go on planting seeds destructive to your meditation.

That's the function of the communion of the seekers. Alone, perhaps you will find yourself very weak against the mind, but when there are so many people meditating and creating an ocean of meditative energy, you also feel the strength and you can put the mind aside. The mind may be ten million years old, it does not matter. It has no correspondence with reality.

Bernie Bernstein returns to his business in New York after a holiday in Miami where he enjoyed the company of a gorgeous blonde called Suzy.

Bernie has been back in his office for a few days when Fagin Finkelstein the lawyer pays him a visit.

"I am here," begins Fagin, "on behalf of my client, Suzy Lamour."

He then opens his briefcase and pulls out a stack of glossy photographs of Bernie and Suzy in all the various positions of their lovemaking.

"Well, Mr. Bernstein," smiles young Fagin, "what do you think of that?"

Bernie looks from one photograph to the next in horror and then in amazement.

Eventually he reaches a decision.

"Okay," he says, pointing at two of the photos, "I'll take two of this and two of this."

The mind finds some way, however stupid, to get out of the reality. But the reality does not change; in fact, you should learn to get out of the mind, and the reality changes tremendously. It changes because you can see it now as it is. It is not according to any theology, any religion, any philosophy.

Existence is so vast and philosophers are so small that their efforts are going to be found stupid. They may find some small fragments of reality and make out of those fragments great systems. But existence does not need a system created by your mind but an experience by your very being.

The being is not very far away – just a little distance. Only one station on the way, from the mind to the heart and from the heart to the being, and you have arrived. It is not a long journey, and you don't need any vehicle. You can simply slip inward. The mind will try to persuade you not to do such a dangerous thing because "I am always here to help you; without me, you will be helpless." Tell the mind: "Shut up! You have helped me enough and I don't need your help any more. For the first time I want to experience helplessness."

You have arrived at the heart which is still the same as it was when you were born, innocent. It still wonders, it still feels the mysterious, it still loves. It is still the music of the depths of your being. But don't get stuck there. You can be a poet, a painter, a dancer which is far more beautiful than being a mathematician or a physicist. Don't get stuck there, just one step more: enjoy an overnight stay, drink the beauty of the heart, thank the heart and enter your being. And the heart never prevents, but helps, shows you the way.

Once you are at your being, the whole universe of reality opens up. You cannot find a single contradiction, you cannot find anything against anything else. Everything is supportive to each other; the whole existence is a cosmic, organic whole. And the moment you realize, "I am also one with this tremendous unity," the ecstasy that arises remains with you for eternity. But a little effort is needed to get out of the mind, because you are also convinced that your mind is a great help, is a great defense. It is nothing but an imprisonment – and a very small prison.

You are almost like a bird in a cage. Certainly the cage protects, but it has taken away your whole sky. It protects, but it has destroyed your joy and your dance in the sky, in the sun, to far away. Against the whole sky, this defense of a small cage – it may be of gold – but it cuts your wings, it kills you. Encaged in a golden cage, you are not the same bird flying in the sky in freedom; you are just a showpiece. The moment your freedom dies, you have died too. The moment your wings are cut, you are only nominally alive.

Osho,

Is there some spiritual passion of the heart that needs to drop away, as has the driving force of body passions? There is essentially such longing to reach my fellow travelers. When it does not happen – the nearer the friend is to my heart, the more I fall off center into an anguish that feels like something dying in my hands or something left unborn.

Seeing paradise lost, the dream of growing and soaring up together with another – is that my soul's agony to go astray?

All passion is of the body; there is no passion of the heart. Yes, there is compassion of the heart and there is a tremendous difference between the two. Passion is lust and ugly; compassion is love, beautiful, spiritual. But people go on living in fallacies, they go on thinking their body lust is their love. The mind knows nothing of love because it does not appear in the curriculum of any university. It is not part of mathematics, physics, chemistry, geography. Love simply does not exist for the mind. Love exists in the heart.

But you never reach the heart, you remain in the body, dominated by the mind. The body has only lust; it is nothing spiritual, it is very earthly. It is simply a biological strategy to continue the species, to create children.

The people of the head need to descend from the mind into the heart because all our social systems and educational programs are based on a very cunning device: they avoid the heart. Don't bring the heart because there is no place in any subject, there is no department in any university where love is being taught. On the contrary, every effort is made so that your whole energy moves into the head and remains closed there. It never blossoms like a flower.

Everyone has a heart, and certainly a right education will be divided into three parts: education for the body, because the body has a mystery of its own; education for the mind, because the mind has its own great strength as far as inquiry about objects is concerned; education for the heart, for love – which is completely denied. If you ask a physician or a doctor where the heart is, he will say, "There is no heart, there is only lungs and a pumping station for blood, for purifying blood; it has nothing to do with love, music, poetry."

And the physicians are not deceiving you, they are themselves deceived. The heart which the mystics have been talking about is not the pumping station. The lungs are part of the body, but just behind the pumping station… An invisible force. All forces are invisible. No one has seen electricity. Have you seen electricity? Perhaps you think you have seen it. You have seen only the expression of electricity.

It happened…

The man who worked the most on the subject of electricity was Thomas Alva Edison. He had gone for a holiday to a small village on the sea beach. They had a small school there, and just by coincidence he saw something was happening and inquired. They said, "The students have made things. It is their annual festival. And people are coming and going to see the things that the students have made."

So having no other work, he walked into the school. The school children had made an electric train, a small train: push the button and the train makes a circuit.

Edison just jokingly asked the student who was showing it, "What is the force that makes the train move?"

The boy said, "Electricity."

Edison said, "Have you seen electricity?"

He said, "I have not seen it, but perhaps my teacher – he is a graduate of science – he may have seen it."

So he called his teacher. The teacher said, "Seen electricity? I have not seen electricity. I have seen only the effects of electricity: it can become light, it can drive engines, it can do many mechanical things, but what is it? Perhaps our principal who is a postgraduate in science may have seen it."

The principal was called. And the principal said, "Forgive me, no one has ever asked. Energies cannot be seen. You can see only their effects."

Edison laughed. He said, "Don't be worried. Don't look so worried. My name is Thomas Alva Edison."

They said, "You are Edison? You have created so many electrical devices and you are asking this question?"

He said, "I am asking because I myself have not seen what electricity is."

Love is not part of your body system. Love is a hidden source in the body of pure energy which can make anyone rejoice, can quench the thirst. And unless your energy called the heart, blossoms, you are not perfectly alive, you are just a robot.

The mind is a computer. Just the other day I received the news that in Japan for fifteen years they have been keeping the head of a monkey – without the body – wired with all kinds of nourishment that the brain needs. And because they have been successful, now they are going to try on human beings. Just your head is enough; then mechanical lungs and mechanical wiring, blood that is needed for your brain – reaching through the wires, being purified by the mechanical lungs and you will be perfectly alive.

And the strangest thing is that you will feel love, you will feel emotions, you will be angry if someone insults you. You will talk, you will answer questions which have been taught to you before this calamity, this scientific calamity happened to you.

This whole body has to be understood as a robot. Behind it is another body referred to in the esoteric schools as the astral body. The heart is part of the astral body. That's why love is such a nourishment. That's why love makes you so alive. That's why love gives your legs a dance – and if you allow it to fill your robot, for the first time you will feel what life is. And behind the astral body is your real being, your immortal body.

You are asking if you have "…some spiritual passion of the heart that needs to drop away." Don't jump ahead of yourself. All that you have to do is to drop out of your mind. And that does not mean that you have to cut your head off. That simply means you need to change the route of the energy that you are continuously giving to the mind, and divert it toward the astral, the heart.

The heart has no passion, but it has tremendous compassion. I am using the word *compassion* because *love* has been contaminated. People have used the word *love* almost synonymously with *lust*. Just say to someone, "I love you," and there will be no problem. But if you say, "I lust for you," there is going to be trouble. Then be prepared for the police station: "This man is dangerous."

In fact, when you say, "I love you," that's what you are saying. But a little homework is needed before you reach the bedroom, before lust can be accepted – it must not be announced! The very word seems to be somehow animalistic. Animals have lust – and you are human beings. But the reality is that all the introductions, the parties, the meeting on the beach, the gardens, the presents, ultimately lead you to the animal.

Without all this introduction, if you are a very direct man, you will go to jail: "Why bother about this ice cream? Just let us do the thing." No, that is not human. Humanity has to be a little sophisticated: first hold the hand, first talk about beautiful things, poetry and music. All the time you are thinking of something else, but you have to create this camouflage. To be straightforward would mean going to jail.

The heart has been completely ignored; society does not need it. It is the need of the individual and society does not need even individuals, it needs only personalities. It needs bogus people, obedient, always ready to follow an order, always ready to be enslaved.

A man of heart is a man in revolt – revolt against anything that is ugly, revolt against anything that is simply mechanical. Society does not want individuals because they will create trouble. So from very childhood, it starts destroying individuality. And the best way to destroy the individuality is to let them pass around the heart, not through the heart. All our educational systems are managed in such a way so that you can move without ever being aware that you have a heart. I am using the word *compassion* because *love* has become mechanical. Everyone is "loving" – it has lost its depth.

A woman said to her husband when the hero in the movie kissed the heroine very lovingly, very romantically, "Look, you never do that to me."

The man said, "That is only a film, it is not reality. And moreover, who knows whether that man is married to someone else or that woman is married to someone else. No one is certain about these actors – and anyway, it is all acting. Do you want me to act?"

The woman said, "I know the woman personally. She is married to the hero in actual life."

The man said, "My God, then the hero is really an actor. To be so loving and so romantic to your own wife… I cannot do it. It is too difficult."

The moment you remember that it is your own wife and what are you doing… It looks as if you are doing something nasty. The movies, the films, television, the poets and literature have all reduced and contaminated the word *love* – polluted it and destroyed its beauty. That's why I am saying the heart has compassion. Compassion is the purest love which gives and asks nothing in return. You don't have to renounce it. You have to go deeper into it. You have to become it. Because by becoming it, you will come closer to your being.

Mendel Kravitz opens a new business and wants an international staff. So he hires Klaus, a German, Paddy, the Irishman, and Wu, a Chinese.

"Klaus," says Mendel, "I'm putting you in charge of production. I want you to make things efficient around here. Paddy, you will be in charge of personnel. Make sure the morale stays good. Wu," he says to the Chinese, "I am putting you in charge of supplies."

A couple of weeks later, Mendel is touring the business and finds Klaus and Paddy together.

"Everything is going smoothly?"

"Ya!" says Klaus. "Production is up double."

"Everyone's getting on great," says Paddy. "People are all liking each other."

"How is Wu doing in supplies?" asks Mendel.

But neither of them have seen Wu since the first day. Mendel starts to get worried and looks all through the factory.

As he is walking between some large stacks of boxes, suddenly Wu leaps out and shouts, "*Suplise*!"

It has been a good morning. You listened silently to things which are very essential to your spiritual growth, and you laughed heartily. More than that is not needed: a good laughter and a deep silence together are enough to transform you. You are on the right path, unless you get stuck somewhere. The path is simple and easy, and all that it needs is a let-go – either in silence or in laughter, either in music or in dance. Remember the most spiritual words in existence are *let-go*.

6

To Be Free, Your Beliefs Must Be Destroyed

Osho,
Many of your sannyasins, some of whom have been with you for many years, have left you to follow the teachings of channels or psychic clairvoyants.

I have visited some of these people, partly out of curiosity and partly through the recommendation of friends, and have found nothing that comes even close to the love and benediction in being with you.

Osho, what is the attraction to these dead masters or so-called entities when you are here, a living enlightened master?

The question you have raised has many layers and a simple answer won't be justified. But I would like to go into it as deeply as possible because it is something of much concern to each of you.

I am not in any way a bondage. I do not create a program in you, a belief system. I don't ask you to surrender; in fact, I don't ask anything from you. All I want is to help you to be yourself. This is one of the reasons why a few are bound to leave me because they are in search of someone who can take responsibility for them. But they are not aware that the moment you lose your responsibility you also lose your freedom. The moment you surrender to anyone, dead or alive, you destroy yourself – you commit suicide as far as your individuality is concerned.

But there are people who will feel much relief; relief in being free of responsibilities. Someone has taken the burden on himself; he is your savior. Now it is easier for you just to believe in him. There is nothing easier in the world than belief, because you don't have to do anything at all.

With me there is no possibility of any belief. I will destroy all your beliefs so that you can be a freedom, a bird on the wing in the open sky. But very few people are in search of freedom. Those who are not in search of freedom are bound to leave me; it is natural. And I don't prevent anyone because even to interfere is against my approach and my respect for individual dignity.

Secondly, there are many who are not interested in understanding existence, in understanding their own being. But like small children, they are very much interested in puzzles, esoteric ideologies, occult phenomena. Anything that is irrational, illogical does not mean that it is truth, does not mean that it is going to give you your innermost being and its treasure. There are thousands of esoteric schools, theologies, theosophies and they are very interesting in a way – but they are interesting because you are retarded! They look very magical and there are people who exploit your retardedness.

The founder of the Theosophical movement, Madame Blavatsky, was found guilty of strange kinds of things; you cannot call them crimes, you can simply call them fraud. She had a servant named Damodar. While she was traveling by train she would be in first class and Damodar would be in third class. Suddenly Damodar would fall flat on the floor of the compartment, unconscious, foaming.

Naturally, the train was stopped, people gathered and then Madame Blavatsky would come and do some abracadabra. Damodar would immediately open his eyes and everyone would see "What a tremendously spiritual powerful woman." And no one knew that he was her servant and that was his only job. Finally, in a court case Damodar was forced to admit that he had played a part in many kinds of fraud.

Beautiful letters still exist that were written by Blavatsky herself. She made a special ceiling… Her followers would sit in Adyar, Madras, with closed eyes in the dark night. And with no light because divine masters don't want to be seen. Damodar would be hiding and would slip a letter down from the ceiling. A light would be brought in… The letter was coming from Master K. H.

Those are beautiful letters; they are now collected and published. There was no need… The letters themselves are significant, but this way they became very mystical. Now the followers were not just reading letters written by human hands, but by a great master who is the guide of all those who are in search of the ultimate truth.

I have been to the place in Adyar from where those letters have been dropped, and the gullibility of human beings is strange. The writing is clearly human, the paper is material, the ink is material, and looked at closely, anyone could have figured that it is the writing of Blavatsky herself and no one else. But when you want to believe you become blind. When you want to believe you don't listen to any rationality, your own reason; it just feels good to believe.

Blavatsky created one of the greatest esoteric schools in the world: the Theosophical movement. And the reasons people believed in that movement were neither rational nor mystical, nor based on spiritual experience. In a certain way they were cunning, fraudulent, but very sufficing, very satisfying, very gratifying.

Just today one of my secretaries, Anando, informed me that a nice French gentleman is here. Nothing is wrong with the person, he just believes that he can heal spiritually. And there are thousands of "spiritual healers" in the world. If they are really true there should be no need of any hospitals. Naturally, because he does not understand much English – he is French – all the French sannyasins immediately gathered around him and he talked about me.

These are the ways people are tricked. First he said, "Your master has the biggest spiritual aura that I have seen in my lifetime." Naturally you feel very gratified: your master has the biggest aura. He has to have because he is *your* master, he is no ordinary master!

He must have heard – it is all over the world in every newspaper, in every language – that I have been poisoned in America, and the poison has affected my body badly. So he said, "Your master's aura is the biggest, but on his left hand, just on the top of the left hand there is a black hole." Now, there he missed! The problem is with my right hand, not with my left hand! And the poison cannot create black holes. But just this mistake reveals what he was trying to do. Everyone knows that I walk like a drunkard. Now, nothing can be done about it; I have been walking that way my whole life. I am a man who is utterly drunk.

So he said, "His aura is great, but the energy of the aura is not flowing into his legs. I can heal him and I have come here to heal him."

Naturally my people would think that this is good if someone has come from France, from far away to heal me. But I receive dozens of letters from this corner or that corner of the world saying that their desire is to heal me. Why this desire? They don't want to learn something here; they don't want to heal themselves here. The simple arithmetic is that if I allow anyone to heal me then all of you will naturally think that the greatest healer has come. These people are not necessarily cunning, are not necessarily deceptive; they may authentically believe that they are capable of healing.

Just a few days ago, Doctor Shyam Singha came from London. He was once my disciple, but because he was doing things which are absolutely against humanity, sincerity, truth – he was exploiting people in my name – I had to expel him from the sannyas movement. He was moving around the world, telling sannyasins that he can do this, he can do that. And all that he can do is to manage to take as much money from people as possible. He was exploiting on every excuse in the name of healing: in the name of opening your chakras, in the name of raising your kundalini, in the name of cleansing your past life and its evil effects!

When so many people reported that he was exploiting simple people, I had to debar him and announce in the papers that he does not belong to the sannyas movement. And I had to inform him that he cannot enter the campus. He has been here twice, but was turned away from the gate; he was not allowed in. He must have seen the news that I have been poisoned as a great opportunity.

No one knows who has made him a doctor! He does not have any qualifications for it – but there are many doctors in the world and they go on healing people, homeopathically, naturopathically, spiritually… The names are many but the business is the same.

So he wrote a letter asking if he can come and heal me; if I would simply send my signature on my letterhead so that no one prevents him at the gate and he is allowed in the campus.

I am not sick, and I don't need any healing. The poison was given to me two years ago. And because it has not been able to kill me, the man who was responsible for prosecuting me has been fired from his job as Attorney General of Oregon. He has been fired because he could neither manage thirty to forty years of jail punishment for me, nor a good dose of poison to kill me, nor to put a bomb in my room and destroy me.

One of my attorneys was here just a few days ago. He said, "That poor government attorney tried hard; he did his best." But I have not committed any crime – all is fiction. He had a list of thirty-four crimes that I was supposed to have committed. It would have needed at least one thousand years in jail.

"That long," I said, "I would not be able to live! You should consider the fact: one thousand years of jail? It is hilarious; just think of something practical. The whole list is an absolute lie."

They could not give me the poison in such a dose that I would have died in the jail. It became clear from the statement of the United

States Attorney General Ed Meese that they did not want to make me a martyr. They were afraid that if I were to die, then another Christianity will be born; then another religion, another fanatic fundamentalist group of people will gather in sympathy with me.

The court ordered that I leave the court and go to the airport immediately. My airplane was waiting; I had to leave immediately. Perhaps they were afraid that if I died before leaving, the sympathy of the whole world would be with me, and against Ronald Reagan and his company. They could not give the whole dose, out of fear; otherwise one dies within twelve hours.

That's what the experts from England have informed me; they have presumed that the poison given to me was thallium. It kills within twelve hours, but if given in small doses it takes time. It may kill within six months, but now even that time has passed. The poison is out of my system.

Existence cannot be so cruel! There is no black hole on the left hand. So please, next time when you talk, remember: my right hand has some pain, but that too is not something that needs spiritual healing. It is a physical thing and it needs physical healing; no spiritual healing is needed. And as far as the spirit is concerned, it is never sick; it is intrinsically healthy and whole. It is the body which is bound to become sick and someday old and someday it dies. But there have been spiritualists of all kinds who don't understand that there is an immense difference between spirituality and physical existence.

I have heard about a young man whose father was a member of a Christian Science group.

In England there has been a very influential group and in America also: Christian Science. The young man was asked, "What is the problem, your father has not been seen for three weeks?" They were meeting every Sunday.

The young man said, "It is difficult; he is very sick."

The old man said, "Nonsense, sickness is only a belief, imagination! And he is an old member of our group. We don't believe in sickness, just remind him, 'You are not sick!'"

He said, "I will remind him."

After two weeks they met again. The old man said, "What happened, he has not come?"

The young man said, "What can I do? Now he believes he is dead."

The body has to become sick, the body has to become dead also. One should think of experiencing the spiritual, the eternal, the immortal. One should not waste time on such stupid ideologies, which have been prevalent all over the world.

There are people, simple people, who immediately think that miracles can happen. And the greatest problem is that if you are very trusting something can happen. Seventy percent of sicknesses are illusory; they are only because you believe you are sick. That's why seventy percent of people are helped by any kind of medical approach other than allopathy. Even simple sugar pills work, the scientific name of which is homeopathy.

I used to live next to a Bengali fellow…

He was a great homeopath, but he himself used to go to the hospital when he was sick.

I asked him, "What is the matter? You are such a great homeopath, you have treated so many people." And it is true, he had.

He said, "I have treated them, but I cannot treat myself; I know they are sugar pills. Someone who does not know and believes in me may be helped."

And it has been found that seventy percent of people are helped by any kind of medical approach, except a very few stubborn people who are determined not to be healed whatever happens. They torture doctors, they torture allopaths, they torture homeopaths, they torture spiritual healers, they torture everyone. They are very inventive; they go on finding new diseases, even diseases for which the doctors don't know the name.

Because of this homeopathic doctor, I used to sit in his dispensary. A woman used to come almost every day, and the moment the woman would come, he would say, "My God, this woman is not going to die. She has no disease, she is perfectly healthy, but she goes on reading medical periodicals and finds new diseases. Even I don't know… When she tells me that this kind of disease is happening to her, then I know. But it makes no difference because I have only one medicine whatever the disease."

There was a doctor who was tired of a young man because every day he was standing there. He was poor, he could not pay, and the doctor had tried in every way to convince him, "You are perfectly healthy."

But every day something new. One day it is stomachache, one day it is a headache… The doctor said to me, "What should I do? It seems cruel because he is poor, an orphan, uneducated, unemployed."

I said, "Do one thing: send him to me and just tell him, 'He is a very difficult person; he knows, but he does not want to waste his time, so he is very secretive. But he has the quality that if he touches water, the water can heal anything, but he will not touch it. But remember, remain insistent. Sit in front of his door.'"

He came nearabout nine o'clock in the evening and said, "I am suffering badly from stomachache."

I said, "I am not a doctor and if you are suffering, suffer. Why should you bother me? When I have stomachache, have I ever come to you and tortured you?"

He said, "No, you have never come."

I said, "That makes it simple; just go home."

He said, "It is strange, I have been told by Doctor Barat, the famous doctor, that you have a power, a spiritual power. If you can give me a glass of water and touch the water I will be healed."

I said, "I cannot do that."

He said, "Why can't you do that? I am not asking much. I can bring my own water, I can bring my own glass; you simply touch…!"

I said, "I cannot touch it at all! Why should I lose my spiritual power?"

He said, "Now you have accepted that you have spiritual power."

He ran home and brought a big bottle full of water.

I said, "I am not going to do it because a stomachache is not something immortal, it will disappear sometime. It will teach you patience, suffering, acceptance, and it will give you great qualities. I cannot disturb your life."

He said, "You seem to be a very hard person. Can't you just touch my bottle?"

I said, "I cannot touch it."

Twelve o'clock in the night… I used to live with my aunt; she was listening from her room. Finally, she came out and said, "You are also almost insane! If he wants it to be touched, just touch the water and get rid of him. Wasting time for three hours. I have been listening – there is a limit!"

I said, "No one can convince me, simply go and sleep!"

She said, "I cannot sleep because this man is sitting there."

The man said, "This is a good opportunity." He touched the feet of my aunt and said, "Just help me, he seems to have no heart at all. Three hours and I am suffering so much from stomachache."

I said, "Listen, I can touch it, but you have to promise me not to tell anyone because I don't want a queue the whole day, I have to do something else too."

He said, "I promise, absolutely promise: in the name of God I will never tell anyone."

I touched his bottle. He immediately drank the whole bottle and he said, "My God, I have never felt so high, not only is the stomach completely cured, other small diseases are gone, and I feel so much power."

I said, "Remember the promise."

He said, "Just one thing, my mother is very sick."

I said, "You have started."

He said, "No, I will not tell anyone, I will just fill the same bottle."

I said, "You can do that, but don't bring anyone here and don't bring your bottle again! Once I have touched it, that's all!"

And you will be surprised to know that he became a healer instead of being a crackpot hypochondriac. He would fill the same bottle with new water. But because I had touched the bottle, even though the water went on changing, he was curing everyone. People started going to his home from faraway villages, and he enjoyed it very much. He came to thank me.

I said, "You should not come here."

He said, "No, I have not come to ask anything, but just to tell you that the bottle is working."

I said, "Cure as many people as possible."

After many years I passed by that village again. By that time he had become a very famous healer.

Doctor Barat, a very famous doctor, said to me, "What have you done? Because I used to have migraine once in a while and I had to ask that stupid boy, 'Will you give me some water from your bottle?' And it is a miracle – the migraine disappeared."

I said, "It is spiritual healing, but never tell anyone about it."

He said, "But I had never thought that you really have that power. I was just joking and just wanted to get rid of that fellow. And now whenever I have any trouble, instead of my own medicines, I send my car to find that boy. He comes in the car with the bottle – just a cup of water and it works!"

I said, "It has to work. Spiritual power."

The question is if you trust, then anything… Only thirty percent of diseases cannot be cured by your trust. They are really diseases; they need right diagnosis and right treatment. I don't want any kind of stupidity here. I have heard of a few people who have already started feeling great well-being, experiencing "spaces that they have never known." My librarian, Kavisho… Because she is French she has almost become the leader of other sick people.

I warn you: just forget all about this "great space." Don't corrupt my simple people. And you yourself, I don't think that you are a cunning person; you believe that you have spiritual powers, but you don't even know what meditation is. You have not encountered your own being. So you are simply wasting your time in spiritually curing people. First find yourself. That's exactly what Socrates said: "Healer, first heal thyself." First know thyself.

Unless you know yourself, all is fiction: your sickness, your health, are both meaningless because the reality is the grave. Perhaps someone will die from disease and someone will die with spiritual healing. It makes no difference. The only difference that makes a difference is that when death comes, you are absolutely alert and aware of your immortality in your innermost being. That is the only real healing: real being.

These are just childish games, and because people want something great to happen to them, anyone can convince them: "Look, great things have started happening." Great things happen, but not through anyone else. You have to follow the path absolutely alone. The people who may have come and left must have found that I am not a man to nourish your stupidity in any way. I am not the man to help you believe in great things: in God…

I am not the man to make you believe that your heaven is certain. On the contrary, I start destroying your beliefs and people become afraid and escape. Those who have left will repent because they will have fallen into someone's hands who will satisfy and gratify whatever the desire, but that is all imagination. I am interested only in an authentic experience that makes you free from the mind and from body, not in anything else; anything else does not matter.

Police Officer O'Leary is cruising around in his patrol car one night. He is on the lookout for trouble. He sees two little old ladies in the front seat of a Chevrolet convertible, parked in a used car lot. The car lot is closed so O'Leary drives up alongside the Chevy and asks, "Are you two ladies trying to steal this car?"

"Certainly not," says one of the ladies, "we purchased the car this afternoon."

"Well," says the cop, "why don't you start it up and drive out of here?"

"We don't drive," replies the other little old lady. "And besides, we are waiting. We were told that if we bought a car here we would get screwed."

People are just waiting in used car lots. This is not that kind of place...!

Herschel Goldberg, arriving home from school one day asked his father, Hymie, if he could take their dog Petunia for a walk.

"No," says Hymie, "you can't because she is in heat."

"What? What does 'in heat' mean?" asks Herschel.

"Don't be worried about what it is," replies Hymie. "Anyway I have just thought of a way to fix the situation."

So Hymie goes into the garage and gets a rag, pours some gasoline over it and then wipes Petunia's tail with it.

"Okay," says Hymie, "now you can take her for a walk."

Herschel is delighted and disappears down the street. But an hour later he returns without Petunia.

"What happened?" asks Hymie. "Where is Petunia?"

"Well," replies Herschel, "everything was fine for a while. She was playing with me and my friend Irving when all of a sudden she ran out of gas. So now Irving's dog is pushing her home."

7

Trust, Even When Deceit Is the Law

Osho,
I am leaving the ashram soon to go back to a small Eskimo community, where I currently work and live. I have this longing inside to share with the Inuits the glimpses I have of your vision. My mind says, "Who am I to pretend that I can be of any help to them?" I am afraid of falling into the same trap the Christian missionaries have fallen into with them.

Osho, is this just another mind trip to be aware of and let go?

It is one of the crimes against humanity to be a missionary. A missionary is a hypocrite. I don't want you to be a missionary; I want you to be a mission – and there is a great difference between the two.

The missionary is simply trying to convert the mind of the other person into a certain doctrine, religion. But a man who is simply sharing his heart and his being with no desire to convert is not a missionary, he is a mission. He is a living flame which can put the whole community in which you live afire. And particularly simple people like the Eskimos don't need to be converted, they need to be loved. They need more light to be brought into their lives, more understanding. Strangely, when you go to the simple people like Eskimos, you are not only sharing yourself, you are also learning much from them – much that humanity has forgotten.

The ancient people who are still ancient, who have not entered the contemporary world, have much to give you. But the missionary is not there to learn anything, only to teach. Learning is insulting to him; he is a man of knowledge. He knows more than the Eskimos. But there are dimensions which the poor, the simple, the primitive people know, of which you have become completely unaware. There are communities in the world still…

One community deep in the Himalayan part of Burma has never known any war in its whole history. It is impossible for them to fight, but they are primitive; they are not civilized people. If Sigmund Freud had gone to that small community, he would have been shocked to know that no one dreams. And because no one is repressed, there is nothing to dream.

First you have to repress things which are important and natural; you have to be against the natural and the instinctive, only then can you create dreams. That which has not been lived in your waking hours will have to be lived in your sleeping time. But if you are living totally, without repressing anything, then certainly you will not have any dreams. Your sleep will be a tremendous silence.

Missionaries have reached that community too. They could not believe that those people don't dream: "Perhaps they are lying or perhaps their dreams are so deep that they forget completely when they wake up in the morning." But deep research has shown – and there are very simple methods to know whether a person is dreaming or not – that those people do not dream.

Once in a while if someone has dreamed, they have a strange ritual: when someone dreams he goes to his elders and tells them his dream. Sigmund Freud, Adler, Jung should forget that they are the founders of psychoanalysis. These people have practiced psychoanalysis for thousands of years not knowing that it is psychoanalysis. And it is not done by one person, but by all the elders of the commune.

The person relates his dream and the elders discuss the meaning of the dream. They are simple people; their dreams are simple.

If someone has dreamed that he has beaten a young man of the community in his dream, the elders decide, "You should go to the young man with sweets and flowers to ask his forgiveness, because you have beaten him in the dream."

You will laugh at the whole thing because what happened in the dream has nothing to do with the young man. But those people are right. They may look illogical, but they are certainly right: you beat someone in your dream only because you are carrying some unexpressed anger. And whether that anger becomes action in reality or in dream does not matter; you have to ask forgiveness for your anger.

For thousands of years they have been doing this kind of psychoanalysis and it has helped the commune tremendously. When you go to someone to ask for forgiveness with flowers, with sweets – they are poor people – and the man says, "There is no need because it was only a dream. You have not beaten me..." But the other man will say, "It does not matter whether I have beaten you or not, but the desire to beat you *must* have been in me and it is enough for me to come to you for forgiveness."

Naturally, these people in Burma have never fought. Our world needs continuous war because people are so full of anger and rage – and they cannot find anybody to express it to. It has been observed that in wartime people look very happy. Strange. People are being killed, thousands of people are being massacred, but there is certainly a very alive breeze. People look less dusty, less dead. If it were possible, they would get up and ask for the morning newspaper even from their graves – so much excitement! Otherwise, life becomes dull.

Those people in Burma have lived without fighting, but that does not mean there is no excitement. There is excitement of a totally different quality: they dance, they love; their dances are beautiful. On full-moon nights the whole commune gathers together and dances almost the whole night. Their songs have become more and more refined by each generation. Their music has become more and more spiritual. There is excitement but that excitement is of love, poetry, sculpture, dance, music; it is not of war.

Certainly, the people who feel excitement in war are not civilized. These people of Burma may be uneducated and they may not know the geography of the world and the history of the world, but in every sense they are far more civilized than the so-called civilized people.

When you go to the Eskimos – I don't know what kind of work you are doing there – I hope that you are not doing some kind of missionary work because that is a crime. Those people are simple and they are living their life beautifully. Don't unnecessarily drag them into Christianity, into the Catholic church. Don't force things on them: celibacy and life-negative attitudes; they will be destroyed.

Just today there was a news item from America. A survey has been made by psychoanalysts, and it has been found that two-thirds of patients like to talk to computers about their problems, their dreams. Only one-third of the people want to talk to human beings – the machine is preferred to man. It was shocking, but it reveals a truth: that it is very difficult to find a man who is nonjudgmental. The machine is at least nonjudgmental. Whatever you say it will listen, it will record; it will not condemn you even by its gesture. But to talk to a man about anything, it is impossible not to come across his prejudices.

Everyone has judgment, and when people have judgments they lose their innocence. Everyone, in the name of education and civilization has lost his childhood. Those Eskimos are still living in man's past ages, in mankind's childhood. If you can learn something from their innocence, learn. And if you can share something from your meditation and from your love, share.

Don't take your Bibles to them; take your guitars. Don't take your principles and theologies; take your dances. And don't only be a teacher but be a learner. Don't think yourself superior to those poor primitive people. If you can do this much and not feel superior, then you can only learn something from them. There is so much to learn from every direction if you are available – particularly from very primitive people because they are still uncorrupted by the priests, by the politicians. They are as simple as the animals, as the birds.

You are going into a beautiful situation, but remember not to become a missionary. Share me but don't convert. Transpire but don't convert. Let them become acquainted with the laughter, the silence, the meditation that is happening here. But remember that it is not a religion and we are not here to destroy someone's dignity and make him part of a cult. You will have to be very aware, because old habits die hard.

Our education, our society, our civilization, everything has penetrated deep in our minds knowingly or unknowingly. Whenever you come across someone who is innocent, childlike, you immediately jump and try to convert him in the name of giving him maturity – and there are thousands of beautiful names. But in fact what you are trying to do is destroy the person, his individuality, and impose your own personality on him. It is an ego trip. So unless you are alert and aware of your own mind, it is very difficult not to be a missionary.

Ronald Reagan is visiting India and is met at the airport by Rajiv Gandhi. As they are driving away in Rajiv's limousine, Reagan notices a lot of people shitting by the side of the road. He is disgusted and asks Rajiv if this is common practice in India. Rajiv is very embarrassed and replies that he is trying to educate the people to use a proper toilet, but it will take time for the program to be one hundred percent effective.

On a return visit, Reagan and Gandhi are driving through Washington to the White House when Rajiv notices a man shitting in the street. He points this out with some satisfaction to Reagan. The president is furious and orders his secret service agents to arrest the man. A few minutes later the agent returns.

"Well," snaps Ronald Reagan, "did you arrest him?"

"No, sir," replies the agent, "we could not."

"Why the hell not?" bellows Reagan.

"Well," says the agent, "it was the Indian ambassador."

Osho,

Is the master coming to the disciple or is it the other way around? I would like to be more open to you; to open my heart to you more, to feel you more, but no effort from my side seems to work out. So I console myself that it's you who will enter me, somewhere, suddenly. Is this an illusion?

It is always the master who comes, but it is not necessarily that he will find the disciple's heart open. Most often it is closed. So your question is really not a question but two sides of the same coin. The master comes but the disciple has to be ready to receive, the disciple has to be open. If you are hoping that, whether you are open or not the master will come suddenly, somehow, you are hoping in vain. Even if he comes he will have to return. You will not give way; you will shut your door and lock it from inside.

People are very afraid of opening their hearts. The fear has reasons rooted in our upbringing, because whenever we have opened our hearts, we have been punished or we have been exploited or been deceived. Naturally, we have learned to be on the defensive, to keep the heart closed so no one can deceive us, no one can come close to us. It is a defense measure. And in a society where everyone is competitive, it is natural to defend yourself; otherwise you will be exploited. Someone is going to step on you and go beyond you, use you, misuse you in all possible ways.

There is a place in India; it is one of the biggest railway junctions. I was waiting in my compartment; the train would leave in one hour. It was waiting for some other trains to come.

A man, a beggar, came to me. Seeing me alone he said, "My father has died. I need some help."

I gave him one rupee and told him, "If someone else dies, you can come back. I am here for at least one hour."

He looked at me very surprised, but he could not resist either. After ten minutes he came, "You were right. My mother died."

I said, "I knew. I knew someone else would die. In these coming sixty minutes, almost your whole family is going to die!"

He said, "Why are you saying that?"

I said, "I had nothing to do… What is going to happen is going to happen; I am going to lose at least ten rupees." I gave him another rupee.

He looked again and again at me thinking, "What kind of man is this?"

I said, "Listen. Rather than coming again and again, take all of these ten rupees. Let them all be dead!"

He said, "It is not right to say that."

I said, "But you will have to come."

He said, "That's true. I cannot resist. But you are a strange man. My whole life I have been a beggar. Not my whole life, but as long as I remember. My family have been beggars for generations. My father was a beggar, my grandfather was a great beggar – it is just hereditary – but we have never met such a man; you are unbelievable!

"In the first place, people don't give anything. They simply say, 'Go away! Ask someone else. We have nothing to do with your father. If he has died, he has died. Why should we be bothered?' And you are killing my whole family, and you are giving me the rupees in advance!"

I said, "Go and look at your family. If someone is still alive, come back because all are going to die. Sometimes a few people die one time, two times, three times… People are unbelievable; for example, by the time you are back here your father may have become alive again."

He said, "Are you mad? My father alive? He is dead."

I said, "He will become alive. All will become alive. Just go home."

He said, "If you say, I will go and see."

I said, "Go and see and come back because they will die any moment – if not today then tomorrow – and I will not be here."

After a few minutes he came with those ten rupees and said, "Take these back."

I said, "Why? Have they all become alive?"

He said, "Don't humiliate me! They have always been alive. No one has died. As far as begging is concerned, every day I have to say that someone has died. But for the first time the whole family has died – and in advance! No, I cannot deceive you. You are a very simple person."

I said, "I am not a simple person. I am just enjoying. Ten rupees are not much of a problem…to kill your whole family. If you have some relatives…"

He said, "You want to kill my relatives too?"

I said, "Anyone! Relatives, neighbors – if they are not dead I will give you in advance. Just go and have a look."

He said, "You are mad and I cannot cheat a mad person. I am not that bad. I cheat cunning people but not a man like you. You are too ready to be cheated."

I said, "If you want, I can come with you to count how many have died because you may not be able to count that many. How many can you count? How well educated are you?"

He said, "That is true. I can't count much."

I said, "I can come with you. This train cannot leave without me. The driver is my friend; I will tell him, 'Wait. Let me first go to this man's house and see how many people have died and how many are going to die.' In fact, in this world, whoever is born is going to die, so why not take the advance?"

He sat on the floor in the compartment with tears in his eyes. He said, "I have never returned money to anyone; I am returning ten rupees. And you are ready to come with me to count whether they are dead or alive! You are ready to give an advance for those who are alive because they *will* die!"

I said, "One thing is certain; don't take ten rupees if you are feeling hurt. Take at least one – for you!"

He said, "But I am alive."

I said, "You are alive; everyone is alive – but you *will* die! And at that time it will be difficult for me to find out who you are, where you live, why you lived and why you have died; too many troublesome problems. Just take one rupee and leave me."

He said, "No, I cannot take anything from you. The train is full of people. I will manage from all those cheats. They are cheating others so there is no problem in cheating them. But it hurts to cheat you, although I am a beggar. Even though I am a beggar, I have a certain sense of humanity."

I said, "It is up to you, but I am here for one hour. If someone really dies, you can come without any fear. These ten rupees are yours, deposited with me. I will return them with interest. But come within one hour. After that I will be gone. But I often come on this route, and I am easily recognizable."

He said, "That's right, because I can neither forget you, nor forgive you!"

I said, "Why can you not forgive me?"

He said, "You tricked me. You have taken your ten rupees back!"

This whole world is full of people… I have a friend who used to live with me…

He was a professor, but he never liked doing any kind of teaching because he could never manage to wake up early to get ready to reach the class in time. Every day it was a problem. The principal would call and the vice-chancellor would call, and finally he resigned.

He said, "This is all nonsense. I can manage without it."

I said, "How are you going to manage?" – because he used to live with me.

He said, "First, I will live with *you*!"

I said, "This is great! And when you become bored, tired, because I don't want to give you any more money?"

He said, "I will move. I have many friends all over the country." And it is true. He had many friends. He had qualities to create friends: he was a very good chess player, a very good conversationalist, very good in many games, very handsome. Falling in love, falling out of love was very easy for him.

I said, "But how long?"

He said, "How long? I don't think I am going to live more than seventy years. For seventy years this whole world is available!"

Fifteen years after he left me, he met me in New Delhi. I said, "How are things going?"

He said, "Perfectly well."

He was continually borrowing money. I said to him, "It is strange that you go on borrowing money. What about returning it?"

He said, "Everyone knows that I never return it and there are other people from whom I borrow. I never borrow from the same person again. I use that money to create the atmosphere to borrow more money from someone else!"

Just before I went to America, he came to see me. He was perfectly happy. He said, "In this world where everyone is deceiving everyone else, not to deceive is to be stupid. Just don't deceive the same person again, because that is not right. When there are other new pastures available, why go on harassing one person? I never harass, that's why people give me money because they know that once they have given me money they are free from harassment!"

In this world it is natural to be close-fisted and closed-hearted, continuously afraid that someone is going to cheat you. All kinds of frauds are all around, but one thing has to be understood: if you can trust – even in this world where deceit is the law – your trust will open the doors of the mysteries of existence.

Just a few days ago I talked about the French healer who has come here. Now he is a sannyasin – certainly a man of great understanding. I had criticized all kinds of channeling, healing as frauds. They *are* parasites, but this is true about only ninety-nine percent. There is one percent which is certainly capable of all these things that I condemned, but it is very difficult to find that one percent.

The day I said this, poor Kaveesha's channeling had to stop because people said, "My God, we have been cheated! This Avirbhava as high priestess and Kaveesha, the channel... These people were cheating us!" They were not cheating you. They are simple people, very simple.

You know Avirbhava; every day she screams – not that I am going to hit her or anything. I do nothing to her; I just make the gesture and that's enough. Rather than giving me trouble, she herself shrieks! She knows that if she is not going to shriek, I *am* going to do something! But she is simple and Kaveesha is innocent. They were not representing anyone; they are simply in tune with me.

When you were putting your questions to Kaveesha, she was simply reflecting me, not some dead master. And whenever she found that nothing was coming through, she was simple enough to accept that nothing was coming, no answer was coming; or she would ask me the next day, "Someone asked this question. I waited for your answer, but nothing came so this is their question..."

But people are idiots! Just one day before I criticized the healer, the class was crowded and they were feeling so happy with Kaveesha. And because I criticized, *they* started criticizing – just parrotlike, without ever trying to make any distinction. But the man whom I had criticized did not take it badly as a personal criticism. He understood perfectly that what I am saying is true for ninety-nine percent of the people who are doing it,

I am not against healing, but if I appreciate healing then those ninety-nine percent of the people are also appreciated. So my difficulty is in not sacrificing you to the ninety-nine cheats and frauds. Because the one percent will understand perfectly that he has not been criticized because he has not been cheating. Rather than being against me or going against me, he remained. And he wants to remain here.

Even after my criticism he became a sannyasin. That shows the authenticity of a person. He may have a healing power which healers very rarely have. It is nothing unnatural, but something unique. If a person's aura – the energy that surrounds his body – can surround you, it can heal you without the healer making any effort. I am going to make arrangements for him to have his healing department.

Don't desert poor Kaveesha – she is a rare woman. It is almost impossible for her to cheat you or to deceive you; there is no reason. She knows how to love, and love can heal you. Love can answer your questions, because love in a certain way joins the person with the universal sources of energy. If you are with a master, certainly you are immediately in tune with the master. It is possible to have your heart dance in tune with the master.

When I am speaking, I am nowhere. I am simply allowing existence to speak. And those who love me, if their love becomes so overwhelming that all defense systems are broken, then what I am saying will be said by them too. Every sannyasin finally has to become a master. It has never been tried before. Masters have been very afraid of disciples who can become masters. Those were not real masters. A real master finally transforms all his disciples into masters. The day when you will all be in tune with existence in the same way I am in tune, that will be my day of rejoicing.

Use Kaveesha's energy; it is nothing to do with all kinds of frauds who go on moving around the world. No fraud can stay here! Just a single criticism and he will be lost. And use this new sannyasin's healing energy.

This commune should be aware, alert, loving, open then you can see with clarity whether the other is real or false. You cannot decide it just by intellect; only intuition, only your heart can feel the authentic, the real, the false. The master comes – somewhere, suddenly, sure – but you have to be ready, otherwise his coming will be useless.

This is the world in which you live...

Herbie, the Texan cowboy, is visiting New York for the first time and decides to go to a high-class whorehouse. He pays the fee and is confronted by two doors: one marked Blonde, the other Brunette. He chooses the Blonde, goes through the door and finds two more doors. One says, Big Tits; the other, Little Tits. He chooses Big Tits, goes through and finds two more doors. One says, Fancy Fuck; the other says, Real Screw. He chooses Real Screw, goes through the door and finds himself back on 42nd Street.

Mendel Kravitz, the wealthy American businessman, sends his daughter, Kathy, to Europe to get some culture and maybe meet a rich husband. A few months later she writes and asks her father to send her a book on etiquette. "She must be meeting all the right people," says Mendel to himself. After a few more months she asks Mendel for another book on etiquette.

There is no doubt, thinks Mendel, she is meeting royalty – perhaps Prince Edward. Then two years later, Kathy comes home. Mendel Kravitz meets her at the airport and he is shocked when she arrives carrying a small baby.

"Whose baby?" he asks.

"Mine," replies Kathy.

"And the father?" asks Mendel.

Kathy shakes her head, "I don't know, Papa," she sobs.

"What?" cries Mendel. "I send you two books on etiquette and you don't even know to ask, 'With whom have I the pleasure?'"

8

Back to Nature or Forward to Supernature?

Osho,
In a recent discourse you gave your total support to genetic engineering. I am very much in trouble. For me, such engineering is against nature. Who should be in charge of creating that superman? Often a so-called genius was later regarded as the Devil. And people like Hitler, Stalin or Reagan are only possible because of all the others supporting them.

Genetic engineering is also against my freedom of self-development.

Could you please explain to me this science which bothers me?

Genetic engineering is going to be opposed by almost everyone. But before I say anything on genetic engineering I would like to remind you that every development, every evolutionary step in mankind's life, has been opposed in the beginning as being against nature.

Do you think man should go back to nature? Just see the implications of it: you will be hanging from the trees, jumping from one tree to another. Even if it had been proposed to the monkeys that by genetic engineering a better kind of monkey could be produced, they would have been offended. It would be against nature.

There is a long history of great names who have been against nature, but they are the people who have created all the facilities and all the comforts and the intelligence that you have. And they were vehemently opposed at every nook and corner.

In Russia now they have many fruits which are "against nature." They are a crossbreed, just as by crossbreeding animals, far better animals can be produced than their mothers and fathers. In Russia they have been trying to crossbreed many fruits, trees, animals, and they have been immensely successful. In fact, without your knowing it, you are enjoying so much that is against nature: your railway trains, airplanes, clothes, medicines, health, longer life than your predecessors, can all be called against nature. Even a simple fountain pen is against nature; nature has not produced it.

Leo Tolstoy was one of the most significant thinkers of the West. He was so against the very idea that anything should be produced which is not natural that he became a guru to Mahatma Gandhi. Mahatma Gandhi accepted three masters. On the top of his list was Leo Tolstoy. He was one of the richest men of the world at that time, but lived like a beggar, as if to be a beggar is natural and to have riches is against nature.

Why is it that to be a beggar is to be natural? In fact just the contrary should be the case, because we don't see beggars in animals. Have you ever met any buffalo begging? They are absolutely natural people. They don't use cars and trains – unless you force them. Then too they try to resist in every way.

Mahatma Gandhi's second master was an American philosopher, Emerson, who also "went back to nature." His third master was an Indian, Shrimad Rajchandra. But they were all his masters because they agreed on one point: going back. But where do you draw the line? How far back is natural? All these philosophers of "back to nature" have not been able to give a clear-cut answer, except Mahatma Gandhi. His "back to nature" means when the spinning wheel was invented – but that is not nature. The spinning wheel is as technological as any technology, it is just primitive.

When a man can produce a thousand times more with a small machine, why should he bother with a spinning wheel? It takes eight hours per day to spin if you want enough clothes for the year for one person. So everyone is spinning and everyone will go bananas because you cannot eat, you cannot do anything else; there is no time! You have to sleep too, but just making your clothes will take your whole time! But even clothes are not natural. No one pointed out to Mahatma Gandhi that even clothes are unnatural, because no animal uses clothes except for a few dogs in England – and that too against their will. It is absolutely unnatural to force them to wear clothes. Ladies take them for walks, and you know dogs – every tree creates a tremendous urge in them, which is natural… No one has planted it in their minds. Perhaps they are watering the tree just to help it grow faster. But the lady is embarrassed.

So the first part of your question has to be understood: every new thing is opposed. For example, in India, birth control is opposed by all the religious leaders for the simple reason that it is not natural.

I was very friendly with a *shankaracharya* – who, in Hinduism, is almost similar to the pope – and he was very much against progress, science, technology. I heard that he had a heart attack so I went to see him in the hospital. And I asked him, "What about your philosophy?"

He said, "This is not the time."

I said, "This is the time! What is this cardiogram? Something produced by nature, grown by the trees? What are all these instruments that the doctors are using and the medicines that are being given to you? This is the time for it to be decided whether you are a man of your word or you just enjoy talking. When it comes to yourself then forget all about it."

What is wrong with birth control? The Indian religious leaders have many arguments.

One very famous Hindu leader, Karpatri…

Just by chance we were traveling in the same compartment and we started discussing birth control. He said, "Don't mention that word; it is absolutely against nature. Just look, Rabindranath was the thirteenth child of his parents. If they had used birth control there would not have been any Rabindranath."

I said, "Agreed, that means every father and mother should produce at least thirteen children in search of a Rabindranath?"

In India there are people who have twelve children, thirteen children, fourteen children… But the Rabindranath does not appear.

"So can you give me a guarantee?"

He said, "Why should I give any guarantee for anything in which I'm not involved? It is unnatural to prevent children whom God is sending."

I said, "Who told you that God is sending them? God has been practicing birth control from eternity. He has given birth to only one child, Jesus Christ. If you have learned something from God, learn birth control. He could have produced millions of children – but he is a wise man, it seems. And that too he managed without getting married, via an agent, the Holy Ghost. So the blame goes to the Holy Ghost; God is completely out of it. But the Holy Ghost seems to have learned birth control because in the two thousand years since Jesus Christ, he has not tried again."

He said, "You always bring strange arguments. I am not a Christian and I don't know the Bible or the Christian God."

I asked him, "Then tell me about the Hindu gods. How many children has Shiva produced – two? That's what the Indian government has been saying, 'Don't produce more than two!' Brahma has not produced any, being wiser!"

He said, "I have never thought about it."

I said, "You don't understand anything of the whole process of the birth of a child. One million people die, then one child is born – and that too once in a while. Every time you make love you don't create children, otherwise every woman would be carrying so many pregnancies together. Once she is pregnant then you cannot do anything to make her more pregnant; the door is closed. People come and knock – and not a small crowd. In each love affair, loving a woman, millions of male sperms rush to knock on the doors. But if the doors are closed, their life span is only a few hours. So much violence is happening."

You will be surprised that Mahavira, who was teaching nonviolence – his concern about celibacy was not the concern as it is of other religions. His concern was that in each love act you kill millions of people without even knowing it! Just think of a man, normally… It seems in his whole life he can kill four hundred million people. All Adolf Hitlers and others don't matter; even normal people are killing! So birth control will not make much difference. In one million, if one more is added, it will not make much difference.

I told Karpatri a story…

A very famous noble emperor, Akbar, was bringing swans from the Himalayas. It The lake is called Mansarovar; it must be the highest point where a lake exists of the purest water. And strangely, the biggest and the whitest swans live in Mansarovar. They come to India when it becomes so cold. For nine months it is frozen: you can drive on it without any fear; it is solid rock. For only three months it melts. So for three months those swans go back to Mansarovar. Akbar had seen those swans – and they were so beautiful.

He said, "Make a beautiful marble lake in my garden. Make every arrangement so that those swans don't have to go to Mansarovar again."

The lake was made and it was the season when the swans would be coming soon. He said, "It is not an ordinary lake. It is a royal reception, so inform the whole capital that tomorrow morning they fill the whole lake with milk. Bring as much as they can, at least one bucket each person."

Birbal, his friend and adviser, laughed.

He said, "Why are you laughing?"

He said, "In the morning you will see why I'm laughing. I know what is going to happen!"

And in the morning it really happened… Everyone thought, "Early, in the darkness before the sun rises, just one bucket of water will be lost in the millions of buckets of milk. Who will be able to figure it out? And anyway, I cannot be caught because it is very difficult to see the difference between water and milk when they are mixed with each other."

But human minds think in the same way. Everyone had the same idea, "Why waste a bucket of milk?" A few were so cunning they even went without water, just buckets, so that everyone would know they were going, and in the dark they would pour nothing and just come back home.

When the sun was rising, the king and Birbal came to see, because it must be a scene: a lake of pure milk. There was no lake of pure milk; it was just water. And also, it was not completely filled because many cheated – in fact everyone cheated.

Birbal said, "Now you know why I laughed! When you were saying that, the same idea arose in my mind as that in the millions of people of the capital. It is going to happen that the lake would be of water. If it is *pure* water, thank God!"

I told Karpatri, "I cannot believe in the God which you believe simply for the reason that if he was a little saner, only one sperm, a good sperm, a Rabindranath Tagore, would have been the right thing."

What is the need for so many idiots, the crowd, Adolf Hitler and Ronald Reagan…? These are all God-created; these are not natural. What is natural? And when man creates something, why do you call it unnatural? Man is nothing but an extension of life energy. If you say a flower is natural, then the invention of a man is the flower of his genius.

There is no question of being unnatural about genetics. The fear I can understand. But every new thing creates fear, and once you become accustomed, you completely forget that there was a day when it was a new thing. Do you know that when electricity was invented, no one was ready to have an electric lamp? "Who knows, it may burst and put the whole house on fire." Now you are not afraid.

You will be surprised to know that even at the beginning of this century there was a case in an American court against a man who wanted to make a bathroom attached to his sleeping room. It was a new idea, unnatural! The bathroom and the latrines have to be in the backyard, far away. And Indians are even more natural!

In my childhood I used to insist, "Make a bathroom in the house." Everyone tried to convince me that it is healthy and natural to go out by the side of the river, in the open air, under the open sky, the sun shining: "Why do you insist on an attached bathroom? Are you mad? And the river is flowing..."

But it is the same river as people are defecating all over where they are washing themselves, buffaloes are swimming, washermen are washing their clothes. All kinds of things go on happening by the side of an Indian river. It is a scene worth seeing. And then people take the same water to drink! It is natural, it has always been so, it is not an invention. Remember, genetics creates the same fear: Who will control it? You are not afraid of medicine, of who will control it. You trust the doctor – a doctor you don't know at all – that he will not kill you, that he will not cheat you, that he will not keep you sick as long as possible.

Your question is: "Who is going to control it?" My idea is simple: there should be a world academy of scientists with different departments. Genetics will be the most important department, and scientists should be trusted. There is no other way. Either trust a blind force of biology or at least trust a human being who is a little conscious and understands his responsibility.

You don't ask when you produce children. Who are you trusting? Who is sending all these children? It is a blind biological force, certainly natural, but the scientist is also natural. And whatever he produces is of a far higher value because it is coming from consciousness.

I want to make meditation an absolute for all students, whatever the subject they may be studying, so their awareness becomes more and more clean and clear. And out of that clarity we can create a beautiful world. Those scientists, if they are also meditators, will not create atomic bombs to destroy. They may use atomic energy to move trains so they don't pollute the air. They may use that atomic energy in the factories so they don't pollute the air. Rather than killing man, the same atomic energy can be a tremendous help to save man and his future.

It has been raised again and again that if genetics falls into the hands of men like Ronald Reagan, and he decides what kind of people should be produced, then there is certainly danger. But if Ronald Reagan decides that Charles Darwin and his theories should not be taught in the universities, you don't see the danger. If President Truman decides to drop atom bombs on Hiroshima and Nagasaki, you don't see that politicians should not exist at all, that they are dangerous.

You have to understand the whole implication of my proposition. Meditation should be the central subject for every branch of knowledge, and particularly branches like genetics which are very important, which are going to produce new generations, new men. A new world should be in the hands of very clear, silent, loving people. So don't just think of genetics, also consider that we can add meditation side by side as an essential part of education; otherwise I can understand your difficulty.

Any intelligent person will think, "If genetics is in the hands of Joseph Stalin, Adolf Hitler, Benito Mussolini, what will be the fate of the world?" They will create slaves, idiots. But anyway ninety-nine percent of idiots are already created – just that one percent of freaks prove to be geniuses. And because they are so rare, politicians grab them. They cannot even go to receive a Nobel Prize – just the fear that if they go out of Russia they may never return again. There are many Russian scientists still in Siberia. Their only crime is that they won the Nobel Prize.

So I can see… But that is happening anyway: all the arms are in the hands of these people. And now, nuclear weapons are in their hands and you are not worried, and you are not taking any action on your part; they can destroy the whole world without any difficulty. So what more can they do? But genetics can be freed, in fact the whole of science can be freed from their hands.

All of education should be one worldwide system. There should be only two languages: one, the national language, your mother tongue, and one, English, the international language. It is accidental that English has become the international language, although it is not spoken by more people than other languages. For example, Chinese is spoken by more people than English, but it is confined to China. It cannot become an international language although it is spoken by more people. Spanish is spoken by more people than English, but Spanish cannot become an international language.

It is not a question of more or less, it is a question of having found by coincidence that English has become a worldwide understood language. Teach English as an international language to every child, and his mother tongue, because however you learn the language which is not your mother tongue, something is missing. In your mother tongue there is something poetic, more loving, more juicy. The variety should not be killed.

The international language will remain as a technical language for intercommunication for the whole world. All the armies should be surrendered to the UN, a world government, a real world government. Up to now, two bogus world governments have been in existence. One was the League of Nations, but without any armies it was impotent. And the same is the situation of the UN; it is a little better but not much.

The UN or any name you can give it, a world government, can function only if national governments surrender their armies, their arms. Those who don't surrender their arms and armies should be boycotted by the world government. They cannot stand against the world government; they will have to surrender. It is better to surrender gracefully. They will have their government, they will have their internal guards; a national force which can manage internal affairs, but they will not have nuclear plants and millions of people engaged in the unnecessary exercise of killing man. Man dies automatically… I can't understand: do something that does not happen automatically. Man dies sooner or later, so what is the hurry? If he lives a few more days, let him live!

These millions of people who are in the armies are a sheer wastage; they are not doing anything. Their use only comes into force when there is war; in peace they are of no use. A world government with all the armies will slowly start dissolving armies, making them peaceful citizens, useful, creative, because at least up to now, there is no other known world with which any war can happen. A war of the planets is a faraway possibility. Perhaps after millions of years there may be a possibility of a war between two planets. Right now we don't even know that anyone else exists in the whole existence – most probably we are alone.

A world government, a world language, a world education system – and you will create the barriers which will keep science and its discoveries from being misused. Nations can remain as provinces, so they can enjoy a little politics, but it will be just like you see kings and queens on playing cards: formal. They don't have actual force; they can't do anything. In their own country they can control the telephones, railways and whatever is necessary for the country. The world government can be an umbrella that takes over all the responsibility of defending them. There is no need because there is no one else who is going to attack you, and there is no need of piling up arms, new arms.

The whole scientific energy can move into sciences like genetics. According to me, genetics can be the most important part that science can play because it can create a new kind of human being, healthier; their very program is of no sickness. It can make human life long enough, as long as they want. It can drop not only diseases but old age too. The possibilities are so tremendous that we should put our fear aside, and we should take cautious steps that genetics is not being used against humanity, but for humanity.

Anyway if you don't do anything, then what you are afraid of is going to happen. Genetics cannot be prevented from developing; every government which has enough power is interested in it, so your fear, your paranoia will not help. If cautious efforts are made, and if there are worldwide protests and movements for sciences like genetics not to be put in the hands of nations but into a world community of the scientists themselves, there is much less possibility of any danger.

And always remember, it is going to happen. These "back to nature" people have always been talking; even they themselves don't go back to nature. Mahatma Gandhi was against railway trains. Now, railway trains are such good people – they have never done any harm to anyone! He was against the telephone, he was against the radio, he was against anything that can make you comfortable.

I stayed just a few hours in his ashram. He was dead, fortunately. His son was in charge of the ashram. It was not an ashram but a slum. I told him, "This is a slum. This is not an ashram."

When nighttime came he said to me, "There are many mosquitoes and because we believe in nonviolence we cannot kill them with Flit spray or anything else."

I said, "My God, that means I am going to be eaten by your mosquitoes – then I am not going to stay!"

I asked him, "How do you manage?"

He said, "Mahatma Gandhi found a very natural thing."

That "natural thing" was kerosene oil. Kerosene oil is not a natural thing. It has been discovered; it was not always there. There were times when there was nothing else except wood for the fire. And there were times when there was even no fire; you cannot even believe that fire is an invention, it is not nature.

Mahatma Gandhi forced those poor twenty or thirty people who were in the ashram – mostly widows, because in India… This is the only ashram where you will find neither a widow nor a widower. Once in a while one becomes a widow; that is another thing. Niskriya is sitting behind... Once in a while he becomes a widower. And when a German becomes a widower he stays one for at least a few days – but it does not last long!

...so a few widows, a few old people who had nothing to do, whose families didn't want them – they are of no use – and Gandhi taught them to put kerosene oil on their faces, on their hands, on everything that is uncovered.

I told Ramdas, his son, "Just think about it: these mosquitoes are more intelligent than you. They don't come close to the kerosene that someone has spoiled their food with. How can you sleep with the smell of the kerosene all over the place?"

He said, "I know it looks stupid, but it is part of going back to nature. We cannot use mosquito nets, that is a far too advanced technology" – mosquito nets! – "and we cannot use mosquito nets because what will happen to the poor mosquitoes? So we have found a middle course. If they are daring enough they will rush in and eat their food. If they are cowards; it is up to them, we are not responsible. We have every freedom to paint our faces with anything we want."

Mosquitoes cannot bring a protest march to say that this is not good, this is going against nature. It is going against nature because no animal paints itself with kerosene oil to avoid mosquitoes. Where are you going to draw the line? And what is the need? New challenges should be accepted with all their dangers. Intelligence requires that we should take the challenge and that we make defense measures against the dangers and the risks; otherwise nothing can happen.

Back to nature? No! I say, forward to supernature. It is also natural. Nothing unnatural can happen. Whatever happens is natural. The question is only of whether you are going back or going forward. Go forward!

We can create millions of new fruits, new vegetables. Just that old cabbage...and one goes on eating, one never bothers about whether something should be done about this cabbage. Just those old fruits that Adam ate – apples. In all these years you have not been able to make something better. The mind is so orthodox, so afraid of the new; particularly when it comes to man he becomes very shaky. That's what is making you afraid; otherwise there is no problem. We should take the risk, making every arrangement that nothing goes wrong. Even if it goes wrong, so what? Anyway everything is wrong. One more thing added...

Just now I was talking about Niskriya and here he is with his question; some problem has arisen: "Osho, the other morning I heard you say that the man of the heart rebels against social conditions. To me, flirting is one of these conditionings" – he does not want to flirt! It's strange. Then what will you do with your life? Just eating cabbage? Once in a while search for the cauliflower! It is not flirting; it is just intelligence. I have never thought, even in my imagination, that when I am talking about dropping old conditions, flirting is also part of them. This is how people hear what they want to hear.

He is saying, "I don't want to behave diplomatically when approaching a woman." Then it is better not to approach a woman, because diplomacy is nothing but the art of approaching a woman. The woman will try to escape. Make a thousand and one excuses, but be strong – and never go backward!

But Niskriya is saying, "Even if I decided to flirt – and I tried it – I could not because it is not me!" Niskriya, you cannot do it because it is you! Just seeing you any girl will start running.

I have heard, people are asking in the boutique, "Can we have a picture of Niskriya?" – just to make the children afraid.

Niskriya, do whatever you want to do with your camera, flirt, talk, and mostly that's what you are doing. You don't need a woman. A woman will be a great disturbance. Niskriya is so totally devoted to his art. A twenty-four-hours-a-day cameraman! He has no time for a woman. But just seeing others… This flirting is like an allergy.

He says, "But how can I fulfill my lust – which I always enjoy very much as a natural part of myself – without buying ice cream and telling sweet lies?" It is a difficult question, Niskriya. I will have to talk to some women who look like witches. They may be ready to flirt without ice cream. There are a few. Because you are continually looking through the camera, you don't know who is around. Once in a while just look around. The moment you see a woman who looks like a witch, that is the woman! There is no need to be diplomatic; there is no need for any ice cream. Just go to her and say to her, "I want to take a photograph of you." That will do!

9

Transforming Passion into Compassion

Osho,
As far as my experience reaches, compassion between man and woman seems to be a rare thing. The other morning I heard you say that the mind creates walls and intelligence creates bridges. Osho, can you say something about the way from passion to compassion? Also, for two months now I have given my very best in relating to Niskriya. Have you got a little joke for us?

Your question is almost as ancient as man. It is certainly a very rare phenomenon that passion between man and woman turns into compassion. It turns only into hatred, because it was not passion in the first place. In the very first place you had given a wrong name to something which was not love; hence when that experience which you have called love, passion, disappears, what is left is not compassion, is not friendliness, is not gratitude, but sheer hatred.

The psychologists have started talking about marriage as an intimate hatred. You are together because you fulfill certain biological needs of each other, but otherwise, you are as far away from each other as two stars can be. If love is authentic, if it is not just lust but a spiritual harmony, then certainly this passion is going to bring compassion in your life. And the transformation of passion into compassion is the whole evolution of man into a Gautam Buddha. But you are right that it rarely happens. It could not even happen in the case of Gautam Buddha himself.

Gautam Buddha renounced the world, his kingdom, his palace, his wife whom he thought he had loved so much. After twelve years he came back. Enlightened, he realized that he had not been human to his old father, to his loving wife, and to the one-day-old child. So as he became enlightened, the first thing was to go back to his kingdom and ask forgiveness.

There is a beautiful story…

The moment he initiated his cousin-brother, Ananda, into sannyas – Ananda was older than Gautam Buddha – Ananda said to him, "After initiation I am no more. Your word is my life, your order is my way. Before initiation I am still your elder brother, hence I want three conditions to be promised now because later on I cannot ask anything from you, you will be the master."

Gautam Buddha said, "What are those three things? I don't have anything to give – just this begging bowl."

Ananda said, "I am not asking about things. I am asking about something else. The first condition is that you never send me anywhere away from you to spread the word, the message. Second, I will be with you the whole day, and even during the night I will sleep in the same room where you will be sleeping. And the third thing, if I ask any question or if I bring someone who wants to ask you any question, you will not refuse, you will have to answer."

Gautam Buddha said, "There is no problem in it. It is okay. Get initiated."

But he had not realized that this was going to create many problems. But the worst problem happened when he came back to his home after twelve years. Ananda was with him just like a shadow.

Gautam Buddha said, "I know you have the right to be present with me wherever I go, but you can understand, you have that much intelligence: the woman I loved twelve years ago and left without even telling her that I was going away – obviously she must be very angry. She is from another royal family. She will not show her anger in front of you; that would be against manners, etiquette. I would like to unburden her of all her anger, rage. But it is up to you. I am asking you if you can remain a little behind, just outside the door of the palace. Let me see my wife…"

There was a moment of silence but Ananda understood the situation and allowed Gautam Buddha. And he was right, the wife was very angry.

She said, "My anger is not that you renounced the world. If you wanted to renounce it, I would never have prevented you. My anger is that you did not trust me. You did not say a single word and in the middle of the night you escaped. That has been hurting me. Just as you belong to a warrior race, I am also the daughter of a great warrior. We send our husbands to war with prayers, with garlands, touching their feet; not allowing even a tear to come in the eyes because that may prevent them, may be destructive to their lifestyle and their life pattern.

"If you had said to me that you wanted to renounce the world in search of truth, I would have been dignified. You disrespected me. You damaged my dignity. My anger is not that you left; my anger is that you did not tell me why."

Buddha himself had never thought about it, that the cause of anger would be of not saying to his wife…

And the wife said, "If you had loved me enough, you would have trusted me. I would have sent you with prayers in my heart that you should succeed and be victorious in your search, but you did not allow me the chance."

Gautam Buddha said, "You are right. I have come to ask your forgiveness. Forgive me. What I used to think was love was not love. Now I know what love is. But I wanted to wait until you have unburdened the rage that you must have accumulated day and night in all those twelve years, in your loneliness."

The wife looked at Gautam Buddha with tears in her eyes because she could see that this was not the same man who had left her. He looked the same, but everything had changed: such silence, such presence, such eyes and so much compassion.

She said, "Before I ask to be initiated also – if I cannot be your wife, at least let me be your disciple – your son has been waiting for twelve years and I have been telling him, 'Wait. Someday he will come back.' And you have come, but you have come so transformed – so luminous is your being."

And the son was standing just by her side. She pulled the son in front of Gautam Buddha and said, "Ask your father for your heritage. He has given birth to you – what else has he to fulfill his responsibilities toward you?"

The son asked him and Gautam Buddha said, "I have your heritage." And he gave him his begging bowl and initiated him into sannyas. He said, "There is nothing which is more valuable. I was waiting for this moment, when I would be really capable of loving you. But my love is now so far away from the love that people talk about that I cannot even use the word. I use the word *compassion*. I take you both into my compassion. I have nothing else to give, but I am giving you my very heart and my very experience."

What we call love is not love. And the test comes only when love starts disappearing; then you suddenly see it was not love. You were simply full of lust – a physical, biological attraction. You were not a master of your love, you were only a slave, driven by blind forces of biology. Certainly such kinds of passion cannot become compassion. If you want your love to grow into compassion then first let it be love! You cannot hope. You sow the seeds of marigolds and hope for roses. Your flowers will show what was hidden in the seeds.

You are saying to me that for two months you have been very interested in relating to Niskriya, and ask, "Have you got a little joke for us?" You are a joke unto yourself – why torture poor Niskriya? I have heard that the whole day many women have tortured him. He is a man of a very different quality; he is doing Vipassana. And he had to appoint a secretary to write down the name of all those women and tell them, "When I have time I will see them. Right now I am doing Vipassana."

The Vipassana teacher, Pradeepa, has informed me that his Vipassana is strange. He goes on looking into the camera, but his attention is very clear!

You can torture anyone else – he will be tortured because he has asked for it. And I have told him that there are many witches, but he does not want even to waste time or ice cream. I have given him a simple technique: just take a photograph. Or there is even no need to waste the film; just make an effort as if you are taking the photograph and tell the witch, "You are very photogenic" – and that will do! And you don't have to go very far. A witch is sitting just by your side.

[*And there, a little to Niskriya's right, is the most irresistible creature. Dressed in the flowing black garb of a witch, she turns to Niskriya and begins to caress him.*]

And this is the joke for you...

Hymie Goldberg has a row with his wife, Becky, and goes out drinking. Late that night he stumbles into the local all-night deli and hunches over a bowl of noodle soup. Hymie notices a Chinaman sitting at the next table, and still being in a bad mood, he picks up his bowl of noodles and dumps it over the Chinaman's head.

"This is for Pearl Harbor," says Hymie.

"But I am Chinese, not Japanese," says the man.

"Chinese, Vietnamese, Japanese – what's in a name?" says Hymie.

As Hymie goes to pay his bill, the Chinaman suddenly hits him over the head with a salami sausage. "That," says the Chinaman bowing, "is for sinking the Titanic."

"But," shouts Hymie, "the Titanic was sunk by an iceberg."

"So," says the Chinaman. "Iceberg, Goldberg, Greenberg – what's in a name?"

Komala, you can torture anyone – what's in a name? For two months continuously you have been harassing a silent man, who has no time at all. From one morning till another morning he is concerned only with photography.

When my other photographers have a session they ask me to "somehow avoid Niskriya." I say, "Why?" They say, "If Niskriya comes he does not bother about anyone else. He jumps from this corner to that corner. He does not care that other photographers are also present. He stands in front of someone who is photographing, he crawls on the floor…!"

I also wondered what he was doing when he started crawling one day. He was finding the right angle. He does not bother about anything that people will say. He is such a devoted photographer, you could say he is a born photographer. He has been doing that for his whole life. He came here tired of photography, and finally, he saw such a great opportunity. He forgot all about… Brought all his equipment, his whole studio! He had come here to meditate, but where is the time?

Now these kinds of people – scientists, mathematicians, artists, painters – are not interested in anything else. Their whole interest is in their art. It is possible that once in a while, casually, they may have run out of film or the camera is broken, and then they may think of a woman. But more than that you can't expect.

There is no need to wait two months. Here things happen so fast that people don't even ask each other, "What is your name?" Because what is the point? Tomorrow you will have to ask someone else, "What is your name?" Just do the thing and be on your way. Niskriya has to be saved, but it will be very difficult now.

One witch has even written, "It will be good to open a witches' coven, so anyone who cannot find a woman can come to the witches' coven." I like the idea! It will be an interesting place. In India it has never existed; only England has known witches' covens. They still exist there. They are arising, spreading again.

So I am already looking for a place, and perhaps people like Niskriya can go – just to take photographs! But don't torture him. And just now I have told you that a witch is sitting by his side. She will follow him; she is not going to leave him – camera or no camera. You can have a good look!

[*By this time the glamorous creature's hands are weaving and dancing all around Niskriya.*]

Osho,

Ten years ago I came to your feet and found that unknowingly I was already there. Have I ever been somewhere else in my life or in any life? Isn't it that this thirst of ours has created your smile to show us how existence smiles?

I don't know what the question is or if I have any more questions, for they are quenched day after day by your love and my gratitude. But then why did I say to myself, "Jump now"? And yet, I look back once more to my passion and to its old songs and dreams.

Beloved master, can you really promise me that passion is always transformed into compassion?

My God! Sarjano… Has everyone gone mad? You are also in the same trouble! But your passion is different. It has nothing to do with ordinary, blind natural forces. Your passion is what has brought you to me, which even makes you feel that perhaps you have always been here, or even in other lives too. You are asking, "Isn't it that this thirst of ours has created your smile to show us how existence smiles? I don't know what the question is…" There is no need to know what the question is. Just know the answer. This silence is the answer. This love is the answer. This feeling of a thirst being quenched is the answer. Who cares about the question?

The whole of humanity can be divided into two categories: the majority has questions, and the minority has answers. It is very rare to find a person who has both. I have never come across anyone, living or dead. By the time a person reaches the answer, questions disappear. Questions are just like darkness: when you reach the light, they disappear – not that they are solved, they simply dissolve.

In this quenching of the thirst, day after day, certainly a love and a gratitude arises which says to you "Jump now." But the old, the past, is heavy. To drop it, even though it is meaningless, needs a lion's heart, because one has identified oneself for long, too long, with things which you are not. And now suddenly, you have to drop all those identities of many lives.

It is not only difficult for you, it is difficult for everyone. But however difficult it may be, it is not impossible. If it has not been impossible for me, why should it be impossible for you? If hundreds of mystics around the world have been able to drop the whole past and have never looked back, you are also capable of the same courage – you have just not tried it.

But you go on looking back. You say, "And yet, I look back once more..." How many times have you looked back, and how many more times are you going to look, again and again, "Just once more"? The past that has been is no longer there, and that which is, is herenow. You need to jump without hesitation. A slight hesitation, a split second's hesitation and you have missed it.

But you say, "And yet, I look back once more to my passion and to its old songs and dreams. Osho, can you really promise me that passion is always transformed into compassion?" I have described clearly that if your love is hiding lust, it cannot be transformed into compassion; there is no way. But if you have *really* loved, even without your becoming aware, one day you will find your love has become more and more lovingness, your passion has become more and more compassion. Just the right seed is needed and the roses are going to blossom. But learn to forget and forgive the past.

The present has greater dreams and greater mysteries to open their doors for you; you will not be a loser. The past is gone already; you cannot do anything about it. And if you have dreamed in the past, and if you have sung and danced in the past, what prevents you to sing and dance in the present? If those songs of the past, and the dances and the love affairs of the past are preventing it, then they are not your friends. They are your enemies; they are unnecessary luggage. Drop them without thinking even for a single moment whether to drop or not to drop. Just drop them. The present is the only reality.

If you can make the present your only reality too, you will have greater dreams, greater dances, greater passions, greater love. And then, certainly, a man who lives in the present is capable of moving from love to compassion, from passion to compassion, without difficulty and without effort.

In fact, it is not right to say that he is capable, the right thing will be to say that it happens on its own accord. Just be in the present. It is such a fire that it burns all that is rubbish in you. And it is such an opening that you cannot exhaust the songs and the dances. Once you know the *real* diamonds, you will automatically forget those old stones that you used to think were diamonds. To cling to the past is dangerous because it does not allow you to be in the present, and all that existence has is in the present. The past is only memory and the future is only imagination. The present is the only reality.

All that I mean by meditation is to be in the present – no past, no future. Just let this moment be all, and you have come in contact with the heart of the universe. Great will be the blessings, and unknown treasures will be open to you. And things which are unsayable will be heard by you, will be lived by you.

Now, something religious…

One day while on holiday in Italy, Hymie Goldberg finds himself traveling in a train compartment with Pope the Polack, Mother Teresa and a beautiful young orphan girl. Suddenly the train enters a tunnel and the compartment is plunged into darkness. Then everyone hears the sound of a kiss, followed by a slap across the face. When the train leaves the tunnel, everyone looks at each other in stony silence.

Mother Teresa thinks to herself, "One of these filthy guys kissed my orphan, but she, being a good girl, slapped him."

The girl thinks to herself, "One of these guys tried to kiss me, but in the dark kissed Mother Teresa instead, and she of course slapped him."

Pope the Polack thinks, "That Jewish jerk kissed the girl and she slapped me instead – the bitch!"

And Hymie thinks to himself, "I hope there is another tunnel soon so I can kiss my hand and slap that Polack idiot again!"

10

Reflect but Do Not React

Osho,
More and more, I see how my energy is either going very high or very low, and how sometimes I get very excited, come down again and then feel embarrassed about what happened during this state of excitement.

Do you have a knack to give me for how to watch when the excitement comes, not to get carried away and not to get identified with depression, and how to find my grounding and balance?

Latifa, the mind is almost like the ocean, waves upon waves. Some waves are higher, and between two waves there is a depression. There are two ways to get out of this continuous up and down process. The easiest is when you are ecstatic, that is the moment to be aware. Awareness becomes more difficult when you are in depression, in agony. When you are flowing with joy, blissfulness, that is the moment to be aware, but people do exactly the opposite. When they are happy, who cares about awareness? And when they are in anguish, then certainly they start thinking it is time to be aware and get out of anguish. But no one has ever been able to get out from anguish directly.

First, one has to get out from ecstasy. In the first place, the downs will not come if you can be aware of your joyful moments, and the depression. The door to get out from is ecstasy. So this is the simplest way. Be happy and be aware. Rejoice and be aware. Love and be aware.

Don't put awareness aside saying, "This is a kind of disturbance; I am in such a great ecstasy." Awareness becomes like a disturbance – it is not. It may appear like this in the beginning, but soon you will see it will take your ecstasy to higher peaks. Ultimately awareness and ecstasy become one. Then those downs, those depressive moments, those agonies disappear.

The second way which is unnecessarily followed by a few people is difficult, but your being German, perhaps the second may be right for you. Try to become aware when you are suffering – and it is not only you, many people around the world throughout history have tried that. If there was no suffering, they created suffering just to be aware of it. They would fast, that created a suffering; they would live naked in the cold winters without clothes, that created suffering. Man is very inventive – he will torture himself in many ways.

Once in a while, a person has become aware from that experience also; it is unnecessarily inhuman, but almost all the religions have been preaching it. Whatever is difficult is appealing to the human mind and whatever is obvious and simple, you tend to forget. But here, you are not in Germany. And even in Germany, you are not going to be German. Once you are with me, you have to drop all these diseases of being German, of being Indian, of being Chinese... Just being human is enough.

I teach you the easy. I am not in favor of any kind of unnecessary torture. If it is inevitable that is another thing, but we have even been trying to make inevitable suffering into a transformation. To me, the easiest door is whenever you feel joyful, dance, sing, and while dancing and singing, be aware. Don't be lost and don't be identified.

The old habit of the mind is to be identified with anything. The mind gets immediately identified with whatever is happening. The mind does not function like a mirror, it functions like a film. Whatever comes in front of it becomes imprinted on it. The mirror remains empty. People come and go, ups and downs, but the mirror does not lose itself in any identity. Here, I teach you celebration, rejoicing, because I know that is the door closest to your ultimate awakening. A man full of joy is close to existence. The greater his joy, the less is the distance between him and the heart of the universe.

In your agony you are alone; the heart of the universe is far away. Your agony has created the distance. So when you are in agony – it is human and once in a while it happens – remain alert. And if you have been able to remain alert when the dance was descending on you and flowers were showering on you, it won't be difficult at all to be aware when something has gone wrong. You can be a watcher: standing aside, unidentified.

This is the way of the mirror. And this is the way of those who have known human nature more deeply than your so-called religions, psychoanalysts, wise people. But it is up to you. If you enjoy self-torture, then choose moments of misery for the practice of awareness. But if you are understanding and intelligent, you will choose the easiest and the closest way.

Anyway, whatever you choose, the result is the same: awareness will make you free from identification. You can try both; a few people get lost when they are happy. Perhaps for them it is difficult to be aware when they are happy. The mind says, "What is the need of awareness? In such a blissful, happy moment, don't bring religion in. You are young, you are healthy, you are in love, what is the need for the church at this moment?" Yes, when you have become old, one foot in the grave you remember God – but it is too late. Then you pray to God – but it is too late.

Just the other day, Anando showed me a picture of a very famous Christian missionary, an old man of thirty years' standing. He had been giving television sermons, and millions of people were listening to him every Sunday. Now he has been caught coming out of a prostitute's house. He did the right thing: he appeared on television, tears in his eyes… I looked at the picture and I could not believe that at his age he is weeping. Millions of viewers felt sympathy for the old man, and he is saying, "I will ask God to forgive me, and ask you to forgive me. I have been going to prostitutes all these years. Now for three months as a penance I will not speak." But most probably during these three months he will visit prostitutes. What else will he do? God is always available. Today, or three months afterward, you can ask forgiveness.

But with me there is no God. No one can forgive you and there is no point of any prayer. *You* have to change. *You* have to understand the mechanism of transformation and it is very simple. In an early morning walk when the birds are joyous, the trees are glowing in the sun, and you are feeling a peace, become alert.

Whatever is happening should not happen in an unconscious state; just be conscious. That does not mean that you have to be verbally repeating inside yourself, "Look, the birds are singing. Look how the trees are happy. Look, what peace is prevailing." Then you have destroyed everything. You are not to verbalize. You have to experience. And whenever you find the moment which is worth rejoicing, in that moment, be alert. Slowly, slowly your alertness will become part of you. The work of alertness is to destroy identification.

Once in a while you will be down – dark clouds, life seems to be meaningless for any reason. Your alertness gained, strengthened, crystallized in moments of joy, will come to your help. You will remain far away and you will know deep down: "All this is happening but not to me, only around – and it goes on changing. My awareness remains just like a mirror, only reflecting but not identifying."

But old habits die with difficulty, with great effort; we have been taught them from the very beginning. If there have been other lives before, we are carrying conditionings, calculated by scientists to be at least ten million years old. And the most dangerous conditioning as far as awakening is concerned, enlightenment is concerned, is identification.

Within a split second, you get identified, you forget that this too will pass. Just wait a minute. The old boyfriend has left? Feel blissful: "What a great opportunity." That's what I have been teaching: let the old go because the new is coming. It will take a little time. In that space, it is up to you to be miserable or to be awaiting with alertness. But it goes on every day. In the morning, your mood is bad and you know that this mood has been bad many times before; it does not remain, so why bother? Let it be bad. Why be concerned? Why give any attention to it because every attention is nourishment? Just watch, let that old mood get shocked: "What is the matter? Latifa has been always welcoming. Something has changed. She is sitting silently, not even bothering that there is an old bad mood."

But you don't remember your own life and its pattern. These ups and downs are not happening to you, they are only happening in the mind – and you are not the mind. You can stand aside and watch the whole game. Choose any way, but drop the old habit of falling into the same trap again and again. One time you can be forgiven because you were moving in an unknown territory, but the second time if you fall into the same trap, and the third time, and the thousandth time… Then it seems that you have decided to fall into the trap whatever happens. It is not the trap, it is your decision – or perhaps you are not at all conscious and just stumbling in your darkness like a somnambulist. Even they do better.

But this old habit has to be changed. And there is no question of any effort to change it. Don't decide, "I will change." A simple understanding, a simple clarity of the whole situation and the old changes. But even grown-up people behave like small children without maturity, without really proving that they are grown up. All that seems to be is that they are growing old, not growing up.

Little Ernie's parents are horrified. Their four-year-old son is just learning to talk fluently, which is charming, but he uses the word *fucking* in almost every sentence – which is very impolite. They try every strategy to get him to stop, but nothing seems to work so they try bribery.

They tell Ernie that he can go to Janet's birthday party if he stops swearing. His father warns him that he has asked Janet's mom to send Ernie home at once if she hears the filthy, disgusting word.

On Saturday at two-thirty Ernie sets off, but at three o'clock he is back again in tears.

"I told you not to use that disgusting word," his father cried.

"I did not use the fucking word," shouts Ernie. "The fucking party is not till next fucking Saturday."

If we look at our own behavior, you will not find much difference. The same thing goes on and on. Let understanding prevail – a simple understanding. Just be aware of this silence. Don't use words inside; don't judge. Let whatever is happening simply be reflected. And this has to be the method used to get unidentified with your ups and downs, and bring a balance to your life.

Osho,

It is said that all situations and people we run into are like a mirror to us. Do I attract them unconsciously as well as accidentally? When someone is aggressive toward me, how can I distinguish whether it is me or him who causes it?

Life is very interdependent. It is very difficult to decide who is responsible for what. In truth, we are all responsible for whatever happens; we contribute in some way to it. If someone becomes aggressive toward you, rather than thinking in the ordinary way that he is aggressive, start thinking from the point, "What is in me that is making him aggressive? He is not aggressive to everyone." He is not aggressive to the trees; he is aggressive toward you. There must be something you are doing, some way you are behaving that creates aggression in him.

You may not be doing it to him. That's what I mean, it is so interwoven. Perhaps you remind him of his father who used to beat him, and he was so small that he could not do anything. And when he sees you, he is not aggressive at you, you are simply symbolic. He is aggressive at his father who is no longer in the world. So rather than reacting to his aggression, which will make things worse, try to understand. Ask him, "Why are you aggressive to me? Is something wrong in me that hurts you? Have I done something to you? Because I am not aware of doing anything to you. There must be some other reason for your aggression."

That should be the way of the man of wisdom. And if you ask that person, perhaps tears may come to his eyes and he will start asking your forgiveness: "You have not done anything, you just remind me of my father. When I was small, I was beaten so much that I used to think that when I become big and strong, I will show this man. By the time I was big and strong he was dead. So something has remained incomplete in me. The moment I see you, that sleeping aggression comes to me. Forgive me, you have not hurt me. It is not your problem, it is my problem."

If people start behaving in this way, we will create a totally different kind of life – saner. You fall in love with a woman – have you ever asked why you have fallen in love with a certain woman when there are so many women around? You never ask. Perhaps she reminds you of your mother? Perhaps the way she walks reminds you of your mother, and you loved your mother so much that the same love is revived again.

Before becoming a fool and falling in love, make a little analysis of what you are doing and why you are doing it. Perhaps that will save great misery in the world. Unconsciously, without understanding your inner sleeping desires, your tendencies, you fall in love with a woman, but you don't know – you will not be able to love her because she is not your mother. And as you come closer, you will see, "My God, she is not my mother." Naturally, that woman has not married a son; she has married a husband. She cannot behave the way your mother may have behaved.

She may be expecting you to behave like her father whom she loved. And some trait in you… Those traits may be very small, very simple: perhaps your mustache is exactly the same – and that's enough, it triggers the memory of the father who is no more. She has fallen *in love* with you, but not with *you*. If, before acting, people try to understand that whatever they are doing must have a reason within themselves and that the other is not obliged to fulfill it… The woman may have the same hairdo, that does not mean she is the same kind of person. If you love the hairdo, you can purchase one from a shop which deals in wigs, made just exactly according to your mother – worship it, love it. That will be more sane because that wig will not hurt you, will not demand things which your mother has never demanded. But a new woman, where the only similarity is the hairdo, is not going to fulfill your desires. You are searching for a mother.

Now, psychologists are very concerned that most problems are because we are brought up by parents. So the girl starts loving the father and the boy starts loving the mother – which they will never find in their life. And for their whole lives they will miss the woman they are seeking or the man they are searching for.

Your question is significant. It reminds me of George Gurdjieff. He was only nine years old when his father died. And his father must have been a man of great wisdom. They were poor people. He called Gurdjieff close to him and said to him, "I am sorry I am not leaving any heritage for you. I am leaving you alone in this vast world of competition, violence, greed. I want to tell you one thing; my whole life's experience is contained in it. Perhaps you may not understand now, but keep remembering it; one day you will understand."

And the advice was very simple. The advice was that if anyone is angry at you, don't react immediately, don't start fighting. Listen silently to what he is saying. Be very calm and cool. When he is finished, tell him, "Please give me twenty-four hours to think over what you have said and then I will come with my reply."

A strange advice but of tremendous psychological implications. Gurdjieff said in his old age that this simple advice changed his whole life because, "Sometimes I would find that the person's anger had nothing to do with me. I didn't even have to reply to it; it was not addressed to me. Perhaps he was angry and it was just a coincidence that I happened to be close by; or I would find that what he was saying was right, I had done something wrong." Then Gurdjieff would go and ask for forgiveness saying, "You were right."

Gurdjieff says that it shocked people. They said "What kind of boy is this? Even if you hit him, he says, 'After twenty-four hours, I will come to give you the answer. And if I don't come that means I don't have any answer for it. That means it is not a question addressed to me.'"

I have told you a strange anecdote…

In a world psychology conference, a very famous psychoanalyst is delivering his thesis, his findings. And just in the front row, an old psychoanalyst, famous in his own way, is sitting beside a beautiful young woman. She is new but has produced papers of tremendous insight into human behavior. She has been conferred honorary DLitt's from many universities. But she is so young and so beautiful.

She was attracting his attention, distracting him, but more than that – that old fellow was playing with that young woman's breasts. That is too much, and just in front… How can you read your thesis?

The psychoanalyst becomes angry. He says things which are not relevant. Even the conference thinks, "What has gone wrong? He has always been a very consistent thinker, but he is looking very disturbed." And his disturbance is about this old man: "This idiot is playing with the breasts of the beautiful woman." And certainly a deep desire is there that he would have liked to be in his place.

This whole combination of things, and his whole paper was disturbed. He even forgot what he had come to say. He could not complete the paper. In the middle of his thesis, he left the podium and went directly to the lady and said, "You don't object to this old idiot who is playing with your breasts?"

She said, "It is his problem. He is doing no harm to me. He is very soft, very nice. Why should I bother about his problem?"

It looks strange, but it is true; the problem is of the old man. And the young lady is certainly wiser than both the fellows. "Why should you be disturbed?" she asked. "You are not playing with my breasts; he is playing. It is his problem. I am not disturbed. There is no harm. In fact, he is being very respectful to a beautiful woman, but why are you disturbed? Certainly, deep down, you are thinking, 'If I had been by the side of the woman…'"

Where can you find such a woman with such understanding? – that you play with her breasts, and she does not know you and she allows you because she understands…? That poor fellow must have suffered in his early life. Perhaps he was not breast fed.

All the painters, poets, novelists go on continually painting breasts. Strange, because the breast is simply a mechanism for the child to be nourished; it is not for old men! Women all over the world who have become a little liberated are against breast feeding because it distorts their breasts. It distorts the roundness of the breast because the child goes on pulling it downward – and the child has to do it; he is milking the mother – and the breast becomes long.

Existentially, a long breast is very necessary for the survival of the child. If the breast is really round, the child cannot survive because he has such a small face. If he starts milking, his nose will close, he will not be able to breathe; either he can milk or he can breathe. In either case he is going to die. So naturally, he goes on pulling it longer – and no woman wants long breasts; certainly, they don't look aesthetically beautiful. So there are many devices to keep at least the appearance of a round breast: bras… And even if a few women have to lose their breast in cancer surgery, they will replace it with a rubber breast which is far more perfect, looks really beautiful, but it has to be under the clothes.

A man entered a circus manager's office and said, "I have something to offer."

The manager said, "I am tortured by so many people. What have you to offer?"

He said, "I have a very beautiful woman."

The manager said, "Can she dance?"

He said, "Dance? Just see her act and you will forget all about dancing."

The manager said, "Okay. Tonight, bring your woman."

The woman had such long breasts, so heavy that she crawled on the stage and then tried to stand up.

The manager said, "But where is the dance?"

He said, "This is far more difficult than any dance. And you can see that everyone is laughing. No one has laughed at any dance."

And then the woman went down again. She could not stand carrying that much weight.

There are women who are trying to make their breasts bigger with injections or smaller with injections. But this concern with breasts is as ancient as you can conceive: old statues, but the same concern… So you may be interested in a woman whose breasts look rounded, but they may just look rounded and behind the clothes it is rubber, not real breasts. So it is perfectly good on the sea beach to talk romance and poetry and have film dialogues. But just on the first night of the honeymoon, everything is going to be a disaster. When you get hold of the breasts, they will both come off in your hands. And the woman can go to sleep telling you, "You can play with them."

There are problems, but the problems come from within you and then they are projected on other people. The same is happening to other people. They have problems, they have repressed desires, they have incomplete experiences. And if by chance it happens that you fit with something in their psychological poverty, either they can fall in love with you, they can be angry with you or they can hate you.

There are people who say, "I hate certain people – just seeing them. They have not done anything; I have not even talked to them, but just to see them is enough for me to hate." It cannot be enough to hate but perhaps your experience of the past, of a certain man has damaged the image inside you, and that image fits completely with this man. Naturally, hate arises, love arises, anger arises.

But the man of understanding always looks inward to find what the cause is: "Why am I doing it?" If it is not harmful to the other, and if the other is also willing, that means the other also is expecting some experience of the same kind. Then things go perfectly well; otherwise, every moment problems arise. And you can create actual situations in which you can see how problems arise.

For twenty-four hours, watch your judgments of people. Are they good or are they bad? Just watch from where your responses to people are coming. Are they coming from them or are they coming from within you? This whole world with all its misery and suffering is within you. This whole world can be a world of bliss and benediction if your inner being changes.

This is my definition of a religious person: he has changed his inner being, cleaned his inner being so he becomes just a pure mirror, reflects but does not react. He feels compassionate, even for those who are full of anger, he feels compassionate for those who are sad, miserable, destroying their life by drinking alcohol or using other drugs. All that he feels is compassion. And out of that compassion comes a response: if he can help, he helps.

You cannot create a reaction in the man of wisdom; he never reacts. This is the difference between these two words – they look similar – *reaction* and *response*. Reaction is blind and unconscious and it blames the other. Response is conscious and clear and sees things as they are. If he is to blame, he accepts the blame; there is no need to fight. And if he is blameless, then too there is no need to fight: "It is your mind; I have nothing to do with it."

I must have received thousands of letters from around the world. A few people say they love me. And they have not even seen me; they have not even read me. From where is their love coming? Perhaps their whole lives they wanted to be in revolt, and hearing about me they see their desire fulfilled – someone is in revolt. But it has nothing to do with me. It is their own desire, their own projection.

There are thousands of others who go on condemning me for strange reasons. Just a few days ago, a man wrote an article in which he said, "If Osho had not been controversial, he would have been accepted as the greatest intellectual of the last part of this century."

I asked Anando to write a letter to him and to inquire, "Can you tell us of any great man, just a single name will do, who was great and not controversial?" He has not answered. Then we published the letter, but he is hiding; there is no answer. Every great man, Gautam Buddha, Zarathustra, Lao Tzu... To their contemporaries, they were the most controversial people. Only people who are making shoes, who are cleaning the streets, are not controversial.

The moment you say something original, it hurts many people because their prejudice comes into a clash with the original idea. They can't see that they are not angry against me, they are angry because they are prejudiced. If they were people of silence, they would have balanced thoughts about both: "Who knows, perhaps the original idea is right? It has to be given a chance." And certainly it needs to be respected because I am not imposing my ideas on you, I am simply expressing. But everywhere there seems to be thousands of locks on every mouth.

And it is all nonsense talk which says, "freedom of thought." There is neither freedom of thought nor freedom of expression. These people who have been condemned as controversial are the cause of the whole evolution. The noncontroversial, the mediocre, the retarded have not contributed anything. They have destroyed much, but they have never contributed anything. So whenever something happens, remember, first look within yourself. Perhaps what is being said is right, and if it is not right then it is none of your concern, it is someone else's problem who is projecting it on you.

Just to break your silence because sometimes it becomes too heavy...

Paddy and Sean go hunting together in the Oregon mountains. After a while, Sean stops to take a piss, and a rattlesnake bites him on his prick. He calls out to Paddy and tells him to go to the nearest village and ask what to do.

Paddy runs off and after half an hour runs breathlessly into the doctor's office and asks for advice.

The doctor says, "Take a sharp knife and make an opening in the wound and suck out the poison."

Paddy rushes back and as he approaches, Sean calls out, "Paddy, hey, Paddy, what did he say?"

"I am sorry," replies Paddy, "but he says you are going to die."

Little Ernie asks his dad, "Dad, is it true that God exists everywhere?"

"That's right, son," replies his father, still reading his newspaper.

"Is he in the garage?" asks Ernie.

"Yes, son," replies his father, "he is in the garage."

"Is he out in the garden?" asks Ernie.

"Yes, he is, son," replies his father.

"Is he under mummy's dress?" asks Ernie.

"Yes, he is everywhere," snaps his father getting a little irritated.

So little Ernie looks in the garage but he can't find God. He looks out in the garden but he can't find God there either.

So he goes into the kitchen and crawls under his mother's dress.

"Ernie," she cries, "what are you doing?"

"Quiet, mum," says Ernie triumphantly, "I have just caught God by his beard."

11

Fearlessness: The First Requirement to Go Inward

Osho,

I read a poem of Rumi the other day which went: "Move within, but don't move the way fear makes you move." Around the same time I awoke from a dream in tears and all I remembered was looking at myself in a mirror, face-to-face, and my eyes were full of fear. Sometimes in meditation I touch a blank horizontal space with no reference point for who I am and this same fear is there. Can you help me to understand and make friends with this fear?

The words of Mevlana Rumi are immensely significant. There have been very few people who have moved and transformed as many hearts as Rumi. In the world of the Sufis, Mevlana Rumi is the emperor. His words have to be understood not as mere words, but sources of deep silences, echoes of the inner and the innermost songs. He is the greatest dancer the world has known. Twelve hundred years have passed since he was alive.

His dance is a special kind of dance. It is a kind of whirling, just the way small children whirl; standing on one spot they go on round and round. And perhaps everywhere in the world small children do that and their elders stop them saying, "You will become dizzy, you will fall, you will hurt yourself," and, "What is the point of doing it?"

Jalaluddin Rumi made a meditation of whirling. The meditator goes on whirling for hours, for as long as the body allows him; he does not stop on his own. When whirling, a moment comes and he sees himself utterly still and silent, a center of the cyclone. The body is moving around the center, but there is a space which remains unmoved; that is his being.

Rumi himself whirled for thirty-six hours continuously and fell, because the body could not whirl anymore. But when he opened his eyes he was another man. Hundreds of people had gathered to see. Many thought he was mad saying, "What is the point of whirling?"

No one can say this is a prayer; no one can say this is a great dance; no one can say in any way that this has something to do with religion, spirituality. But after thirty-six hours, when they saw Rumi so luminous, so radiant, so new, so fresh – reborn, in a new consciousness – they could not believe their eyes. Hundreds wept in repentance because they had thought that he was mad. In fact he was sane and *they* were mad.

And down these twelve centuries the stream has continued to be alive. There are very few movements of spiritual growth which have lived so long continuously. There are still hundreds of dervishes. *Dervish* is the Sufi word for sannyas. You cannot believe it unless you experience, that just by whirling you can know yourself. No austerity is needed, no self-torture is needed; just an experience of your innermost being and you are transported into another plane of existence from the mortal to the immortal. The darkness disappears and there is just eternal light.

His words have to be understood very carefully because he has not spoken much; just a few small poems. His statement, "Move within, but don't move the way fear makes you move" – is so beautiful. Don't move the way fear makes you move. Move the way love makes you move. Move the way joy makes you move – not out of fear because all so-called religions are based on fear. Their God is nothing but fear and their heaven and hell are nothing but projections of fear and greed. Rumi's statement is very revolutionary: Do not move because of fear. All the religions say to people, "Fear God!"

Mahatma Gandhi used to say, "I do not fear anyone but God." When I heard it, I said that this is the most stupid statement anyone can make. You can fear everyone, but don't fear God, because God can only be approached through love. God is not a person but the universal heartbeat. If you can sing with love and dance with love; an ordinary activity like whirling out of love… Joy and celebration are enough to reach the innermost sanctum of the being and of existence. You have all been living out of fear.

Your relationships are out of fear. Fear is so overwhelming – like a dark cloud covering your life – that you say things which you don't want to say, but fear makes you say them. You do things which you do not want to do, but fear makes you do them. A little intelligence is enough to see…

Millions of people are worshipping stones carved by themselves. They have made their Gods and then they worship them. It must be out of great fear because where can you find God? The easier way is to carve God in beautiful marble and worship it. And no one thinks that this is sheer stupidity, because everyone else is doing it in different ways: someone is in the temple, someone is in the mosque, someone is in the synagogue; it does not make any difference. The essential thing is the same, that what you are doing is out of fear; your prayers are full of fear.

Rumi is making a revolutionary, an extraordinary statement: "Move within, but don't move the way fear makes you move." Then what is the way to move within? Why not move playfully? Why not make your religion a playfulness? Why be so serious? Why not move laughingly? Just like small children running joyously after butterflies for no special reason. Just the joy of the colors and the beauty of the flowers and the butterflies is enough. And they are so immensely happy.

In your every twenty-four hours find a few moments which are fearless, which means in those moments you are not asking for anything. You are not asking for any reward and you are not worried about any punishment; you are simply enjoying the whirling, the going inward.

In fact, in the beginning it may look just a little difficult. As you move a little inward you become automatically joyful, playful, prayerful. A gratitude arises in you that you have never known before and a space opens up which is infinite, your inner sky. Your inner sky is not less rich than the outer sky: it has its own stars, its own moon, its own planets, its own immensity. It has exactly as vast a universe as you can see outside. You are just standing in between two universes: one is outside you, one is inside you. The outside universe consists of things and the inside universe consists of consciousness, of bliss, of joy.

"Move within, but don't move the way fear makes you move," because fear cannot enter inward. Why can fear not enter inward? – because fear cannot be alone, and inward you have to be alone. Fear needs a crowd, fear needs companionship, friends, even foes may do.

To be alone, to go inward, you cannot take anyone with you; you have to be more and more alone. Not only can you not take anyone, you cannot take anything either: your wealth, your power, your prestige – you cannot take anything. Inside, you cannot take even your clothes! You will have to go nude and alone; hence fear cannot move inward, fear moves outward. Fear moves toward money, fear moves toward power, fear moves toward God; fear moves in all directions except inward. Fearlessness is the first requirement to go inward.

You are wondering how to make friends with the fear. One has not to make friends with darkness, death or fear. One has to get rid of them. One has to simply say good-bye forever. It is your attachment; a friendship will make it even deeper.

Don't think that by becoming friendly with fear you will become ready to go inward. Even the friendly fear will prevent it; in fact, it will prevent it more so. It will prevent you in a friendly way, it will advise you, "Don't do such a thing. There is nothing inward. You will fall into nothingness and returning from that nothingness is impossible. Beware of falling into your inwardness. Cling to things."

Fear has to be understood – you don't have to make friends – and it disappears. What are you afraid of? When you were born you were born naked. You did not bring any bank balance either, but you were not afraid. You come into the world utterly nude, but entering like an emperor. Even an emperor cannot enter the world the way a child enters. The same is true of entering inward. It is a second childbirth; you again become a child: the same innocence, the same nudity, the same nonpossessiveness. What do you have to be afraid of?

In life you cannot be afraid of birth. It has happened, now nothing can be done about it. You cannot be afraid of life; it is already happening. You cannot be afraid of death; whatever you do it is going to happen. So what is the fear?

I have always been asked even by very learned people, "Do you never get concerned what will happen after death?" And I have always wondered that these people are learned. I have asked them, "One day I was not born – and there was no worry. I have never for a single moment thought, 'When I was not born, what kind of trouble, what kind of anxiety, what kind of anguish did I have to face?' I was simply not! So the same will be the case: when you die, you die."

Confucius was asked by his most significant disciple, Mencius, "What will happen after death?" Confucius said, "Don't waste time. When you are in your grave, lie down and think over it, but why bother now?"

So many people in their graves are thinking! You will think that there seems to be no problem: in every cemetery, and there are millions of cemeteries, people are simply lying. They don't even get up to inquire, "What has happened, what is the news today?" They don't even change sides. They are so relaxed. And when people die, others close their eyes out of fear: "The poor people will go on seeing in the grave." It makes you afraid that thousands of people in their graves are looking – "Close their eyes."

I had a distant aunt who was unique because she slept with one eye open. She had to because that one eye was false. Whenever she used to come to our family, I would frighten people. Whenever she would go to sleep, I would take them to her and say, "Look, this is what happens: even when she is alive one eye is open. In death you try to close people's eyes, but don't believe it. They will open their eyes and look around, 'What is happening?'"

Fear of what will happen when you die is unnecessary. Whatever will happen will happen. And anyway you cannot do anything beforehand. You don't know, so there is no question of doing some homework, getting ready for the kind of questions you will be asked or what kind of people you will meet; learning their manners, their language… We don't know anything; there is no need to worry. Don't waste time.

But it is fear, fear that something is going to happen. After death – and you will be so alone; even if you call from your grave, no one is going to hear. People close the grave completely just out of fear. If you leave some window open and dead people start looking out from there, they would make anyone afraid!

Just now, I have heard that there is a new phenomenon in America called The Couch Potato Movement. It was created for people who sit at home all day and watch TV. It was started in 1982, but has recently become a great phenomenon: the home-video revolution. The Couch Potato Movement has published two books: *The Official Couch Potato Handbook* and *The Couch Potato Guide to Life*. It also has a newsletter, *The Tuber's Voice*, with a circulation of eight thousand.

Mr. Armstrong, the founder of the movement is spreading the Couch Potato gospel: "We feel that watching TV is an indigenous

American form of meditation." He says, "We call it Transcendental Vegetation."

People can do anything out of fear. They can even become a member of The Couch Potato Movement. Just sitting for seven and a half hours per day just like a potato on the sofa, and growing fatter and fatter and fatter. Once in a while they get up to go to the fridge; otherwise, they are doing so much Transcendental Vegetation. It has never been done on such a vast scale.

Why would people watch television the whole day? One has to look into the psychology. These people simply don't want to know anything about themselves. These people are trying to avoid themselves by watching television. Television is a substitute; otherwise, having so much time, you will have to look inward. And that is a fear. Inward...? But the fridge is outward. Inward...? But the boyfriend is outward. Inward, you will not find anything. You cannot go shopping... You will just get drowned in nothingness.

This being drowned in nothingness creates fear. But the problem is that this fear is only because you don't know the beauty, the bliss, the joy of drowning in nothingness. Because you don't know the ecstasy that opens up as you fall inward. It needs a little taste. I don't want you to believe, I want you to experiment. If thousands of mystics have experienced something inside, at least hypothetically, you can also have a look. Perhaps there may be something that you are missing.

There is no question of fear, just a little intelligence is needed – not friendliness with fear but an intelligence: the adventurer's heart, the courage of those who go into the unknown. They are the blessed ones because they find the meaning and the significance of life. Others only vegetate. Only they live.

A Frenchman, a Jew, and a Polack are each sentenced to thirty years in prison. Each man is given one request that will be honored by the jail warden.

"A woman," asks the Frenchman.

"A telephone," says the Jew.

"A cigarette," says the Polack.

Thirty years later the Frenchman walks out with the woman and ten kids.

The Jew strolls out carrying a ten thousand dollar commission he has made during the time.

The Polack walks out and says, "Has anyone got a match?"

Just don't be a Polack! Thirty years of holding the cigarette, waiting: "When the door opens I will ask has anyone got a match."

The first thing is that you don't need much to enter your own being: a little intelligence, a little sense of humor, a loving heart. Serious people go on standing outside with long English faces.

I have heard that an Englishman got out of a train. His wife was waiting outside with the car to take him home. She asked, "What happened? You are looking very pale."

He said, "Don't ask. Such a long journey and I had to sit the opposite way in which the train was going, and it always makes me sick. If I sit facing the same way as the train is going then it is good; otherwise I become very sick."

The woman said, "You could have asked anyone, 'This is my problem, please can you change seats?'"

He said, "I also thought about it, but there was no one in the seat in front. Whom to ask? And without asking..."

Father Murphy wants to raise money for his church and he has heard that there is a fortune to be made in horse racing. However, he does not have enough money to buy a horse, so he decides to buy a donkey instead and enters him in a race. To his surprise the donkey comes third. The headline on the sports page reads: "Priest's Ass Shows."

Father Murphy enters it in another race and this time it wins. The headline reads: "Priest's Ass Out Front."

The bishop is so upset by this kind of publicity that he orders Father Murphy not to race his donkey again. The headline reads: "Bishop Scratches Priest's Ass."

This is too much for the bishop. So he orders Father Murphy to get rid of the donkey. He gives it to Sister Theresa. And the headline reads: "Nun Has Best Ass in Town."

The bishop faints. He then informs Sister Theresa that she must dispose of the donkey. She sells it to Paddy for ten dollars.

The next day the bishop is found dead on the dining room table with a newspaper clutched in his hand. The headline reads: "Nun Sells Her Ass for Ten Bucks."

Just a little sense of humor, a little laughter, a childlike innocence – and what have you got to lose? What is the fear? We don't have anything. We have come without anything, we will go without anything. Before it happens, just a little adventure inward to see who is this fellow hiding behind the clothes, inside the skeleton; who is this fellow who is born, becomes young, falls in love and one day dies and no one knows where he goes. Just a little curiosity to inquire into one's own being. It is very natural; there is no question of fear.

Sisters Agnes, Theresa, and Margaret go out from the convent for a walk. They enter the local liquor store and order a bottle of bourbon whiskey.

"Sisters," says the owner, looking concerned, "you should not be drinking hard liquor."

"It is not for us," explains Sister Agnes, "This is for Mother Superior's constipation."

He sells them the whiskey and the nuns leave. Later as he closes the store and walks down the street, the owner finds the nuns sitting under a tree, gulping in turns from the bottle.

"Sisters, I'm shocked," he says. "You told me that booze was for Mother Superior's constipation."

"It is," says Sister Theresa. "When she hears about this she will shit herself."

12

Camels Don't Like to Go to the Mountains

Osho,
Why is it that through the ages, filthy corrupters, rapists of this beautiful planet, people who betray their own mother for power and wealth, are given the right to regale themselves in such an ostentatious manner so as to live freely; so to say, in their presidential palaces or princely retreats – not one but many – and a man of your light, height and far deeper understanding in every way is permitted only to breathe this stinking, polluted air which does not at all contribute to your physical health?

Osho, forgive me if I am being jealous, but it is disgusting and appalling to see the abnormality of it. In the past days I have seen their faces and heard their voices and it is sickening. Is this our fault? Is this a situation deliberately created by this silent intelligence to separate the cream from the curd?

If it be my decision, you are the one to be in every possible network media around the globe talking about Mendel or Horowitz, showing to the world the glory of existence that lives in your presence. Because to you the blessings and love were given in their highest form and abundance and not raped and forced to abide with their manipulators, like the son-of-a-bitch Reagan and his kind have been doing for so long.

> Forgive me if I am mistaken or serious about it, but in the past two weeks what I have seen in the world has made me sad and now I know less than I ever did.

Your question is so long that by the time I hear the end I have forgotten the beginning! Somehow because I have tried to remember the beginning, the middle is missing. You are certainly a great writer, but have compassion on me. Question exactly, telegraphically; otherwise it becomes difficult to answer your question in its completion, but I will give a try.

The first part seems to be why the corrupted people are in power and in the palaces. I have quoted Lord Acton many times who said, "Power corrupts…" But he does not have the deeper understanding that corruption leads to power also. You have to be corrupted enough to be in power. Our minds are continuously forced to reach somewhere, to eminence, to become a president or to become a prime minister; only then have you fulfilled the meaning of your life.

This continuous teaching from parents, teachers, everyone pushes you toward all that gives power: money, position, prestige. And it is true that when you have power, by that time you are so corrupted… That has been your ladder to reach, and now you have immense power in your hands and no one to prevent you. What are you going to do with the power – more corruption or perhaps bigger goals ahead?

The past has been dominated because of will to power. We have not been taught love, we have not been taught noncompetitiveness, we have not been taught humbleness, simplicity, just to be oneself. We have been dragged by great forces on every side to faraway powerful positions. Corruption leads to power. And in return power gives you more capacity to corrupt.

The past as a whole is ugly and criminal. Just because there has been a Gautam Buddha, a Lao Tzu, a Kabir does not matter. The past is so vast that these people can be counted out. The mainstream of humanity has been moving on wrong paths; you are always in a crowd and the crowd loves to worship powerful people, to praise powerful people. The crowd is very willing to be enslaved by power, because power takes away its responsibility without the understanding that this also takes its freedom. But one wonders what you are going to do with your freedom?

For example, all the constitutions of the world talk about freedom of expression. But do you have something to express? So what is the point? For ninety-nine percent of people it is meaningless; they don't have anything to express. And who cares about the one percent? They will be crushed. In fact the person who should have been praised and loved will be crushed.

The psychological background has to be remembered: mankind has never praised anyone who was contemporary, expressive, creative, had something to say. The crowd has been against these people because in a certain sense their presence becomes an insult. Their very presence humiliates you.

There is an Arabic proverb about how camels don't like to go to the mountains. They love the desert. In the desert they are mountains. It is very humiliating being close to a mountain and to realize that you are nothing – not even a particle of dust by the side of the Everest. It is better to avoid. They have chosen the desert where they are great people.

It has to be remembered that even your so-called powerful people don't want to come in contact with a man of authentic power; a power that arises within and is not borrowed from others, begged from others. There are a few people, certainly, whose sources of power are intrinsic. Even presidents and kings and queens look like nothing but beggars in front of them, because their power depends on others. A power that depends on others is not much of a power, but it is easier to attain.

People choose easier ways and people choose to imitate. People want – are taught and conditioned to want – to become someone special. And that specialness can come: either you are a president or you are the richest man in the world. This whole system of teaching people has been basically wrong. No one should be condemned for it; they are all victims. But the time is ripe and there is intelligence enough to see the point and change the whole programming.

A child should be respected, not for his obedience, but for his intelligence. And if his intelligence makes him a rebel, that is perfectly in tune with existence. A child should not be given concepts, beliefs, baptism because you don't have any right to force your own burden, your own unconscious conditioning on a pure consciousness. A child should not be Christian, Hindu or Mohammedan…

If you really love your child, you will protect him from being contaminated by any belief system. You will protect him from all that corrupts and from all that takes him away from himself, from all that destroys his individuality and makes him a hypocrite. But who loves so much? People think it is love, that if you are born a Christian, your children should be Christians. It is not love. It may be anything else, but certainly not love. Love will leave the child to grow according to his own intrinsic capacities. Give him the sky; give him the opportunity. Give him the freedom. Give him the nourishment. Give him the courage to be himself.

That is still a dream and a hope. Perhaps one day it will happen because doubts about humanity's past have started arising from many sources. We have lived unnecessarily under a very dark night, when the whole sun, the flowers, the trees are our birthright.

So the first thing is that you should not be angry because anger is not understanding. You should be very understanding – whatever has happened has happened. You should be a scientific, impartial, objective observer, so that you can know why it happened and find ways that it is not repeated again.

The second part of your question continues "…and a man of your light, height and far deeper understanding in every way is permitted only to breathe this stinking, polluted air, which does not at all contribute to your physical health." This too is part of the whole programming of the mind of the past.

For almost two years the Indian government has been denying that they are preventing sannyasins to reach me. But just the other day in San Francisco, the Indian consul in a press interview said clearly: "Osho is a criminal and not only a personal criminal, but a corporate criminal, and he should not be allowed anywhere. In India we have to accept him, but we are making every effort that people from all over the world who are interested in him and love him, should not reach him."

This is the first time that they have at least accepted that they have been preventing sannyasins from coming to India. They have sent many sannyasins back to their homes from Indian airports. Sannyasins had to learn to tell lies that they are not sannyasins, "Who is Osho? Do we have to go to him? We have come to see the Himalayas, the Taj Mahal. We have never heard...!"

And I knew this was going to happen. That's why I told you to drop the outer symbols of sannyas completely. Still, they interrogate for hours, even when a person is saying, "I have not come for Osho. I don't know him and why should I go to Pune? What is there?" But politicians are suspicious people. They were interrogating in such a way that somehow they could get the idea that the man *was* going to Pune. This being unsuccessful, they started asking, "Have you come to India to learn meditation?" Now meditation has become synonymous with me. Innocent sannyasins were not aware that "meditation..." – and they are finished! They have to return home from the airport; they cannot enter the country.

We have reported this to the government, and the government denied it saying, "We are not doing anything. Why should we prevent people?"

And this man from San Francisco... I remember him because he came to see me. After twelve days, when the trial was over and I was released from the jail, he asked me, "Rajiv is very concerned about your health and well-being. In what way can we be of help to you?"

I said, "You have come a little late – and perhaps consideredly. I am out of jail, now what can you do? You can force me into jail again; that is the only help that is left."

He said, "We have been watching."

I said, "Watching won't help. What were you watching for? A man is arrested without any warrant. He is not given a reason why he is being arrested; no evidence is given." Just a list of names was shown to us, and of the six people who were arrested not one of those six people was on the list. And he was made aware that we are not the people…" You should arrest *these* people; you have the list. You are arresting the wrong people. You don't have arrest warrants" – and the Indian ambassador was watching!

One of my secretaries was sitting in Washington continuously for twelve days, insisting to the Indian ambassador, "This is absolutely ugly that you are silent – it is a conspiracy. If an individual citizen of your country is arrested without any reason, who has not committed any crime… What is your purpose here? You should interfere."

He went on promising, "I will. I am in constant contact with Rajiv Gandhi. I am in contact with the American government and you need not worry." And they did not do a thing!

And this same man now says, "We are trying to keep Osho in such a situation that he cannot move out of India" – obviously. Twenty-one countries have passed laws that I cannot enter those countries; four other countries are going to pass… I have not even asked to enter their countries. In India the strategy is that I cannot go anywhere even in India, because then the Indian government has its own ugly ways of doing things.

I first wanted to be in the Himalayas rather than in this polluted place. I remained there for one month. They immediately deported all the foreigners who were with me and informed me that I could not purchase land because I don't live in that state. Unless I am a resident of a particular state, I cannot purchase land. And they provoked their followers to protest that I should not be allowed to live there because if I live there people will start coming and everyone's morality will be in danger, religion will be in danger. Their golden past will be in danger.

Just one day ago, a friend from Delhi informed me that I should leave India because the Indian government is thinking of arresting me. Their reason for arresting me is that I have paid four hundred thousand dollars as a fine and from where did I get that money? I myself don't know! I sincerely have no idea who the sannyasins were, from all over the world, who gave that money.

I left India and went to Nepal because the king of Nepal was very interested in me, in my books; the prime minister of Nepal was interested. The prime minister came to see me, but he said, "It will be very difficult. Although it will be against our wishes, we cannot allow you to remain in Nepal because we are a small country and are in constant danger to be taken over from India. They have done this in Sikkim; they can do it in Nepal, and we don't have armies or anything. We cannot even give a good fight. So the king wants to inform you that we love you, we love your teachings, but we are unable to risk the whole country."

I decided that it was time that I should go on a world tour to see which country has the courage to accept a man who has nothing but ideas which can create a better humanity and a better world.

In a few countries which you would think are powerful countries, like England, I was not even allowed to stay in the airport lounge overnight. And I asked the airport officer, "My pilot has done his twelve hours and he cannot do more, otherwise it will be against the laws. We have to stop and we need to refuel."

The officer said, "I understand, but orders from the ministry of home affairs are that you should not be allowed to stay at all, even in the lounge" – from where you cannot enter England; it is an international airport.

I said, "Then do you want me to sit here the whole night?"

He said, "The only alternative that has been offered from the top is that if you want to sleep, you can sleep in the jail, and in the morning you can leave."

Going around the world was a tremendously great experience, seeing that all these corrupted and powerful people will not allow anyone who can be a danger to their power, who can expose their ugliness.

The Attorney General of America made the statement in a press interview: "Osho should be *only* in Pune. And we will try in every way to make sure that no one reaches there. First, no one will be given a visa if he is going to Pune. Secondly, Indian immigration at the Indian airports will make sure that no one enters." He exactly said, "This is our way of silencing him."

I said, "This is good. This is my teaching: to silence people." But I don't go to so much trouble for silent opportunities. I also create a world where people can be silent, but my meaning of silence and his meaning of silence are different.

Immediately the reporter asked, "Do you mean you are going to assassinate him?"

He said, "No. Our purpose is served: the commune is destroyed. We could have jailed him for his whole life, but that would have made him a martyr and the people who love him would have loved him more. And the things that he is saying will create a greater movement. So we don't want to do that. That's why we allowed him to go. Now we will try to create all the barriers... Our ways of silencing him are very sophisticated." But they don't know that my ways are far more sophisticated!

As far as pollution is concerned, the whole world is becoming polluted. And unless those industries, railway trains, airplanes, rockets are run on different methods so that they don't pollute the air, there is no way... In fact, this small campus you are sitting in is the most unpolluted situation. You will not find this silence in New Delhi or in Washington.

But their fear of me continues. It has been two years since they destroyed the commune in America. First they had not allowed us to sell it, so that it became less and less of value. And people must have started stealing things from the commune, because how long can we keep protecting a commune of 126 square miles? First we had sixteen people. Then we reduced it to eight; it was unnecessarily expensive. Then we reduced it to four; now we have reduced it to one.

One person is guarding a commune spread 126 square miles. And there is proof that burglars are taking things away. Just in front of the Mandir in the commune we had our symbol of two birds. Someone – this you can see is utterly stupid – has made holes by shooting bullets into the birds. Those birds are just painted, but such is... These people would have liked to kill all of you. They would not dare! Now they are shooting painted birds which were our symbols.

Just the other day, one man has been caught as a murderer and he confessed in the court that he was offered the opportunity, at whatever cost, to bomb the house where I lived in the commune. He went there, but seeing that it was too well guarded he did not dare. But his statement shows that people were trying to kill me; now they are trying in a psychological way. They are preventing any news media from reaching here; the Indian government does not give them permission.

We received letters from many television stations saying, "We want to come and see what has started again, what is going on in the ashram, but the Indian government says, 'You can come, cover the whole of India, but you cannot go to Pune. You come to India only with that contract'"

Camels are very afraid of the mountains. It hurts... It hurts their egos. But you should not be angry. You should try to understand because this has been the whole history of mankind. If we want to bring a new world, a deep understanding of the old will be helpful. Don't repeat the same things. Ambition should not be taught. Things are very subtle. You may not find them if you simply look at the ultimate consequences.

My father was right: whenever I came home after taking an examination and came first, he would say, "That simply proves your class consists of idiots, otherwise how could you come first?"

I said, "You are a strange person: people teach their children to try hard and come first. I don't try at all and come first – and this is the reception you are giving me?"

If you want to change the face of humanity then very small things, in detail, should be changed. Children should not be taught to be competitive. There should be no examinations; no one should pass and no one should fail. The change should be radical.

If someone fails, it should never be shown in that person's records. The teacher's salary should be cut. What had he been doing for two years? "You wasted two years on a course that can be taught in two months – and still a few people have failed. The responsibility is yours." He should be demoted, his salary cut, and those six children who have "failed" should never know. They will pass to another class without any distinction as to who is first and who is second. The teacher in the following class should just be made aware to pay more attention to those six people, so that they can also be brought up to an equivalent level.

It looks like a strange idea, but without this you cannot destroy competitiveness. All children should come out of schools and universities feeling equal. No inferiority complex, and politics will disappear, the desire for power will disappear. The whole educational system should make it absolutely compulsory that everyone meditates. Twenty years of education is a long time. In twenty years if you cannot teach people Vipassana, being silent and looking inward, then there is no hope. And people who come out of universities humble, silent, peaceful, will create the same kind of society. It will have a flavor of its own, a fragrance of its own.

And certainly this kind of society will choose people out of their silence and clarity, out of their peace, intelligence – not corrupted ones; their world will be gone. It will choose people who are wiser and who can make society a garden rather than a graveyard. The past has been continuously making society a graveyard. Everyone can blossom, given the right opportunity. You will have to look mostly, deeper, into the educational system because that is where competition starts.

When I refused my gold medal for being first in the whole university, the vice-chancellor said, "Why are you doing it? People hanker after it!"

I said, "You can give it to anyone who is hankering for it but I am perfectly okay as I am, I don't want it. I am not in any way feeling inferior, that I have to prove by having a gold medal that I am a superior man who has topped the whole university."

When I encountered the education minister of those days, I said to him, "There is a place vacant in the university and I am ready to fill it."

He said, "Strange. First, you should apply."

I said, "What is the need when I am present? You respect papers more than people?"

He said, "No, it is just a formality. You can just write down… This is the paper; write out the application."

I wrote out the application, but then he said, "What about your character certificate?"

I said, "I have not come across a man for whom I could give a character certificate. Do you want me to ask people who don't have any character for a character certificate? Could *you* write a character certificate?"

He became so puzzled that he said, "Forget it. Just take this letter and join the university. Remember, this kind of behavior is not right. You are suspicious of my character."

I said, "You were suspicious of my character. You started the whole thing. I have not asked about your character certificate because everyone knows!" He was the most corrupt man. He knew it and everyone knew, so he said that it was better to get rid of me.

He was in such a hurry, he forgot that the appointment letter should go through a proper channel. He simply gave it to me, just to get rid of me as quickly as possible. And when I reached the college where I was appointed, the principal looked at me. He said, "You have been appointed just today, this morning – and by the evening you are here and I have not received any information about it? This is very strange. It has never happened."

I said, "Phone the education minister. If he had told me that it had to go through the proper channels and it would take three days to reach and not to go before that, I would not have come. If you don't phone, I am going to phone him."

He said, "No, don't. I will phone him. You go in the other room."

I said, "No. When there is a problem concerning me, I have to be here."

He phoned the minister and the minister said, "I forgot completely. The man is so strange. Beware of him!" And I was there.

And I said, "Listen, have you heard…?"

He said, "I have heard."

I said, "I am a dangerous man and the education minister thinks you have to be careful about me."

He was so shocked by the whole thing; I had disrupted the routine. He gave me more periods than are supposed to be given to a teacher in the university.

I said, "These are too many and if you give me too many, I will conduct them according to my own routine and you will have to face the consequences."

He said, "Let us cut them down. How many do you want?"

I said, "I don't want any! I *love* teaching. I will teach. And I will give you the list of which periods, which classes, I am going to teach."

He said, "Okay, but don't tell anyone."

This whole structure is in a deep need to be completely overturned. But look at small details: one is the educational system; another is the religious system that every family is trying to enforce. Let your children blossom according to their own intrinsic potentiality. It doesn't matter whether they become presidents or they become just flute players. The question is that whatever they become, they should be blissful.

I have heard about a great surgeon who was retiring…

A party was arranged to say good-bye to him. He had served the institution and he was most loved. It was going to be difficult to find a substitute, he was such a perfect surgeon. The party was going on, people were drinking and dancing and eating. Suddenly a friend of the surgeon looked around – the surgeon was not there.

So he went out to see; the surgeon was sitting under a tree. The friend was a famous advocate and he asked, "What are you doing? They are all celebrating and you are sitting here in such sadness."

The surgeon said, "It is because of you. Remember, twenty-five years ago I came to you to inquire – because you had been my friend and the topmost legal expert – what the consequences would be if I killed my wife. And you said twenty-five years in jail."

The advocate said, "What has that to do with today?"

He said, "Today, twenty-five years are complete. Today I would have been free. But you prevented me from attaining freedom. You did not act like a friend but like an enemy. Today I would have come out of jail. You forced me to live my whole life with a woman who was nothing but torture."

The advocate said, "You should think about your art, your surgery, your skill, your fame. If you were in jail you would not have been a famous surgeon."

He said, "I don't care about being famous. What has fame given me? Just those few idiots who are drinking, talking all kinds of nonsense and thinking they are celebrating my retirement? What has fame given me? I wanted freedom!"

If you think about yourself, you will also see if whatever you have become is your inner voice that has been leading you, or outer forces which have been distracting you. They may make you successful but they will not make you blissful, and success is meaningless.

What has happened in the past has happened. We are in a good position because we can analyze all the causes that led humanity into misery, poverty, wars, and we can change it. Revolution can be our religion. In fact, there is no other religion. But everyone has to be very aware and alert about himself because he is the society, he is making the society, creating the society. You cannot save yourself from the responsibility.

An old Indian from Kolkata is waiting at the bus stop with his family of twelve children ahead of him and a blind man behind him. It is late at night and they are waiting for the last bus. Eventually the bus comes and when all the children are aboard, the conductor says it is full, and the old Indian and the blind man have to walk home.

After walking for some time with the blind man tapping the ground loudly with his stick, the Indian says, "You know, if you had a little bit of rubber on the end of your stick, all that noise could have been avoided."

"I know," snaps the blind man, "and if you had a little bit of rubber on the end of your prick, we could have got on the bus!"

Just wait, because Niskriya is coming in…

As a forward to his question: he found the witch and he spent the whole night with her, drinking and all – and now he is finished. Just one night! He cannot be finished in one night, however great the witch may be. Now he has moved to metaphysical questions! He is asking…

> Osho,
> The other day you suggested very charmingly to me, to be only with witches. Does that mean I am a devil?

Niskriya, it shows great intelligence. At last you understand who you are. That is the function of the witch. She has helped you to self-realization! But the question can be taken from some other angle. Perhaps you don't know that the word *witch* is not condemnatory. It is Christianity which made it condemnatory; otherwise it was equivalent to a wise man.

All over Europe there were witches. They were consulted, their advice followed. With the spread of Christianity, people became very arrogant about witches because they were giving an alternative wisdom to people and Christianity wanted to monopolize wisdom. And particularly women, who cannot be wise; only men can be wise. The trend even goes back to Jesus Christ: all his apostles were men, although the old scriptures mention three women.

His mother obviously loved him, and one very beautiful prostitute, Mary Magdalene – her whole life was transformed just by listening to Jesus. A third woman, Martha who was the sister of Magdalene, had just come out of curiosity to know who had changed her sister and her lifestyle; she had almost become a saint. But none of these three were chosen to be one of the apostles.

They loved more, they were more courageous, more cultured. Those twelve apostles were uneducated, uncultured, farmers, fishermen, woodcutters – people like that. The final test came when Jesus was crucified: all twelve male successors disappeared out of fear that if someone recognized that they were followers of Jesus – because they had been hanging around him all the time – then the same would happen to them as had happened to Jesus. And they had seen that there seemed to be no sign of resurrection, no miracle.

They were hoping that angels would come, sitting on white clouds, playing on their harps, "Hallelujah!" And that the whole scene would change. But not even a white cloud came – no harp was heard. They looked all around; the whole sky was as silent as ever. But those three women did not leave Jesus. They were sitting underneath the cross. They were the first to take Jesus off the cross. Still, no respect for them.

All religions of the world are male-oriented and are somehow afraid of women. The greatest fear is that the woman can distract their attention from God. And in fact, there is no God, just their idea that any beautiful woman will be able to distract… They are right!

Gautam Buddha said to his disciples, "Never look at a woman. Avoid! Never touch a woman. Never speak to women." And for twenty years continuously he resisted the idea of initiating women into sannyas. When finally he had to, he was very disrespectful. He said, "My religion was going to last for five thousand years; now it will last only five hundred years. These women will destroy everything." Soon there will be boyfriends and girlfriends – and who cares about Gautam Buddha?

The fear of the attraction of women, the natural attraction, has made all the religions antagonistic. Christianity did the worst. It burned thousands of living women who were known as wise women. *Witch* is the old name for a wise woman. It has no condemnation in it, but because witches were killed and burned and ugly kinds of confessions were made – because they were *forced* to make them…

Just before I went to America, my back was troubling me – it is still troubling me, but now a kind of companionship has arisen. When I came in contact with Christianity, I could not believe that thousands of women confessed. I was always suspicious that it is not possible that those women would confess to be in a love affair with the Devil. But when I was reading I came across a note… Which I have experienced here, because of my back. There is a similar device, a traction machine, so that they can pull your legs and your hands to bring your back into line.

I had never realized that the traction machine was first used for confessions. by Christian churches in Europe. Women were continually being put on traction machines, and I know by my own experience that on traction you can force anyone to confess anything! Just a little more of a pull and you become afraid that your hand is going to go out of joint or the leg will be gone! It is better to tell – who cares about anything in that moment? And they are asking you to confess that you are a witch.

And on the traction machine – that is the only invention Christianity has given to the world – those poor women accepted that they were witches. The implications were that they were in a love affair with the Devil, that they really did make love. To make love to the Devil certainly cannot be tolerated by the Christians;

otherwise there is no problem. The Devil is not making love to your popes. I am certain, on a traction machine, even the pope will say, "Yes. I am a homosexual and the Devil makes love to me!"

I have suffered that traction machine. Because of that suffering I finally said, "I am getting better; now take the machine away." The traction machine cures people. They stop complaining because when you complain, you go to Dr. Hardikar's traction machine. It is better to suffer a bad back than Dr. Hardikar and his colleagues who do a perfect job of pulling you apart!

But the word *witch*, Niskriya, is not bad; it is not condemnatory. It is just the feminine of a wise man, but people have forgotten it completely.

And *devil* also is a misunderstood word. It comes from a Sanskrit root. Hebrew has no root for it, nor has the Greek language nor any other language. Only Sanskrit has the root of *devil* and that is *divine*. *Divine*, *deva*, *devil* – they all come from the same root, *div*, and *div* means light. Hence another name for the sun in Sanskrit is *divakar*. Another name for *day* in Sanskrit is *divas*, and *day* also comes from *divas*. Neither is *witch* condemnatory nor *devil*; *devil* means divine.

So don't be worried, Niskriya. You did well. Everyone enjoyed so much that you could not recognize who the witch was. You were looking again and again out of the corner of your eye to see who the witch really was. It was only late in the night, when you woke up from all that had gone by, that you looked at the witch and said, "My God! This is not a witch; this is a sannyasin!" But you were finished with your fear that no one flirts with you, and whether we should stop flirting completely.

Flirting has nothing to do with religion. It is natural, human. It is not a conditioning of the past; it is just intelligence that one wants to taste all kinds of things. You are not a devil, and now you know the witch was not a witch either. But you will remember the night forever – not only you, everyone who has seen it!

I have heard from the witch herself that Niskriya was looking again and again at the film, asking why I was waving my hand.

"What is the significance, the meaning?" And finally he decided it means flirt! This is a great conclusion, very philosophical! And whenever you want, just tell me. My function here is just to make you as blissful as possible. And whenever Niskriya wants a queue, I have a list of those who are ready to become witches. The witch also liked Niskriya and said that he is a very meditative man…

Just something serious now…

Hymie Goldberg has a tough day at the office and phones Becky to tell her he will be coming home late. Then he goes out to a Chinese restaurant and orders a Big Deal big meal. As plate after plate comes, Hymie notices that the Chinese waiter is always smiling and looking happy. "What is there to be so happy about?" moans Hymie.

"Ah," says the waiter, "I am just thinking about my sex life."

"And what is so special about your sex life?" asks Hymie.

"Well," says the waiter, "I take my time with sex. I put it in, I say 'Excuse me,' I take it out and go to the kitchen for a glass of rice wine."

"And that is it?" asks Hymie, amazed.

"No, no," replies the Chinaman. "I just take my time. I put it in. I say, 'Excuse me.' I take it out and go for some refreshment. I go back. I put it in. I have a wonderful time."

Later when Hymie gets home he decides to give the waiter's idea a try. He starts making love to Becky. He puts it in, "Excuse me," says Hymie, taking it out, "I am going to get a glass of seltzer." Two minutes later he trots back, puts it in and takes it out again. "Excuse me, honey," says Hymie. "I am going to get some blintzes." Just then Becky sits up in bed.

"You know, Hymie," she says, "you fuck just like a Chinaman."

13

Be, Know Thyself, Keep the Measure

Osho,
We poor modern Greeks don't know what the true religion of our ancestors was. So-called scholars have no answer as they are confused by the rich mythology of poets.

However, at Delphi, only three admonitions were engraved on the original temple: Be, Know Thyself, Keep the Measure. Osho, Would you reveal how these three mysterious precepts – including meditation, self-awareness, etcetera, but no god – could constitute the whole religion acceptable to men like Socrates, Heraclitus and Diogenes?

Greece lost its golden age not because of mythological scholarship or poetic imagination; it lost its golden age the day it decided to poison Socrates. It killed its own highest expression of spirit. With the death of Socrates begins the decline of a tremendously beautiful and great civilization which has given the world people like Pythagoras, Heraclitus, Epicurus, Plotinus and many more. The whole Western civilization owes its origins to the Greek genius.

To understand why it has become poor – not only outwardly but inwardly too – you will have to understand that when a civilization kills a man like Socrates, Socrates is not killed, that very civilization is killed. Socrates' death has to be understood because without understanding it, Greece and its intelligence cannot return to the heights it has already known.

Democracy was born in Greece but unfortunately we have not been able, up to now, to tolerate or forgive the giants among us. Their very presence becomes a deep wound in our being. Rather than becoming a challenge, a great invitation for a pilgrimage to the heights of consciousness, it becomes a wound. And it is very difficult to live with that wound. Something has to be done, and the easiest way is to destroy the man who makes you feel small.

The height of Socrates or Diogenes simply makes the ordinary man so inferior. But there are two ways to face this situation and one has never been used. The unused way is that the presence of Socrates or Pythagoras should become a deep certainty that "What can happen to another man can also happen to me. In their heights are my heights, hidden. In their freedom are the seeds of my freedom. In their sky, the stars have become clear – just a little effort is needed and my dark night can also be full of stars." Their presence should become a guarantee of human potential, of human growth, of possibilities which ordinarily look too far away.

But if Socrates can touch those stars, our hands are also hidden in his hands, because no two human beings are essentially different. All differences are nonessential; the intrinsic man is one and the same. But this path has not been chosen. Because it was difficult, because it would have to be proved by traveling to the same heights on the same lonely path, to attain the same light and the same consciousness.

Man chooses the easier. He does not bother whether the easier is truer or not. The easier is to remove a man like Socrates. His removal will take away the wound that his presence creates. Then you can be happy in your ordinariness, then you can rejoice in your retardedness, then there is no one who can hurt your ego.

Socrates was not killed because he had committed any crime. His only crime can be that he attained what is hidden in you. He made reality what is only potential in you; he transformed the seed into a glorious flower, dancing in the wind and the sun. You cannot forgive, the masses cannot forgive such a man. It hurts our ego very deeply.

And the masses are powerful as a crowd. Men like Socrates are alone; they are a majority of one. The crowd could not prove anything against Socrates. Still, he was poisoned and killed. Even in his death he was great, and the people who killed him, even in their life proved to be very ugly, mean and small. But it creates a situation in which no other man will try to become a Socrates because if to be Socrates means to be poisoned by the crowd, then why bother? Keep quiet. Don't annoy and irritate the ordinary and the mundane.

Once this settles in the mind of people, great people start disappearing. Slowly, slowly a country like Greece, which has brought humanity many flowers, became poor on both counts. The outer poverty is not so important because it can be destroyed very easily, but the inner poverty is very difficult. It is not easy to create Socrates, Heraclitus, Pythagoras. We have destroyed the atmosphere in which such roses blossom. By destroying these flowers, we have destroyed the possibility of other flowers who could have blossomed. What is the point, if this kind of treatment is going to happen?

One Christian missionary – a great thinker in his own right, Stanley Jones – used to come to India. I had become very friendly with him just by chance, because the church in which he used to speak was just near my house. I said to him once, "Jesus has promised to come back again, very soon. Now it is too long. You cannot stretch 'very soon' that long – one year, two years but not two thousand years!"

He said, "I had never thought about it."

I said to him, "I have thought about it: he will never come!"

He said, "On what grounds are you saying this?"

I said, "If he is intelligent, then one experience is enough. What have you given the man? – Crucifixion, and you are still expecting him to come?" And I told Stanley Jones to read a book that he had not read: Dostoevsky's *Brothers Karamazov*, one of the greatest books written by any man. But it is so big that very few people have dared even to start to read it. Just the voluminousness of the book prevents them. But it is so valuable that hundreds of Bibles are of no value compared to it. Dostoevsky has written it with his own blood.

In that book one of the characters is Ivan Karamazov. There are three brothers, hence the name *Brothers Karamazov*. One brother is very religious, almost saintly. Another brother is a rationalist, an atheist, absolutely against the other brother – thinks him naive, stupid – and his worship. One day he tells him a story…

He says, "Have you heard that Jesus has come back?"

The other brother said, "I have never heard that. Where is he?"

The other brother said, "You are continuously reading the Bible. You don't have time to inquire what is happening around you. Jesus had come to Jerusalem on a Sunday morning hoping, 'Now, I will be received and welcomed because the last time they were not *my* people. Now I am going among my own people. My own priests, bishops, cardinals, the pope – they will all celebrate my coming. And I had promised the second coming; I have to fulfill it.'"

The crowd was coming out of the church, the morning service had ended, so he stood there under a tree waiting to see whether they would recognize him or not. A crowd gathered around him – they recognized him not as Jesus Christ, but that "He seems to be some crackpot who is trying to pretend to be Jesus Christ." And they started advising him saying, "It is better that you get as far away from here as possible before the bishop comes out of the church."

But Jesus said, "I am Jesus Christ." And they all laughed.

He said, "This is strange. People laughed the same way eighteen centuries ago, but they were not my people. And you are *my* people, *my* sheep, *my* flock."

The people said, "Just get down. Don't pretend. We accept that you are a good actor, but that does not mean that you are Jesus Christ. What is the guarantee? Have you got any certificate, any message from God? It is just that you look like Jesus Christ. Anyone… And there are many who play the part of Jesus Christ in dramas, it is nothing new. Just don't be stupid. If the bishop comes to know, you will be in difficulty."

Jesus said, "Wait. You are ordinary, uneducated people. You cannot understand. But the bishop is *my* representative. He is bound to recognize me." The bishop came out and the crowd gave way for him.

The bishop shouted at Jesus Christ, "You idiot, get down from that platform and come into the church!"

Jesus said, "Have you not recognized me?"

He said, "I have recognized you. Just get in the church."

Jesus followed him thinking, "Perhaps he does not want to recognize me in front of people, or he wants to talk to me privately inside the church."

And inside the church the bishop locked him in a room and said to him, "I will release you only when you come to your senses – and I will call a barber to shave your beard and change your clothes. This kind of thing cannot be allowed. It is irreligious."

Jesus could not believe it. He said, "This is strange!"

In the middle of the night the bishop came with a candle, unlocked the door, fell at the feet of Jesus and said, "Forgive me. I had recognized you, but we are doing your business perfectly well. You are not needed at all. In fact, if you insist, we will have to crucify you – unwillingly – because people like you are always troublemakers. We have managed your empire with great difficulty. Almost half the earth follows you, not because of you but because you have the best managers: the priests, the bishops, the cardinals, the pope. What more can you do? We are already doing it! It is better you go back. Don't make unnecessary trouble; otherwise the second coming will become the second crucifixion."

I told this story from *Brothers Karamazov* to Stanley Jones and asked him what he thought about it. It is fictitious, but I think it has a truth in it – if Jesus comes, this will be the behavior toward him.

I have heard…

One early Sunday morning a young man looking like Jesus entered a church before the bishop entered. The bishop was almost in shock, but thought, "Perhaps he is just a hippie – these hippies are creating so much trouble. Now he is pretending to be Jesus Christ. What is he doing here?"

He approached the young man, and the young man immediately said, "Don't be misguided by your mind. I am not a hippie, I am Jesus Christ. You have been worshipping and you have been asking for me to come, and now I have come. Last time, I had come to a very remote, uneducated part of the world. I thought this time, New York would be better."

The bishop could not figure out what to do. He said, "Wait a minute." He immediately phoned the pope at the Vatican saying, "I am in great trouble. A man whom I think is a hippie, but he looks exactly like Jesus Christ… And who knows? He may be. I need your guidance."

The pope said, "Jesus Christ? Do two things: inform the police and look busy!"

It has not only happened in Greece, it has happened almost all over the world. Judea has not been able to create another man of the quality of Jesus, nor has Arabia been able to create another man of the quality of al-Hillaj Mansoor. And something similar, in different ways in different countries, has created a spiritual poverty.

In India we have not crucified Gautam Buddha, but we have been more sophisticated in destroying him, far more clever. And it is bound to be so because India is a far more ancient land than Greece. India has been in existence for at least ten thousand years.

Gautam Buddha and Socrates were contemporaries, but before Socrates there was emptiness in Greece. There were sophists, but sophists are not seekers of truth. There is not a single figure who can be compared to Socrates. Greece reaches its youth with Socrates – and dies young with Socrates. Much more was possible.

Gautam Buddha was not the first in the line but the last. Socrates was the first in the line. Gautam Buddha was not new to India – Krishna, Adinatha, Neminatha, Rama, Parasuram, Yagnavalkya… And the story goes back at least ten thousand years. Naturally, a far more sophisticated country. It has killed Gautam Buddha, not by poisoning him but by a far more subtle means.

The Hindu scriptures say – and you can see it – that in India, Gautam Buddha's influence has completely disappeared. The whole of Asia became influenced by Gautam Buddha; faraway countries like Korea, Taiwan, China, Mongolia, Japan, Sri Lanka, Mayanmar. The whole of Asia except India became Buddhist. What happened to India?

Buddhism simply disappeared from India as if Buddha had never been born here. The Hindu priest is more cunning than the masses who crucified Jesus and the masses who decided to poison Socrates. The Hindu priest is far more ancient, far more cunning, far more clever; he knows that if you kill someone, then sympathizers will remain. Then there is a possibility that a religion may become consolidated just because the founder was killed.

Christianity is not founded by Jesus but by the cross; hence I have always called it *crossianity*. It has nothing to do with Jesus. If Jews had been a little more sophisticated, as Hindus were, they would have tolerated Jesus. He was not doing any harm. Even if he was saying that he is the only begotten son of God, what is the harm? Let him believe it. All that he needs is some psychiatric help. But crucifixion is not psychiatric help.

Hindu priests have written that God created the world – he created heaven and hell – and he appointed the Devil to dominate over hell, but millions of years passed and no one entered hell because no one was committing any sin. The Devil became tired. He reached God and he said, "I resign! What kind of job is this? I am waiting for millions of years and not a single soul has ever reached. You can appoint someone else."

God said, "Don't be worried. Go back. I will make arrangements so that people start entering hell. I will be born as Gautam Buddha in India and I will corrupt people's minds and they will start going astray from the authentic Hindu religion. Then don't blame me. Hell will be overcrowded and you will have to control it."

Since then, the Devil is perfectly happy and his empire has been growing. All the Buddhists that have disappeared from India are in hell. And this was the strategy: Gautam Buddha was condemned by the Hindus in exactly the same terms, but in a very cunning way.

Socrates was condemned by saying that he was corrupting the youth – and the same was the case with Gautam Buddha, but it was enough just to spread the idea: "He is a god so you can worship him. But remember, don't get influenced by him, don't follow him."

He is certainly a god. And Hindus accept him as one of the reincarnations of God, but his reincarnation is to "corrupt people so that the Devil is satisfied." Do you see the sophisticated way? They don't deny Gautam Buddha's godhood, but they deny his philosophy, his religion. They say it is all corruption, to make people go astray from virtue. It is a strange fact that Hindus have succeeded in destroying Gautam Buddha far more successfully than the Jews with Jesus, or the people who killed Socrates. They have all failed.

A time came just three hundred years after Gautam Buddha's death… Three hundred years afterward, Alexander the Great came to India from Greece. His teacher was Aristotle, one of the disciples of Plato, who was a disciple of Socrates. And he was surprised that Buddhism had almost disappeared. Buddhists were either killed or converted or forced to leave the country. Even in Bodhgaya – where Gautam Buddha became enlightened, and his followers have made a memorial temple – the priest is a brahmin because there was no Buddhist to be found, even to be the priest in the temple.

I have been to the temple. I talked to the priest, the present priest whose family had been there generation after generation. His family have become the owners of the land and the temple where Gautam Buddha meditated, became enlightened, where he used to walk. Every place is occupied by the brahmins, and it has been so for eighteen centuries. You could not even fight the case. And they are *against* Gautam Buddha. They don't believe in his philosophy, but they worship Gautam Buddha because he is a Hindu god who helps the Devil to populate Hell. He is a god, but his philosophy is absolutely wrong and his religion is a corruption. No one in the world has killed a great philosophy like Gautam Buddha's with such subtle and sophisticated means.

It has happened all over the world that man has settled into a kind of mediocre, retarded state of mind. Now Gautam Buddhas don't arise, now Socrates is no longer heard. But because of these people's disappearance from the earth, we have become so poor, we have forgotten completely our innermost being. And this situation has helped the priests – which have the most corrupted, cunning profession in the world; it exploits people.

Your question is very significant. You say that in the ancient temple of Delphi, only three admonitions were engraved on the original temple: "Be, Know Thyself, Keep the Measure." God is not mentioned, heaven and hell are not mentioned, worship and prayer are not mentioned. In fact, within these three words the whole religion is complete. Other than these three words, all is nonessential rubbish which priests have been imposing. The garbage has gathered so much that the authentic is completely lost. Just a single word, "Be," is the whole of religion. The other two are explanations. You *are* – that much is certain. Being is certain – but who you are, for that you will have to go on an inner journey. Hence the second statement: "Know Thyself."

The third statement is of immense importance: "Keep the Measure." Unfortunately, no one has been able to keep the measure. In fact it is very difficult for the so-called scholars to exactly understand the meaning. Why, "Keep the Measure"? For what? A strange statement: "Be, Know Thyself, Keep the Measure." You will have to look...

You are and the world is. You have one universe of your inner being and you have another universe outside you. "Keep the Measure" means: remember the introvert has lost the measure, has forgotten the balance; the extrovert has also got lost. The West has lost balance because it is only extrovert; it only thinks about objective truth – the reality that is available to science. And the East has lost the measure because it only thinks of its own inner world; the outside is condemned as illusory, maya. It does not exist, it only appears. Don't be bothered with appearances. The East has decided for the inner and the West has decided for the outer. Both have forgotten what was engraved on Delphi's temple: "Keep the Measure" – a tremendously meaningful statement.

You *are*, but without knowing *who* you are, it does not have much meaning, significance. Understanding, awareness that you are – just knowing this much, that "I am" – is not enough. It is not much knowing. You have to go into your inner being to explore the vast blissfulness, the peace, the silence, your divineness, your godliness. But don't get lost in the inner. The outer is also divine, the outer is also immensely useful.

Unless science and religion are together, they are going to create some kind of poverty. The West is poor spiritually. It may have immense wealth, all kinds of technology, all kinds of comforts, but what is the use? The whole house is full of things but the master is completely lost. You don't know who you are. And if you insist, "Who are you?" you will think that you are asking a significant question. Others will think, "You seem to be mad. I am a doctor. I am an engineer. I am a businessman… What more do you want to know about me? My family, my father's name, my name – what else?"

And certainly you are not your name; it is just a useful label. You are not just your profession, you are not your job, and you are not your wealth. You are not your knowledge. Then who are you?

In this simple statement, "Be," is hidden the whole art of meditation. It means just being silent without any thought, simply drowning in your own consciousness, deeper and deeper, until you reach the very center. It has to be your own experience; you cannot borrow it. Without knowing it, you will remain poor. You will have many things, but you will not have yourself.

"Knowing Thyself" is the only way to experience the meaning and significance of existence.

Now there are contemporary philosophers in the West, existentialists, who insist that there is no meaning, no significance; man is just accidental, has no essence. These people are very influential today. In fact that is the only contemporary school of philosophers in the West. They represent the genius of the whole West. Their conclusion can only be suicide. If life has no meaning, if life is an accident, then why suffer? Why be miserable? Why be old, why be sick and why go into unnecessary anxieties, anguishes, angst? There is no point.

According to existentialism, you are not needed, you are unnecessarily forcing yourself. You are just like mushrooms, grown up existentially, accidentally, because a cloud rained; otherwise you are not needed. You are not serving any purpose. Existence is perfectly happy without you. The stars will not miss you. Do you think they will miss you? Do you think they will miss if Niskriya is not sitting there like a Chinaman? – that without him everything will be disturbed?

No, existentialists say everything will continue to be as it is. You will not be missed because you are unnecessary. One wonders that people like Jean-Paul Sartre, Jaspers, Heidegger don't commit suicide. Perhaps the only reason is that there is no meaning in committing suicide either. So drag on and wherever you go, in whichever direction you go, you will reach the grave, so what is the hurry? Why dig your own grave? Someone else will dig it.

The West has lost all contact with the inner being and the East is poor, hungry, starving, because it has lost… Remember the third statement engraved in the temple of Delphi: "Keep the Measure." Remain balanced. The outer and the inner should be like two wings: you cannot fly like an eagle in the sky with one wing; you need both wings. Science alone is going to lead humanity to suicide, and religion alone is going to lead humanity to the same goal – suicide, starvation.

Just by the end of this century, in this country alone, five hundred million people are going to die because there is going to be no food. Already half of the country is starved, undernourished. We have just seen one thousand people dying per day in Ethiopia, and now there is another famine – and this is going to be a bigger famine than the last one. Perhaps two thousand, three thousand people will die every day. This is forgetting the immense, the significant balance: "Keep the Measure." These three words are enough.

You are asking that these words may include meditation, self-awareness, etcetera, but no God: How then could they constitute a whole religion? God is not a necessity of any religion; God is a necessity of the priesthood. God has nothing to do with religion. Buddhism has no God, Jainism has no God; there are already religions which have no God.

I don't see any point. If you are truthful, sincere, meditative, alert, and you know yourself; if you know the beauty of your being, the immortality of your soul, the eternity of your existence, God never comes in the way. No one has ever met God.

In those three precepts, "Be, Know Thyself, Keep the Measure," God is not mentioned because God is not needed at all. It is an unnecessary hypothesis; not only unnecessary, but harmful. In the name of God, so much cruelty, so much violence, so many crusades: Mohammedans destroying Christians, Christians destroying Jews, Mohammedans destroying Hindus, Hindus destroying Buddhists. And the reason? The reason is that their hypotheses of God are different.

This is sheer stupidity – to fight for a hypothesis. And for centuries, millions of people have been burned alive, just because their hypotheses of God were different. Such strange behavior has been shown by the priesthood of all religions of the world, and everything becomes possible in the name of God.

Just a few days ago, the Vatican pope gave a declaration to all the Catholics of the world: "You cannot confess directly to God." Strange. You have to confess via the right channel, otherwise the priesthood will be finished. If you start confessing directly to God, then what are thousands of bishops, cardinals, priests going to do? Their whole business is to be mediators between you and no one.

In India there is a place, Surat, where there is a local, small religion, but of very rich people. Their high priest takes the money whenever someone dies and writes a note in the name of God saying, "This money will be delivered to you when you reach paradise." The man dies and the written note is put in the pocket of the dead man, so when he reaches he can cash the money.

I used to stay in Surat in the house of a friend who belongs to that religion.

I said to him, "You must be utterly stupid. All that money is going into your high priest's pocket."

He said, "No, this is not possible."

I said, "Then let us go to your cemetery. We will have to open a grave and let us see whether the card is there, the man is there, or they have reached heaven."

He was hesitant. He said, "But this is very irreligious."

I said, "I don't belong to your religion. You stand aside, I will dig!"

So I pulled out a freshly buried man and took out the note. He had given the high priest three lakh rupees. I said, "Look. The card is there, the man is there, and in all these graves… Whichever grave you want I can dig."

He said, "No, don't. Just get out of here. If someone finds out there will be trouble. Somehow push this man inside the grave and put the card in his pocket. It is none of our business."

But I said, "This is being done everywhere."

Why is the pope insisting, concluding, that it is a sin to confess directly to God? It is a strong statement. You have to confess to the priest and the priest will manage God's compassion and give you some punishment – and punishment means a few dollars!

I have heard…

A bishop and a rabbi were great friends. They had decided to go to the golf course, so the bishop was finishing his business quickly. But there was a long line of confessors. The rabbi was waiting outside in the car. Finally he came into the cabin. The cabin was divided with a small window: on one side sits the confessor, on the other side sits the priest.

The rabbi said, "We are getting late."

The priest said, "I am doing the business as quickly as possible, but people go on and on. When they confess they don't confess in a summary way: just *long* stories. It seems as if they enjoy it. They say in detail, 'I have done a rape. This happened and that happened…' It is a simple thing: you have committed a rape, put ten dollars in the box and get out!"

The rabbi said, "Get ready. I don't know because in my religion this kind of thing does not happen, but no one knows who is sitting on the other side. You go and get ready and I will finish the business."

But a rabbi is a rabbi. Another man came and he said, "Father, excuse me. Again I have committed a rape."

The rabbi said, "Just put twenty dollars in the charity box."

The man said, "But this is too much. Last time it was only ten dollars. Have the rates gone up?"

The rabbi said, "No, the rates are the same – ten dollars in advance. You can commit one more rape!"

Without the priest, who is going to collect these dollars? And where do these dollars go? The pope goes around the world at least three times a year, doing a very stupid thing which he can do in the Vatican as many times as he wants – kissing the earth. He can do it every day; what is the point of going to Australia, coming to India? Perhaps the taste may be a little different, but how much money is wasted? Each tour costs eight million dollars. Even when Queen Elizabeth went to Australia, it cost only three million dollars. When the pope went it cost eight million dollars – and it is coming out of your pockets.

God is not getting anything! God is the creation of the priests to exploit you. God has nothing to do with religion. And the inscription on the temple of Delphi is absolute in those three points. The religion is complete. All else is commentary. Be authentic, true, sincere, yourself – not someone else, not a personality but an individuality; not having a mask but your original face. "Be," and "Know Thyself." Look into your own inner world, of what it consists. It consists of eternity, it consists of blissfulness, it consists of ecstasy. It makes you the richest person in the world. It consists of intelligence, purity, love, compassion – all that is great. But it will not help to make you rich on the outside. It will not create a marble palace because you know yourself. That is the meaning of "Keep the Measure."

And there is no conflict, no contradiction. You can be meditative and you can be creative. In fact you can be more creative if you are meditative. You can create much more on the outside if your own roots have gone deeper in your being. In these three words the whole religion is complete. But the people who have reached these heights, these riches, create antagonism in the mediocre minds.

Socrates was asked by the judge who pronounced his death sentence by poison – the judge must have been a man of some compassion and some intelligence – he said, "Socrates, I am helpless because the majority of the people of Athens want you to be killed. But I can suggest to you a few alternatives: you can leave Athens." Because in those days Greece was not one country, but every city was a state. So Athens was a state in itself, and once you crossed the boundary of Athens, the constitution of Athens or the law of Athens became invalid.

The judge said, "I can manage it. Simply get out of Athens. There is no need… I don't see the point in unnecessarily destroying yourself."

Socrates said, "Death is going to come anyway and moreover I have lived in Athens my whole life. This is the most civilized state in the whole of Greece. If this civilized state cannot tolerate me, who is going to tolerate me? In this old age, to start my academy again or my school somewhere else… And the result, I know, is going to be the same. It is better at least to be poisoned by the most civilized part of the country."

The judge said, "I have another alternative: stop speaking – because they are against you for the single reason that by speaking you corrupt people, you destroy their conditionings. Stop speaking, be silent. It is good in old age."

Socrates said, "I should be silent just because of fear? No. You don't understand me. Without speaking the truth, what is the point for me to live? If I have to live, I have to speak the truth. Don't be worried unnecessarily. If the majority decides to give me poison, perhaps this is the way existence wants to take me back."

A man of tremendous courage… But with him, Greece lost something very essential: the urge to seek the truth. In fact, unconsciously people must have become afraid even to mention the word *truth*. If it leads to death, it is better not to bother about it and never to question the superstitions of the people. Just remain silently one with the crowd; it is safer, more secure. And the moment any community of human beings loses the urge to search and to seek the truth, in a certain way, it dies. It vegetates, but it does not live. It loses dignity.

I have been to Greece and I never went outside my house. Amrito, who was my host, is sitting just in front of me. She had found a very beautiful palace on a small island, just by the sea. Sannyasins from all over Europe had gathered. We had nothing to do with Greece or its politics; we were meditating, we were enjoying, we were dancing, and I never left the house in fifteen days.

I was to be there only for four weeks, but the archbishop of the Greek Orthodox church started sending telegrams to the prime minister, to the president, to the newspapers, stating that I am corrupting people's minds. I had not even gone out of my house.

Finally, he threatened that if I was not thrown out of Greece immediately, he was going to dynamite the place where I was staying with my friends. These are the people who teach "God is love." He was ready to kill people, to burn people alive who have done no harm to anyone. And the reason? – that my stay in Greece is going to corrupt the youth, the same old reasons that were put against Socrates.

I could not believe it: "How can I corrupt the morality and destroy the religion in just fifteen days?" They have created the morality in two thousand years, and if the morality and the religion which has been created in two thousand years can be destroyed by a tourist in four weeks, it is worth destroying!

I was arrested. They did not have any arrest warrant; just the prime minister became afraid that my stay may rock his boat. On the airplane the police officer came and asked to see my passport. He stamped "deported" on my passport. I asked him, "Do you understand law? Are you aware that you are putting a stamp of deportation on a man's passport who has not committed any crime?"

I took his pen and just crossed out his stamp that he had put on my passport. He said, "What are you doing?"

I said, "I am *not* deported. I am simply leaving – sign here!" He became so afraid. I said, "If you don't sign, then tomorrow in the court you will have to sign. Otherwise, tell me what crime I have committed and give the evidence." My passport has become a historical thing! He signed immediately out of fear and stamped again that I was simply leaving Greece, not deported.

At the international airport of Athens there were forty police officers with the chief of the police and all the high police officers – as if I were a terrorist! News media people were present and they wanted to ask me a few questions. I was answering them and I told them that these police officers are the same people, it seems, who must have poisoned Socrates, because the reason is the same. But for me it was too early; at least Socrates had lived his whole life, a long life. He was not a tourist. I myself was going to leave in two weeks. And these people had no arrest warrant; just loaded guns against a person who had not even a paper knife.

The chief of the police came out of the crowd to interfere. I said to him, "I don't like anyone interfering with me. Just go back to your place and keep your mouth shut, because these people are not taking your interview; they are taking *my* interview!"

And I was amazed. He is the chief of the police, and he simply went like a dog, tail between the legs, back to his place! I could not believe it; I was thinking that he would argue. I wanted him to argue because the whole news media was there, television from all over the world. Perhaps he was afraid that if he said anything… "This man seems to be strange! No one tells a police officer to 'Shut up and go back to your place,' so it is better to get behind the crowd."

I asked the men who had arrested me, "Can I stay the night in a hotel in Athens? It is late, twelve o'clock at night. My plane is standing here; in the morning I will leave."

They said, "No. We cannot allow you to stay even a few minutes. You have to leave immediately. That is the order from the prime minister" – just out of fear of an old idiot, the archbishop, who had been protesting from the very first day I entered Greece.

The archbishop had been threatening, "I will bring a protest," but he never did it, so I inquired, "Amrito, find out what the matter is. I am waiting for the protest and it is not coming."

Amrito said, "He will never come because no one goes to his church except six old ladies, so he will look like an idiot leading a procession of a protest consisting of six old or almost dead ladies. He will only threaten. Who is going to carry out the threat that he will dynamite the house – those old ladies?"

Amrito and my other sannyasins and the intelligentsia of Greece, Nobel Prize winning people, are all protesting that this treatment of me has been absolutely illegal, unconstitutional. Their fight continues. I have told Amrito, "Whenever you can manage, next time I am going to come and I am going to invite all the sannyasins from all the European countries. Then we will have a protest and procession against this old idiot, and then we will see what he can do."

But it is strange… When I was arrested I was asleep. My secretary, Anando, was standing outside on the porch. She said to the police officers, "Just sit and we will wake him up. Let him at least change his clothes and then you can do whatever you want."

They said, "We cannot wait."

As I was awakened, I heard them throwing stones against the glass windows, doors. I had no idea what was happening. I simply thought perhaps the archbishop had come with his old ladies – I missed the scene it seems – and dynamite was exploding. But it was just the police officers who were doing it. And they had dynamite too! They have not answered the protest which was done on my behalf by the Greek intelligentsia. The politicians have nothing to say; they are simply silent.

Sitting here, I am fighting in twenty-five countries – wherever my people are – either in the courts or in protests or in parliaments. Perhaps it has never happened: a man who is sitting here, who never goes out of his house, who never even enters this city… But love has its own ways and love has its own weapons. Even though Socrates has been dead for twenty-five centuries, his fight continues. I am part of that fight. It is the same fight, with the same people; just the bodies have changed and nothing else.

Now you have to become also part of this fight. Nothing illegal and unconstitutional should be perpetuated in any country which calls itself democratic but listens to the threats of religious priests. If the country was *really* democratic, just because of his threat the archbishop should have been arrested. He has been committing a crime, or at least threatening to commit it. Rather than punishing him, I have been punished. But I have been punished in so many countries that now I have started almost enjoying it!

It has been too Greek and too serious. For a change…

One day, Paddy, Sean and Mick are going for a drink when, just before they enter the bar, a man comes flying out of the door and falls down the steps in front of them.

"My God," cries the man, "the bartender there is almost crazy. Whatever you do, don't mention his ears!"

The boys are curious, so they go inside and on their way to a table they take a cautious look at the bartender. The bartender is a mean looking character, with a completely shaved head and no ears – just two holes in the sides of his head.

Mick goes up to the bar first and not being able to look the man in the eye says, "Gee, I love your red velvet pants. Where did you get them?" The bartender lifts a huge fist and knocks Mick to the floor.

Sean tries next, and feeling uncomfortable looks down at the floor and says, "I like your shoes. Where did you get them?" The man lifts his huge fists and knocks Sean to the floor.

So Paddy strides up to the bar, looks the man straight in the eye and says, "You wear contact lenses, don't you?"

The bartender takes Paddy's hand and shakes it vigorously, "Thank you," he says. "You are the first person all day who has had the guts to look in me in the eye and treat me as a human being. And yes, I do wear contact lenses. But how did you know?"

"Simple," says Paddy. "You could not wear glasses because you have no ears!"

Old man Finkelstein is determined not to grow old and senile. He hears about a clinic in Switzerland that claims to be able to make you younger. So he packs his bags and leaves on the next plane. At the clinic he is given hormonal injections, blood transfusions, animal implants and everything else that the medical profession can devise.

On his last day at the clinic, the doctor visits him. "Well, Mr. Finkelstein, that's the end of the treatment," he explains. "No more painful injections, no more operations. However, we have to do one or two more tests, so you won't be able to go home tomorrow, you will have to stay one more day." At this old Finkelstein breaks down and begins to cry.

"What is wrong?" asks the doctor. "Are you in pain?"

"No," sobs old Fink, "but what will Mummy say if I am late back to school?"

14

Trust Is the Greatest Miracle in the World

Osho,
I am standing before a door on which is written: Mysteries of Existence. I open it and find myself at your feet. Looking deep into your eyes, I see that suddenly the door is there again. I open it and once more, I am here at your feet.

Osho, how do you manage to be both the door and the mystery on either side?

The feet of the master are only symbolic. What is real is your deep gratitude. What is real is your loving surrender. What is real is dissolving your personality and your ego. If your trust is total, indubitable, then the feet of the master can become the door because gratitude is the door, trust is the door, love is the door.

The same is true about the eyes; there is no mystery, but with the eyes there is a little difficulty. With the feet you are not encountered by another being. No one is there when you look into the eyes of your master. The danger is you may see yourself reflected in the mirror of his eyes. The danger is that the revolution that can happen through the feet will be more complicated if it happens through the eyes.

The eyes are certainly capable of becoming doors to the divine, but you have to remember that everything has to happen within you. To tell the truth, the master does nothing! He is simply there, available, opening many doors; whichever is your choice. His eyes can become doors, his feet can become doors; just his remembrance can become a door. The love that you feel – and the master may be thousands of miles away – can become the door. The whole alchemy of transformation depends on you. Are you ready to be transformed? Then even a single gesture of the master indicates the truth. Then his eyes or his feet are doors to the divine.

The day Gautam Buddha died, he insistently told his disciples, "Don't make statues of me. Avoid making temples for me because they can be deceptive. Your remembrance is enough; it is the authentic temple. Your surrender, your love, your dissolving yourself into the master's being – nothing else is needed."

But people are people; when Gautam Buddha died, they started worshipping the tree, the bodhi tree. Its name became the *bodhi* tree because that is the tree where Buddha became enlightened. With gratitude, love, and the flowers of their hearts, they found that it was as if the one who had left the body was still sitting under the tree.

But life has its own way. Soon they started making temples. In the first temples there was only a carved tree in marble, no statue of Buddha. But the decline started, and it was not far away that soon the tree was replaced by statues of Buddha. The world is so strange that the man who has died with his last wish that his statues should not be made has the greatest number of statues in the world. There are millions of temples in China; one temple particularly has ten thousand statues of Buddha. These are dead flowers. The fragrance does not arise any more. You can call them art, but they are not the fulfillment of the master's final statement.

And he was right that "Within five hundred years my religion will disappear." It was exactly after five hundred years that his temples, statues, priests, and rituals surrounded the whole of the East. But the trust disappeared, the love disappeared, the sensitivity and gratitude disappeared.

You can have thousands of statues; it can be a good collection of pieces of art, but it is not religion. The statue has no heart and you cannot commune with the statue the way you had communed even with the feet of Buddha. Life was flowing in its most beautiful and highest consciousness.

The West has never understood why in the East, disciples touch the feet of the master. They don't understand a simple thing because something invisible, non-objective, has not happened. When the disciple, with total love and humbleness, dissolves himself in touching the feet of the master, the energy that is flowing, the energy that has come to its purest form, thrills the disciple. And remember, energy always flows downward, energy never flows upward.

If the master touches the head of the disciple, that is immensely important but very esoteric, because that creates a circle of energy: the energy is flowing from his hands into the disciple, the energy is flowing from his feet into the disciple. The disciple is almost flooded with the master's being, his ecstasy.

The West has missed a tremendously significant experience. In the West to touch someone's feet looks humiliating, disrespectful. In the East if the master moves his feet and does not allow you to touch his feet, that means you are not prepared, you are not open; the energy cannot move in you. And the master, encompassing the disciple from both ends, turns the wheel of his life to new dimensions. So it does not matter whether it is the feet or the eyes, or just the remembrance or just the heart throbbing with love and gratitude.

The door will open; there is no mystery. It is a simple arithmetic, but not the arithmetic that is being taught to you. It is the arithmetic of the spiritual world, and those who have not tasted the feeling, the fragrance of it, are certainly very poor.

Little Ernie is taken to the dentist's office for a checkup. "It is okay, Doc," says Ernie. "You can take off the mask, I have already recognized you."

The master has no mask but certainly your recognition is needed. When and where, in what situation the recognition penetrates your heart like a ray of light, depends on your intensity of your search. Finally, the day you recognize yourself, you will find that you, the master, the universe are all one. There is no one to surrender to, there is no one to fight against. And then the ultimate peace descends that transcends all understanding – but it does not transcend experiencing.

Don't be analytical. The seeker on the path has to be open, available, nonanalytical, nonrational; not arguing with the reality but just taking it as it comes, tasting it and its fragrance. You are immortals, you just don't know it. The whole universe is yours but you are like small children collecting colored stones on the sea beach. The whole mysterious world is not far away. You need not move a single step toward it; it comes to you if you are ready. Just remember, "Am I ready, ready to open? Indefensible?" Are you ready to allow the fresh breeze of life to pass through you?

The seers of the Upanishads have made the most significant statements. One of their statements addresses you as " *Amritasya putrah*: oh sons and daughters of immortality." Certainly, your body is not addressed, nor is your mind addressed, but you are much more. The body and the mind are both useful instruments, but don't make a cage of them and don't be present in them, and you will know how much blissfulness is possible, how much aliveness is your inheritance. You inherit the whole universe with all its beauty.

The master is only an excuse to show you the path and an example to show that what has happened to him can happen to you – you need not go in doubt and hesitation. Every man and woman has the seed of being divine. Those who have realized it, out of sheer compassion, go on whether you listen to them or not; they go on trying their best somehow to reach you.

The story is that when Gautam Buddha died and he reached the gates of paradise there was great celebration because only once in a while the gate opens, once in a while a man achieves his total potential. But Buddha refused to enter the door. It is a parable; don't think it is a historical thing. But sometimes parables carry more truth than history. Buddha refused on the grounds, "How can I enter paradise when millions of people are groping in the dark and searching in the dark? I will wait until the last human being has entered paradise." The Buddhists think he is still waiting.

Whether he is waiting or not, one thing I know for certain is that existence is waiting and you are postponing for stupid mundane things, things which do not matter, which are simply junk and are delaying the time of your flowering. The spring comes and goes and you remain without flowers. A master is the spring. When the master knocks at your door, drop everything because nothing is more important than to know yourself, to be yourself and experience the great beautitude, the ecstasy that is your birthright.

Two Israeli spies caught in Cairo are put up against the wall and the firing squad marches in. The Egyptian captain asks the first spy, "Do you have a last wish?"

"A cigarette," he replies.

The captain gives him a cigarette, lights it up and asks the second spy, "Do you have a last request?"

Without a word the second spy spits in the captain's face.

"Harry," cries the first spy, "please, don't make trouble."

What more trouble? They are going to be shot dead. What more trouble can you cause? And asking for a cigarette as the last thing shows our minds. Just think that if God appears before you and asks you, "What do you want?" What are you going to ask for? A beautiful car? A palatial house? A beautiful woman? Then you will see with what kind of rubbish your mind is filled.

I don't think anyone is going to say, "I want to meditate, I want to realize myself." These things can be postponed – what is the hurry? Right now, a cigarette is needed, and anyway self-realization will not provide cigarettes, palaces! You don't know what self-realization will provide. The very idea of self-realization does not arise because you take it for granted that you know yourself.

Socrates was right when he said, "Know thyself." There is nothing more important in life to do. Don't waste your whole life in things which you will laugh about later on: how much you wasted, how much ecstasy was possible. And you were smoking cigars, running after women – or vice versa in the case of Niskriya!

Now, the fellow understands that women are approaching him to say, "Don't be worried boy, we are here to take care of you." The Chinaman cap that he was wearing has been presented to him by a woman whom he has fancied for years. And she came herself, seeing the situation that Niskriya had become a hero in a single day. Before any other woman catches hold of him, the woman that he has been fancying for years approached, herself.

Now he is in trouble; he cannot do his work. He is a man of a very one-dimensional, scientific attitude; he does not look here and there. Now all these women are going to disturb him. His real love affair is photography. Now he is praying to me, "Save me. I am perfectly happy alone" – but it is too late.

You go on doing things repetitively in your life – the same things, without ever bothering about the real mysteries, the real meanings, the real significance of your being. The day you become interested in your being, meditation blossoms automatically. And if by chance you come across a man whose eyes become doors to a world beyond, touch his feet and you will be filled with a strange energy and vibration which is a music, a harmony, a synchronicity with existence. The master is only an example of what you can also be.

Two tramps are lying on adjacent benches. One of them is reading an old newspaper: "It says here in a health report that you can exercise over one hundred muscles when you laugh."

"That's typical," replies his friend, "those health nuts take the fun out of everything."

Now even laughter becomes an exercise!

Milarepa, you have the capacity of love, trust, creativity. You are showered with all the blessings that are possible. Don't miss this opportunity. Touching the feet of a master is simply a gesture that "I am ready," that "From my side there will be no obstruction," that "I withdraw all defense strategies." The master won't have to do anything. By becoming open, dropping all defense strategies, the door has opened. The master was just a remembrance of your own future.

The master has never existed in this sense in the West. Teachers have existed, but a master is not a teacher. A teacher teaches you doctrines, theologies, philosophies; a master simply opens the door of your innocence, of your simplicity, of your ultimate awakening.

The master is not a teacher. The master is simply a remembrance: "My God, what am I doing? Here is a man surrounded with an aura of beauty and truth; it is not a time to miss. This man reminds me that I can also be in such glory, in such cosmic blissfulness."

A hotel manager is giving some advice to his staff about how to cope with embarrassing circumstances.

"Suppose one of you enters a room," he explains, "and finds a lady in a state of undress. Anything you do or say could make matters worse, but there is a simple way out. Just pretend you are shortsighted and say something like, 'I'm terribly sorry, sir, I'll come back in a minute.' That will save her from embarrassment."

The next morning a young waiter is on duty taking breakfast up to a room. He knocks on the bedroom door and receiving no answer, walks in. There on the bed, a naked couple are indulging in an energetic bout of lovemaking. Suddenly, they sense the waiter's presence and there is a ghastly silence until the waiter remembers the lecture of the day before. With complete confidence he asks, "Would either of you gentlemen like breakfast?"

Whatever I say to you, don't interpret it, because every interpretation is misinterpretation. Whatever I say, simply absorb it. Let it become part of your being, and you will never be in such an embarrassing situation.

Dr. Bones and Dr. Skinner are out duck hunting early one morning while it is still dark. They hear an owl in the tree above them snoring.

"I'm such a great surgeon," brags Bones, "I can go up there and take out that owl's tonsils without even waking him up."

Ten minutes later, Bones climbs down the tree and holds up two tiny tonsils.

"That's nothing," says Skinner, "I'm so nimble with my hands, I'll climb up there and remove the owl's testicles without him feeling a thing!"

Sure enough, a few minutes later, Dr. Skinner returns with a pair of tiny balls.

Months later, the owl flies over the same tree with a friend.

"Hey!" says the friend. "It is bedtime, let us sleep in that tree tonight."

"No thanks," replies the owl, "I slept there a few months ago and ever since I have not been able to fuck worth a hoot or hoot worth a fuck."

You have to be very subtle, surgical, in removing your ego, in removing your idea that you are separate from existence. It is perhaps the most subtle thing in the world to be able to touch the feet of the master and not feel for a single moment that you are doing something against your being, that you are losing your dignity. But on the contrary to feel that for the first time you have felt the energy which makes you dignified, luminous, and to see that those feet don't belong to any individual. Those feet are simply a device for you to drop your ego, the idea of specialty, the idea of being someone, to just be simple and innocent.

The East has earned much by a simple device of the disciple touching the feet of the master. And when the master feels that the disciple's act is authentic and sincere, he puts his hand over his head and the disciple is flooded with the same energy that is overflowing the master. It is a strange transfer – invisible, but experienceable.

I am reminded of Mahakashyapa, perhaps Gautam Buddha's most innocent and most pure disciple...

He was told by Gautam Buddha, "You are enlightened. You have everything that I have. Now go and spread the word."

Mahakashyapa said, "If I had been alert, I would not have become enlightened. To be close to you, to be able to touch your feet every day and be flooded with your love, your compassion, was enough for me. If there is a way to become unenlightened, I would rather become unenlightened."

Buddha said, "That is difficult. You cannot go backward."

He said, "But what will I do? Each morning when I touch your feet, my joy, my blessing, my ecstasy reaches the highest point. And when you touch my head, it feels as if a shower of roses is falling over me. I will miss it very much."

Buddha said, "You will not miss it. Just do one thing: remember in whichever direction I am, bow down to the earth and touch the feet – and the same thing will continue to happen."

He was so innocent, he trusted and went away. Every morning the first thing he would do was to find out where Buddha was and in that direction – and perhaps that direction was not right, perhaps Buddha was not there, but in his heart, in his trust, he would touch the feet. Tears of joy would flow from his eyes and he would feel a hand on his head. That was an absolute guarantee that he was in the right direction. And the same flowers with even more fragrance would start showering like rain around him.

People said to him, "Mahakashyapa, you have been declared enlightened by Gautam Buddha and you cry? Enlightened people don't cry! What is this nonsense? There is no one and you are touching the feet with such grace. And when you get up, you are almost a different man, so luminous."

Mahakashyapa said, "Distance makes no difference. Love knows no time and no difference of space. It is something that happens within you; the outer is only a device. As far as tears are concerned, they are not the tears of pain or anguish, they are tears of joy, of utter celebration that he has not forgotten. And I feel his hand on my head. That gives me the guarantee that the direction is right."

When he came back to Gautam Buddha, he asked, but Gautam Buddha laughed. He said, "You are so innocent, Mahakashyapa. Everything was happening within you; even that hand was your own. And I know it was impossible for you to find exactly where I am, in which direction, from hundreds of miles away. But because you trusted, the miracle happened."

The greatest miracle in the world is trust. But remember, I am not saying belief. Dictionaries go on confusing people. If you ask dictionaries what trust is, they will say that it is belief, it is faith. It is neither. Belief is always with a doubt hidden behind it. Faith is blind, not your own experience. But trust is your own experience. Once you have tasted the sweetness of trust, you don't need any religion and you don't need any prayer.

I have told you many times, but this story is so beautiful that I love to tell it… Before the Russian revolution – Russia has one of the most orthodox Christian churches. Christianity is such a childish religion that they call someone a saint not in the same way as we in the East call a certain person a *sant*. Although people who are concerned only with words and translations think *sant* and *saint* are the same, they are not. The Eastern word *sant* means one who has realized *sat*, the truth. It is his own realization. And the Western concept of saint is one who has been certified by the church. It comes from the word *sanctus*; he has been sanctified, certified that he is a saint.

But in this beautiful story of Leo Tolstoy…

The archbishop of Russia became very much concerned because people were going more and more to visit three saints. And there were so many rumors and talk about the three saints who lived on a small island in a vast lake. He wondered, "I have not certified them; how can they become saints?" But seeing that thousands of people are going to touch their feet, finally he decided something had to be done, otherwise these three persons would destroy the whole religious hierarchy. Things have to be done in a certain way – Christianity has created hierarchy, bureaucracy.

In the East, one cannot conceive that a *sant* needs anyone's certificate; his own experience is enough. In the East, one cannot believe that even the pope, the representative of Jesus Christ and God, is elected. Is this politics or religion? We have never elected anyone as Gautam Buddha; we have never elected anyone as Krishna. When a person has the experience, the very authority that his experience gives him – he is recognized, has to be recognized, and he is not bothered about whether you recognize him or not. But how can you keep your eyes closed, how long when the sun has risen?

Finally, the archbishop took a motorboat and went to the island to see what was happening.

It was early morning, and seeing those three poor people he said, "My God! These idiots. Who has made them saints?"

He went there with great authority. Seeing that the archbishop himself had come, all three touched his feet. He was very satisfied. He asked, "Who has made you saints?"

They said, "We are poor people. No one has made us saints – and we are not. We just live here under this tree and we don't know what happened, how the rumor went around and why thousands of people come. And how can we convince them that we are not saints? We are not very educated.

"In the beginning we used to try to say that we are not saints – that brought the opposite result. People thought, 'They are so humble; they say they are not saints. They must be. No ego...' So we dropped it. We said, whatever is happening, let it happen. You can help us. Just tell people that we are not saints but poor men. Tell them not to come here because they unnecessarily disturb us the whole day."

The archbishop was gratified and felt that it had been a good act to come, but that he should have come earlier because they had become famous nationwide. He asked them, "Do you pray every day?"

They looked at each other. They said, "Yes."

"What is your prayer? Do you know the Christian authorized prayer?" he asked.

They said, "We are uneducated. We don't know any authorized prayer."

"Then what kind of prayer do you do every day?"

They nudged each other saying, "You say."

The archbishop said, "Say it."

They said, "It is a little embarrassing because we have made it ourselves. And it is a very simple prayer. Please don't laugh and don't tell anyone. Knowing that God is three – God, the holy ghost and the son – and we are also three, we thought we could make a prayer. So we put our minds together and made a prayer: God, you are three, we are also three, have mercy on us. This is our prayer."

In spite of himself the archbishop could not resist laughing, "You think this kind of thing is prayer? Stop all this nonsense. I will teach you the authorized prayer."

But the authorized prayer was long. When he was finished, one of them said, "We cannot remember that long prayer. You have to repeat it. We will try our best. At least you have to repeat it two times more, because we are three and you have to repeat the prayer at least three times. Perhaps then we may remember it."

He repeated the prayer three times. They touched his feet; he blessed them and went away in his motorboat, feeling very happy. Just in the middle of the lake he saw a miracle. All three of those poor people were coming toward him running on the water.

He could not believe his eyes. He had not even deeply believed that Jesus had walked on water – and these fools are running on the water!

They stopped the boat and said, "Forgive us. We have forgotten. The authorized prayer is too long. Can you repeat it one more time?"

The archbishop must have been a man of intelligence. He said, "No need to repeat. Your prayer is right; continue your prayer. I have been praying that authorized prayer my whole life. I cannot walk on water, and you are doing the miracle."

They said, "This is not a miracle. This is our usual practice. We are poor people, we don't have boats or anything and our trust in God is absolute. He is three, we are three, have mercy on us. And he has never failed us. He has always been merciful to us."

Trust opens the door to the uneducated, uncultured. It is not a question of knowledgeability, scholarship. It is not a question of being elected a pope. It is hilarious that God's representative should be elected by human beings. It is sheer politics. If God wants his representative, he should nominate him, but he seems to be so utterly lazy that after six days of creation… What he has been doing, no one knows! He even had to send the Holy Ghost to make poor Mary pregnant – he wouldn't even take that much trouble.

The East understands one thing: truth is your own experience and it comes from your trust. And when it comes, it comes with an authority not derived from any scripture or any representative of God. It is intrinsic in the experience itself.

I only teach you trust, love, compassion, and a way to your inner being – meditation. And whoever you are, whichever religion you have unfortunately been born into, whichever race, it doesn't matter. The color of your skin… I don't know exactly now how much it will cost, but twenty years ago, it took nearly one rupee's worth of color to make a man a Negro. But remember one thing: the Negro is richer than you are. His skin is far richer than the white skin!

We have created all kinds of discriminations and all kinds of theologies, man-made, mind-manufactured. They are not going to help. You have to be very simple, and your religion has to be very simple. Trust life, love life, rejoice life, and existence will take care of you. Existence really takes care – I can forget my watch… At the exact moment it reminds me! Just look at your watch…

15

Dissolve Marriage, and Misery Will Be Dissolved

Osho,
I remember you saying, "Don't surrender to a person, surrender to love." I'm in a relationship with a beautiful and powerful woman and we both definitely don't want to surrender to each other. What does it mean to surrender to love while being in a relationship? I'm quite in a mess.

Prem Avida, I can understand; you really are in a mess and there is no way out. I have heard that there are three rings of love: the engagement ring, the wedding ring and the suffer-ring. Your question makes it clear that you have not understood what I mean when I say, "Don't surrender to a person, surrender to love." And love is never a relationship; this is your problem. Relationship is bound to be a bondage. In relationship either you have to surrender or the other has to surrender.

And you yourself recognize that you are "...in a relationship with a beautiful and powerful woman and we both definitely don't want to surrender to each other." Then just live in coexistence. Live the way all poor husbands are living. Show the world that your wife is so surrendered to you. Who is preventing it? You just have to tell a lie and there is no mess – and surrender to the "powerful and beautiful woman." But remember, the moment a man surrenders to a woman he loses dignity in her eyes. She starts looking here and there for someone who has the guts not to surrender.

You don't seem to have guts. There is no need to surrender to each other. Surrendering to love means to enjoy in the happiness of the other, rejoice in the being of the other; be in tune with each other, dance in harmony.

The question of surrender is political, it is not a question of love. Relationship is not love at all; it means love has ended and the relationship has begun. It begins very soon after the honeymoon – mostly in the middle of the honeymoon. It is not easy to live with another person whose lifestyle is different, whose likings are different, whose education and culture is different. And above all the other happens to be a woman! Even their biology is different.

But one thing you have to understand clearly is that it is the man who longs for domination, and it is the woman who dominates. This is what I call coexistence: live and let live. More than that is all imagination. If you had really known what love is… The basic thing is not to create a relationship. Stand aloof as the pillars of a temple stand aloof, but support the same roof. Don't destroy the individuality of the other, enhance it if you can; otherwise, at least leave it as it is, uninterfered with. Freedom is not to be destroyed in the name of love. Freedom is a far higher value than your so-called love.

The moment you create a relationship you are entering into a contract, a business deal. Love disappears, it becomes law. Now you are not very far away from the divorce court. Unless you are a person who loves to be dominated, who likes to be henpecked – then you have got a perfect woman. Then don't make any fuss, simply surrender, declare, "I am a henpecked husband. I am your poor servant; you are my master. You order and I will follow."

Actually that is what is happening all over the world but no one says it. There are many things which are not asserted in the society.

A teacher asked a small child, "Can you name an animal which changes color?"

The small boy stood up and said, "Colors? I have not only known one, but I live with such an animal who even changes his whole being."

Even the teacher could not understand. She said, "What is that animal?"

He said, "He is my dad. At home, when he goes out he is a lion – just look at his chest and his mustache – and when he comes back to the house, he is just a rat!"

It has a long history which persists in humanity's unconscious. The man is always afraid of a few things. Someone may disturb their relationship. He wants to make a prison cell for his wife, but it doesn't matter; even in that prison there are people: the chauffeur… You cannot make it a hundred percent foolproof prison because then even you cannot enter it. The fear, the jealousy that your object of love… And remember when I use the word *object*, I use it very emphatically. Man has treated woman as a sexual object, not as a human, an equal spiritual being – just a commodity.

For thousands of years women were sold in the marketplace, auctioned. And even today – although the form has changed, the reality remains the same – you prevent your wife from having any kind of friendship with any other man. It is an ugly way. In this vast universe you are not alone. There are so many unique people and your wife is just a human being and it is a human frailty that sometimes she may see someone and a great love may arise in her.

It may be casual, but your fear is very strange, it arises out of your financial mind, your greed. You are afraid – your son has to be *your* son; the empire that you are creating should not go into someone else's hands. You will die one day – your son should receive as a heritage your desires, your ambitions, your riches. Your son has to fulfill all that you have achieved and all that you wanted to achieve.

Your son is a projection of yourself. In a certain way it is true. Your son is nothing but a miniature cell of your being. You will die, but you will live in your children, they will be your blood and your bones. The fear is that if the wife is allowed freedom then it will be very difficult to know whether your son is actually yours or someone else's.

A man was consulting an astrologer. He was very skeptical of the whole thing. Just out of curiosity and to prove the astrologer wrong, he said, "You are talking about faraway things, past lives, future lives. I want to ask you a simple question. This is your test piece: Can you tell me where my father is at this very moment?"

The man closed his eyes and said, "Your father has gone fishing."

He said, "I knew already that you are cheating people. My father is dead; he has been dead for four years. How can he go fishing?"

The astrologer said, "The man you think is dead was not your father. Your father has gone fishing, just go and ask your mother."

To make it a certainty and a guarantee that your son is your son, the whole problem of bondage, contract, relationship, doubts and jealousies, fights and fears… The whole mess has descended on humanity for this stupid reason. When you are in your grave, it does not matter who owns what. Your palace and your money – what difference does it make? Just an ego trip, a very deep ego trip. When I say surrender to love, I am saying that loving is enough, don't make it a relationship. I am absolutely against marriage. Marriage is one of the causes of human misery, one of the most fundamental causes. And unless man drops this whole idea of marriage he cannot drop jealousy, he cannot drop fighting; the wife cannot drop nagging and questioning and inquiring.

A man was tired because his wife would somehow always find out that he had been with a woman. Women have a very intuitive approach toward life. The man may deny, saying, "I have not been…" but the fragrance from his coat shows that he has been with a woman; it is not the fragrance that he uses or is used in his house. Or just a hair on his coat will be enough proof.

So the man consulted a psychiatrist, "What should I do? Every day it is a problem and somehow she finds something and humiliates me, tortures me. Her way of torture is very simple. Whenever I say that I want to make love to her, she turns on her side and says, 'I'm suffering from a headache.'"

This headache has been so much of a problem for husbands. The wife is suffering from a headache, but the real headache is happening to the husband.

The psychiatrist said, "How does she find out?"

The man said, "She has thousands of ways to find out. There is a time limit and if I don't come home within that time limit, then 'Where have you been?' is the first question on entering the house. I have to think continuously where I have been! That question has to be answered and I know that she is not going to believe it because I myself don't believe it. There is no authority in saying it, no sincerity. I cannot look her in the eyes and say that I have been with friends or I have been at the Lions Club.

"The moment I see her, my mind starts getting confused about which answer to give because she is going to find out. One day I said that I had been playing cards with a friend. She immediately phoned the friend and he said, 'I have not seen your husband for months.' I never thought that she would do that! One day she found a hair, a long hair – and that was enough!"

The shrink suggested, "Shave your hair completely, and before you go in the house, take care that there are no hairs on your coat, on your shirt."

He said, "My God! I have to shave my head?"

The shrink said, "Even your own hair may create trouble – and you have long hair."

He said, "First I will try to clean my clothes. First I should go to the cleaners to be certain that there are no hairs."

And when he reached home his wife looked at him, searched about for some clue: Not even a single hair around? She started crying, "This is the end of our relationship. You have started moving with bald women. There is a limit! There is not even a hair on your coat. Where have you been?"

Husbands and wives are continually fighting, fighting unnecessarily and destroying their lives miserably. To be a husband or to be a wife is such a misery that looking around the world one cannot imagine that man is a rational being as defined by Aristotle. If he was rational, at least marriage would have been dropped long ago. But Aristotle himself married two women and they used to beat him. And he is the father of Western logic!

Just a few days ago there was a survey in America showing that women have started to confess for the first time that their husbands beat them. Previously, it was thought that it is an ugly tradition of the poor countries of the East where women are beaten by their husbands.

In countries like India it is prescribed in the scriptures that if you want to live in peace, once in a while, a good beating of your wife is an absolute necessity. But no one has ever thought that the same is the situation in Europe, in America. The only difference is that in the East, it has been a very long tradition, and even religious scriptures give it sanction.

In the West, people used to think that husbands didn't beat their wives, but the reality is coming out. Because of the women's liberation movement, women are confessing that they are being beaten by their husbands. They have not told anyone because of the prestige of the family, but the truth is that it is not only women who are beaten by men, men are also being beaten by women. Although there is no scripture that says that every wife should beat the husband once in a while just to bring him to his senses!

In reality it happens every night all over the world; wives are throwing things at husbands. A pillow fight is almost a religious thing: every day it has to be done – anyway it is good exercise and no one is harmed. Wives go on breaking things, but they always break things which are worthless. They are wiser than men. Even in their anger they keep an alert eye not to destroy something valuable, not to destroy the TV! Old dishes? You can break them. They make a good noise also, a language which is understood in the whole neighborhood.

They throw things at their husbands, but they make certain that they don't hurt the poor fellows; otherwise they will have to take care of them. They never make them a real target. They throw things here and there, avoiding the poor fellows.

But it goes on and after all this fight – as happens in every war – some kind of peace, some kind of treaty and the husband goes out to buy ice cream. And people are living together in this misery without any analysis of where it is coming from. It is coming from private property and the desire to keep the property in the hands of "our *own* children."

Karl Marx used to think that when communism would come, marriage would automatically disappear. He was logically right, but life is strange; it never follows logic. It always goes surprisingly, shockingly, illogically, irrationally. In the beginning years of communism, Karl Marx's theories were tried in Russia. For three years they tried to dissolve marriage, but then finally they found that if marriage is dissolved, misery is dissolved. Then to keep people enslaved is impossible. They are enslaved because they are in such suffering they cannot think of freedom. They cannot be free from their wives – what kind of freedom can they think of? And where is the time?

A man was packing his suitcases and his wife said, "Where are you going?"

He said, "I am going to Paris. I have heard that there you make love to a woman and the woman gives you ten dollars."

The wife said, "Wait, I am coming with you."

The man said, "But what are *you* going to do? What is your purpose?"

She said, "My purpose is to see how you manage to live on twenty dollars for the whole month."

After three years of effort, the Russian government understood that marriage is absolutely necessary to keep the nation. If marriage disappears, the nation cannot remain any longer. The nation will follow because marriage is certainly the unit of the nation. Once there is no marriage, thousands of things will change. And the government became afraid: "Who is going to take care of the children? What will happen to the ancient prejudice of morality? It will disturb the whole structure."

They dropped the idea, thinking that Marx was only a theoretician, he was not a man of practicality. He had not taken into consideration the consequences of his idea. The idea is still great, but just as an idea it cannot be practiced. But the strange fact is that Marx himself never practiced it. He was a married man with children and he lived the same miserable life as every husband and every wife lives.

A world which accepts individuals and their freedom of love has certainly to take care that unless your society, your community wants children, you cannot produce children. When the society wants children, the children will belong to the society and will be brought up by the society.

You can meet your children, you can love your children and it will be far better that the children grow away from you; otherwise seeing the mother and father continually fighting, do you think the children are getting the right direction for their lives? They are being conditioned to repeat the same thing! They will fight with their husbands, they will fight with their wives, because that is how things are; that is how things have always been!

An ancient story says that whenever Adam used to go to sleep, Eve used to count his ribs. She was created out of one of Adam's ribs; one rib was missing. That's okay, but if another rib goes missing then there is danger; there is some other woman in the bushes.

Jealousy is perhaps the ugliest attitude in life. But the way life has been managed up to now, you cannot avoid jealousy. There is jealousy about everything. The wife is worried that when the husband goes out, one never knows where he is going, what he is doing. She takes every care in her own way. On the first day of every month she takes all the money that he earns, so he cannot go anywhere.

A man rushed into his general manager's office and said, "You are such an idiot, and I used to think you were my friend."

They worked in the same office and had the same status. But the first man got a pay raise and his friend, just to make trouble between his friend and his wife, phoned to say, "Your husband has got a raise this month."

The wife waited the whole month. The husband was feeling very happy that she accepted the old salary and she did not know that now he was getting more: "That much I can use for my own purposes."

But the moment the wife took the money she said, "Bring out the rest; you got a raise."

Now he was caught red-handed deceiving his own wife. She took all of the money and she was crying and weeping. The husband had to console her and he was feeling guilty: "I am sorry that I did it, but how did you come to know?"

She said, "Your friend phoned so I was waiting for the whole month to see… You talk so much about trust and faith. What happened to the trust and faith? You were being faithless and what were you going to do with the money? You tell me in detail what was in your mind! There must be some woman – I have always suspected! The way you enter the house always looks as if you are hiding something. Your very face gives the idea of a suspicious, faithless man. Now you are caught red-handed."

And this goes for every point…

I was traveling to Kashmir, and in my air-conditioned coupe there were only two seats. I was there and there was one other person, a woman. On every station a man would come and would bring fruits and sweets.

I asked the woman, "I think your husband loves you very much."

She said, "Yes, we have been married for seven years."

I said, "Don't lie to me."

She became angry saying, "Why are you saying that?"

I said, "No husband will bring sweets and flowers and whatever is available at every station. I can say with guarantee that the man is not your husband." She looked at me.

She said, "Strange, but I have to confess he is my husband's friend."

I said, "If he was your husband, once he had put you in the compartment he would have disappeared. If he had to travel in another compartment he would not have missed that great opportunity. You would have been fortunate enough if he had met you where you were going!"

Whenever you see people, if the husband and wife are together you can immediately see that they are married because the husband does not look to this side or to that side, but keeps looking straight down. The wife keeps an eye on the husband, and both look sad.

We have unnecessarily made such a sad world, when the same people could be so happy. I sometimes think that just a twenty-four hour experiment would be enough to prove what I am saying. Exchange your wives and there will be such joy and such great laughter and singing and dancing. Life will become aflame. Just those twenty-four hours would prove what I am saying: that marriage is a very subtle, psychological imprisonment.

If you really love the woman you say you love, then give her freedom, and in that freedom it is implied that she can have weekends and you cannot interfere. You also can have weekends. It is strange; simple things can make this world very beautiful – just weekends.

But you say that you want a relationship and that neither of you want to surrender. Then why drag me into the trouble? Just fight it out. Sooner or later one starts cooling – the hot affair dies down.

Two small kids were sitting on the steps of a school. The smaller one said, "Every boy has a girlfriend, but I can't find a girlfriend."

The other said, "You are too small to have that such trouble. Just grow up, enjoy your freedom. Once you are grown up you cannot enjoy your freedom. You will find a woman. The real problem is not how to find a woman, the real problem is how to get rid of her."

Getting is very easy – you can ask Niskriya! Now he is trying to get rid of the witch that he has found, avoiding in every way – and that was so joyous. Under the influence of booze, he confessed to the witch in the middle of the night, "This is my greatest life experience." And in the morning all was finished – he is back to his camera. Now other women are torturing him. He himself has invited the trouble; otherwise no one was bothering him. Looking at him, everyone thought that he is a very meditative person.

Just looking at him any woman would bypass him, but now women know that he is a great lover, just he has the face of a meditator. That does not mean anything. He waited long and finally he blurted out. "How long can one wait just because he has got a face which appears to be that of a meditator?" It is not his fault.

Sally Goldberg goes to the doctor to ask for some help in losing weight before her wedding day. He prescribes a course of pills for her.

A few days later she returns to his office, "These pills have awful side effects," she says worriedly. "They make me feel terribly passionate and I get carried away. Last night I actually bit off my boyfriend's ear."

"Don't worry," says the doctor, "an ear is only about sixty calories."

Osho,
Would you please speak about the three rings of love? – the engagement ring, the wedding ring and the suffering?

You seem to be in the same trouble. I have already described those three rings. Just the first two rings are okay. The real problem is the third ring which comes without fail. If you want to avoid the third ring, avoid the first.

Little Ernie is looking through the family photo album when he comes across a photo of his parents' wedding day.

Ernie calls his father over, and pointing to his mother's wedding dress says, "Was that the day that Mum came to work for us?"

Little Ernie is dragged by his mother into the doctor's office. She sits down and says, "Doctor, is it possible for a nine-year-old boy to remove his own liver?"

The doctor roars with laughter. "Of course not," he replies, wiping the tears from his eyes.

Ernie's mother turns round and cuffs Ernie on the ear, "What did I tell you?" she shouts. "Now go straight home and put it back in again!"

Hymie Goldberg loses a lot of money on the stock market and is in a terrible state. He goes to visit his doctor and says, "Doctor, doctor, my hands won't stop shaking."

"Tell me," says the doctor, "do you drink a lot?"

"I can't," says Hymie, "I spill most of it."

"I see," says the doctor and then proceeds to give Hymie a thorough examination. When he has finished he says, "Tell me, do you get a tingling in your arms, aches in your knees and sudden dizzy spells?"

"Yes," replies Hymie, "that's exactly what I get."

"That's funny," says the doctor, "so do I. I wonder what it is!"

Then the doctor refers to his notes for several minutes before looking up and saying, "Tell me, have you had this before?"

"Yes," says Hymie, "I have."

"Well, there you are then," replies the doctor, pressing the buzzer for the next patient. "You have got it again!"

Things are so clear. You can see all around: rings and wedding rings and sufferings. There is not even an exception to be found – there is no question. But because everyone is in the same boat, and everyone grows up with the same kind of people, one starts accepting it as the only reality possible for human beings. It is not so.

Man can grow in many different directions, in many different ways. The way he grows is just imitation. Because other people are doing it, you go on doing it. [*The sound of loud music is heard, coming from a wedding procession happening close by in the neighborhood.*] Do you hear these bands playing? These are leading a few idiots toward the same imprisonment I am talking about. You should go and see! The idiots will be sitting on the horses almost looking like kings, not knowing where they are going.

In India this wedding ceremony has a very strange history. There was a time when people used to go and snatch a girl from other tribes – hence the horse! It is a remnant of all those old days when marriage was the beginning of a war. One tribe would invade another tribe, and steal as many young girls as possible. Even today a sword hangs symbolically at the side of the man who is sitting on the horse, going to the girl's house to get married. The crowd that follows is a reminder that marriage was once an attack by a crowd on another tribe.

No idiot even asks why the sword, and what is its purpose? There is not going to be any fight; the marriages are prearranged. But remnants go on for centuries, and if you go deeply into research, you will be surprised. The horse, the sword, the crowd, the marriage party... It used to be the army. And the band was a declaration: "We are coming. Be ready." It is a war symbol.

Those women were stolen forcibly, violently, and naturally became slaves. Times changed, now anyone can sit on a horse with a sword and go into the street with a bogus crown! If he is alone, people will start throwing stones at him shouting, "Where are you going? Who are you? What is the purpose? Whose horse have you got?" But in a marriage party the same man is respectfully garlanded.

History is a very beautiful study if you go deeply into it. The father of the girl touches the feet of the father of the boy. That is symbolic of defeat: "We are defeated" Otherwise there is no reason for it. And there is no reason for all these fireworks; these are the remnants of bombs and shots. It was a violent affair and it was expected that the woman should love and respect the husband so much that if he died, the woman had to jump in the funeral pyre with her dead husband. She also had to burn, alive. By committing suicide she was very respected. Memorials were raised because she proved to be a true lover. How can she live when her beloved has died!

I can understand it is possible, but I cannot understand one thing: no man ever jumped into any woman's funeral pyre, and no one ever bothered that only the women were expected to love men. In fact while the funeral pyre was still hot and burning, people started thinking about the marriage of the man whose wife had died. Rather than jumping in the funeral pyre, he starts thinking about riding another horse – strange and stupid behavior.

In this century, when we think humanity has become a little civilized, still things go on. And we allow them to go on, although we are also the victims.

Just something for the marriage ceremony…

Wu, the Chinaman has a bad case of constipation. He goes to his doctor who prescribes a course of pills and asks Wu to come back and see him next week.

Wu takes the pills and duly shows up at the doctor's office the next week.

"Did you move yet?" asks the doctor.

"No move yet," replies Wu.

So the doctor prescribes a stronger dose.

Wu comes back the following week and the doctor asks, "Did you move yet?"

"No move yet," replies Wu.

So the doctor gives him a huge dose of pills and a box of suppositories.

Next week Wu comes back and the doctor asks, "Did you move yet?"

"Yes," replies Wu. "Had to move. House full of shit!"

16

All Religions Teach Love and Practice Hate

Osho,
Is it always good to follow the heart or once in a while should a clear mind decide what is to be done? And what to do when they want to go in opposite directions?

Your question is hilarious – to say the least! Let them go on their way. Why should you be worried? The mind is going in one direction; the heart is going in another direction. It is none of your business to interfere. Simply remain a witness and see where these fellows are going. Not understanding the secret of awareness is the cause of your problem. You are neither the heart nor the mind. You are a pure consciousness behind them. And unless you get identified with the heart or the mind, they cannot go anywhere; they don't have their own energy.

You ask me, "Is it always good to follow the heart…?" And I have been teaching you that your heart, your body, your mind, should follow *you*. This is how we go on misunderstanding.

You are not to be a follower of any; you are simply to be a witness. Witnessing the mind moving in one direction and the heart in another is a great experience. Experience that you are neither of them. You can remain above. And they cannot move very far: they need each other's support and finally they need energy from you because you are life, they are only instruments.

Your question is just like this: my left hand wants to follow this side, my right hand wants to follow this side – what am I supposed to do? Of course, to follow the right is always good. Right is right and left is wrong! Not to follow is the secret of freedom, and once your heart and your mind know that you are not a man who is going to follow, they will stop quarreling, they will stop moving because they don't have any energy. The energy comes from you and it comes because you get identified with them, but every identification is wrong.

You remind me of Ruthie Finkelstein who has been having therapy for some time without finding much improvement in her generally depressed and confused state. Finally she tells her therapist that she is going away for a few weeks for a holiday in Greece.

Sometime later the shrink receives a postcard from Ruthie which says, "Having a lovely time, but *why*?"

You cannot even have a lovely time without inquiring why. And that destroys your whole joy. The questions are a disturbance. No question is of any importance. Just to be silent and remain aloof, watch what goes on around in you – in the mind, in the heart – will not only solve this question, it will solve all your questions. But the mind loves to ask! You are saying that you feel very happy following the heart and you know it is always good. Who told you? The heart has also committed as many crimes as the mind.

When a Mohammedan destroys a statue of Gautam Buddha, do you think he is doing it from the mind? It is his heart. When he forces someone on the point of the sword to change his religion and become a Mohammedan, do you think he is following his mind? He is following his heart. The heart has its own conditionings which go deeper than the conditionings of the mind. The heart has always been praised for the simple reason that it gets no chance – the mind goes on playing the whole game and society prepares you not to listen to the heart.

But the Christians who were killing Mohammedans and the Mohammedans who were killing Christians – and they are still doing that – not for a moment does a doubt arise that what they are doing is absolutely inhuman and cannot be religious. If it was done by the mind the question would have arisen, but because it is done by the heart, the heart does not know questioning. They feel with absolute certainty that if a man is killed in a crusade, which they call jihad, then that man has already reached paradise. And your paradise becomes more certain, according to how many people you kill.

These are not mind things. They have entered the heart, slowly, slowly sinking down through the centuries. Just one difference is that the mind always questions if what you are doing is right or wrong. The heart never questions. That's why all the religions want you to surrender, to be faithful, to believe. These are the qualities which enter the heart. I don't teach the mind; for that there are thousands of universities. I don't teach the heart because I know the heart can do things more cruelly than the mind. The mind at least hesitates; the heart believes totally.

I teach you awareness of your being beyond both the heart and the mind. I say unto you to disidentify yourself and they will forget going this way or that way. And for the first time you will be the master and they will simply be servants. You can order them and they will have to follow because without your order they cannot get any nourishment.

As far as your problem is concerned, let each of them go wherever they want. Simply remain centered – above, alert, not being dragged by them and not being influenced by them. Then your purity of awareness will lead you to the cosmic purity of existence. That is the only way of merging with the whole. All else is just an utterly futile exercise.

Your silence will take you to the right path. Neither your mind knows silence nor your heart. Your consciousness will take you in the right direction. Neither your mind knows how to be conscious nor your heart. They are both fast asleep and whatever they do is going to prove stupid and dangerous to yourself and dangerous to others.

If all the crimes that have been committed in the world are counted, you will be surprised that the religions are the fundamental cause of those crimes. They teach love and they practice hate. They teach oneness and they practice discrimination. The religious history of man is so mean, so ugly, that to be part of any religion is to prove that you are retarded, that you don't know what these religions have done.

Old Sam Finkelstein arrives from Russia to visit his relatives in America. On his way to Texas he sits down in a train between two rednecks. He nods in a friendly way but the rednecks sit in stony silence.

Old Sam notices an American newspaper lying on the seat and picks it up. Having taken classes in English for the past few months, he is able to read most of the page, but all of a sudden he turns to the redneck on his right and says in a thick Russian accent, "You look like an intelligent man. Would you be kind enough to tell me what this word is?"

The redneck winks at his friend and without looking at the paper says, "That word is *syphilis*."

Old Sam thanks him and reads on. A few minutes later he turns to the other redneck and says, "You are obviously a man of education. Would you kindly tell me what this word is?"

The redneck smirks, winks at his friend and ignoring the newspaper says, "That word is *gonorrhea*."

"Syphilis and gonorrhea?" cries old Sam. "Ah, my God – that poor Ronald Reagan!"

Don't take any problem, any question seriously. Your taking them seriously makes them important and forces you to find a solution.

Whenever a question arises in you, just be silent and watch the arising of the question. Watch how it becomes more condensed, watch how it becomes more clear – but go on watching. And you will be surprised that just as you are simply watching and not getting involved, it starts evaporating. Soon there is tremendous silence left behind it, and this silence is the answer.

But what do people do? A question arises in their minds – and there are thousands of questions; you will need millions of lives to find the answers for all of them. Still you will remain ignorant, knowledgeably ignorant. And because of the question you start asking others. Perhaps someone else knows the answer; that makes you a beggar. The knowledge that you get from others is borrowed; it is not going to help you at all. One thing and only one thing helps. Watch the question and don't be dragged by it in any direction.

Be silent and see the whole question and what happens to it. It comes and it goes; no question remains there. It is just like a signature on water: you have not even made your full signature and it has started to disappear.

The art of meditation is how to make your questions disappear, not to give you an answer. The answer will bring new questions and there is no end to it. Meditation will leave you in a space where there is no question, no answer, but only a purity, a simplicity – the same you had known when you were born. You were alive but there was no question. You were so full of wonder. Your eyes sparkled seeing a small thing.

In a right society – for which I go on hopelessly hoping – a child's innocence should not be destroyed. And when we have an almost oceanic innocence all around, the beauty and the experience of it are so tremendous and so strong that who cares about stupid questions? In fact they never arise.

I am reminded of D. H. Lawrence, a man of this century whom I have loved much. He was condemned from all corners – not as much as I am condemned, but he prepared the way. He was walking in a garden early in the morning with a small child, and the small child asked, "Uncle, why are the trees green?"

As far as language is concerned, the question is absolutely correct, but you know that it is stupid and you cannot say that it is stupid. If it had been someone other than D. H. Lawrence, who was a man of great sincerity and authenticity, then any other knowledgeable person would have told the child that trees are green because of a certain chemical, chlorophyll.

Perhaps for the moment the child would have been silent: chlorophyll… But sooner or later the questions were bound to arise, "Why do all the trees have chlorophyll? Who goes on giving them chlorophyll? What is the purpose of making all the trees full of chlorophyll? What is chlorophyll?"

But D. H. Lawrence looked at the innocent eyes of the child and said, "My boy, trees are just green," and the boy was immensely happy. The trees are green because they are green – it is not a problem, and the small boy understood it. What can you do? If the trees are green, they are green. It is their problem, it is not our problem. Why should we be bothered?

But as man grows and is filled and fed by all kinds of knowledge and information in the name of educating him, in the name of making him civilized and cultured, we spoil a tremendously beautiful innocence. And there is no need to know why the trees are green. It is perfectly good that they *are* green. If they decide to change, that is their problem, they can change.

But look at people's questions and you will find that all questions without exception are stupid. Although I might say, "This question is very significant," you know I am a contradictory man. It does not bother me, why should it bother you? I am controversial. It has never bothered me; it has bothered the whole world. Strange! These are *my* problems and I don't consider them as problems. They are my unique individuality. Why should you bother? And people get sad…

Just a few days ago Hasya brought news of a sannyasin who had dropped sannyas because, "Osho says many things which are not in the Bible." I am not speaking on the Bible. I don't care a bit about the Bible. But deep down he must have been waiting to be confirmed in his beliefs, to be blessed: "You are right and your Bible is right." And strangely enough, before that he had not read the Bible!

He took sannyas first, thinking that I am talking about the Bible. And being impressed, he went into an utterly boring book, the Bible. No intelligent man can read it from the first page to the last page – no one does it. And what is the problem? Why should I talk about things which are in the Bible? Rather than dropping the Bible, he dropped sannyas. Such is the way of conditioning.

Three missionaries, all nuns, are walking along the street and one is describing with her hands the tremendous grapefruits she has seen in Africa.

Then the second one, also with her hands, describes the huge bananas she has seen in India.

The third nun, a little deaf, asked, "Father who?"

Strange questions – nothing to do with your own being and its growth. But people go on for their whole lives and finally, they become just walking encyclopedias. They know everything, and deep inside at the center is still the same innocence with which they were born. It is not knowledgeable, it is not ignorant; it is simply innocent. And to be utterly innocent is the whole purpose of all meditations, particularly here. I allow you to ask questions so that I can destroy them as much as possible.

Osho,
Just the name of Mevlana Jalaluddin Rumi uttered from your lips sends waves of an unknown force like a wild wind through me. Tears well up with an unbearable feeling of longing. Perhaps I missed Rumi and again, because of the same stupidities, I am missing you. Beloved Osho, can you comment?

It is true: the very word *mevlana* has still, after twelve hundred years, a life of its own. And if you are open, *mevlana* is going to stir strange waves, open unknown dimensions. There have been thousands of masters in the world, but no one's name begins to stir your heart and being with a song and with a juice like Mevlana. And Mevlana simply means the master. In Persian, Arabic and in Urdu, the Mohammedan countries, the word *maulana* is used for the master. But the disciples of Jalaluddin Rumi, who never called him Maulana, must have been great; they changed the whole word. They started to call him Mevlana, "my Beloved Master."

Maulana means a man of great knowledge. It has no juice in it. It is dry, desert dry. Mevlana is a play on the same word but with a slight change. Even those who don't understand its meaning, when they hear "Mevlana" something in their being starts responding to the word. Ordinary words are not that potent, but Mevlana is an exception. It has beauty because it does not say that the person, Jalaluddin Rumi is a man of knowledge. It has some love in it, some trust in it. It does not refer to knowledge at all. It simply refers to *my* heart, to *my* being. Mevlana means "my master," and not just my master but "my Beloved Master."

Since Mevlana Jalaluddin Rumi, no Sufi mystic has been called "Mevlana." No Sufi mystic has stirred so many people's hearts. So I can understand that you say, "Just hearing the name of Mevlana sends waves of an unknown force like a wild wind through me. Tears well up with an unbearable feeling of longing. Perhaps I missed Rumi and again, because of the same stupidities, I am missing you. Beloved Osho, can you comment?"

I can say only one thing to you, Abhiyana: it is possible you may have been with Mevlana; hence a faraway echo of that beautiful man. His dances and his songs, his grace and his peace and his showering of love may be stirring you. You are not here for the first time; most of the faces are perfectly well known. You may have changed your mask, but that does not mean anything, your inner being still shows something that you have carried from many, many lives. And because you have all been here the whole time since eternity, there is every possibility you may have missed Mevlana, and now there is sadness. But Mevlana very gracefully allowed you to escape. I am a different type of man. I will follow you until you get it! This time you cannot go before you get it – not because of you, but because of me!

However stupid you are, the very recognition makes you innocent. Stupid people never recognize that they are stupid, and if you tell them, "You are stupid," you are in trouble. Only a man of innocence can say, "Because of my stupidities I missed something far back. It is a very faint picture or a very faint echo of a song." But this time it is not going to happen because my way of working is totally different from Mevlana Jalaluddin Rumi. I am really a dangerous man!

If twenty-five countries don't allow me to enter, it is not without any reason. Once I get hold of someone I never leave him unless he says, "I have got it! Now let me go home." And you cannot cheat me because I know when you have got it and when you have not got it.

Those who were not worthy, and I could not see any possibility that in this life, however hard I hit them, they were going to open their doors because they were hiding behind the doors and locking them from inside… Finally, I thought that it was wasting time and I should leave this work to some other master who knows the art of entering these people, a real locksmith. I am not a locksmith. The world is vast. How many people can I manage? It is better to let them go. I made arrangements and devices so that those people would disappear to wait for future lives, to be caught by another master of a different quality.

But you don't belong to that category. If even just the word *mevlana* thrills you, you are already ready to sing and to dance and to celebrate existence. To me, other than that, there is no religion. You are a simple person, accepting your stupidity.

Especially for you, a beautiful anecdote to laugh at in the middle of the night when you get them! Right now you can laugh just to keep company, but the real thing happens in the middle of the night when suddenly, under your blanket, your belly starts: "My God, this joke has done something to me!"

A Couch Potato is watching football on TV and eating peanuts at the same time. His wife comes in and somehow manages to distract him, so he puts a peanut in his ear by mistake. He tries everything but can't get the peanut out.

Just then his daughter and her boyfriend Chip come in and find her father shaking his head and sticking his finger in his ear.

"Let me help you," says the boyfriend. "I will put two fingers in your nose and blow in your other ear."

So the desperate Couch Potato lets the boyfriend try, and sure enough, the peanut flies out. The man is ecstatic and goes back to watching TV.

Later that night the Couch Potato and his wife are lying in bed when she asks, "That Chip is really a nice boy. What do you think he will be when he finishes college?"

"I don't know," replies the husband, "but by the smell of his fingers, I think he will be our son-in-law."

17

Love Is Not an Emotion but an Expression of Your Being

Osho,

So often a feeling that I can't describe fills my heart and my whole being. During the other morning's discourse it felt like overwhelming love for you and the whole. But now I realize that the same feeling or a very, very similar feeling also comes up in fear, anguish, throbbing pain, helplessness and frustration.

I am trembling and confused. Can you say something?

There is certainly something similar in very different emotions: the overwhelmingness. It may be love, it may be hate, it may be anger – it can be anything. If it is too much then it gives you a sense of being overwhelmed by something. Even pain and suffering can create the same experience, but overwhelmingness has no value in itself. It simply shows you are an emotional being.

This is typically the indication of an emotional personality. When it is anger, it is all anger. And when it is love, it is all love. It almost becomes drunk with the emotion, blind. And whatever action comes out of it is wrong. Even if it is overwhelming love, the action that will come out of it is not going to be right. Reduced to its base, whenever you are overwhelmed by any emotion you lose all reason, you lose all sensitivity, you lose your heart in it. It becomes almost like a dark cloud in which you are lost. Then whatever you do is going to be wrong.

Love is not to be a part of your emotions. Ordinarily that's what people think and experience, but anything overwhelming is very unstable. It comes like a wind and passes by, leaving you behind, empty, shattered, in sadness and in sorrow. Love, according to those who know man's whole being – his mind, his heart, his being – has to be an expression of your being, not an emotion. Emotion is very fragile, very changing. One moment it seems that is all. Another moment you are simply empty.

So the first thing to do is to take love out of this crowd of overwhelming emotions. Love is not overwhelming. On the contrary, love is a tremendous insight, clarity, sensitivity, awareness. But that kind of love rarely exists because very few people ever reach their being.

There are people who love their cars. Niskriya loves his camera! That love is of the mind. And then you love your wife, your husband and your children – that love is of the heart. But because it needs change to remain alive, and you cannot allow it its changeability, it becomes stale. The same husband every day; it is such a boring experience. It dulls your sensitivity, it dulls every possibility of joy. You slowly start forgetting the language of laughter. Life becomes simply work without any joy; one has to work because one has a wife and children.

I have heard…

An old couple appeared in court. The husband was ninety and the wife must have been eighty-five; they wanted a divorce.

The judge could not believe his eyes. He asked, "At this age? Any moment you can pop off. What are you asking for? What will you do with the divorce? How long have you been married?"

The man said, "It must have been at least sixty years or even more."

The judge said, "I cannot believe how you lived together for sixty years, and now at the end of your life, you want a divorce? Why have you waited so long?"

The old man said, "We had to wait till all our children died! Now is the chance to be free and enjoy life."

Their whole lives they lived together – it must have been utterly stale. But the love that is of the mind is simple: you can change your camera because the camera will not create any trouble. It won't fight you, it won't have tantrums, it won't drag you to court, it won't ask for money. It is a simple thing.

Because of this simplicity, most of the people in the world have moved away from being loving humans to being loving machines, all kinds of machines. It may be a car. Then it is simpler, you can change it any moment; there is no barrier. People have started to love animals. There are dog lovers who are carrying their dogs everywhere. It is better because you can control the dog, you can beat it and still it will welcome you with its tail. It is a joyous experience.

People have other kinds of animals – birds, parrots – and they pay so much attention to them. It is not a simple fact. It shows something deeper about our existence: we cannot love human beings; it is a constant trouble.

A wife had just married and was talking to her friend. The friend said, "This man is a drunkard. You should not have married him; it will be a constant trouble."

The woman said, "No. I will change his habits. It may take a few years, but I will make him docile, obedient. He is a good man."

The other woman said, "You are living in a fantasy. I have had a dog for five years and I have been teaching him with no effect. I tell him that trees are not toilets – he won't listen. I beat him, I don't give him food – he looks very sad. Finally, I also start feeling sympathy for the poor… But he will not change his habits. A dog is so stubborn, and you are thinking of changing a man, and that too, a drunkard!"

The very idea that you will change your wife, change your husband, change your friend, is dangerous. It means conflict from the very beginning. It means it is going to be a struggle, not a joy, not a dance, but a fight. People start drinking just to avoid the struggle that is waiting at home. When they are drunk then it does not matter even if the wife beats them, they are unconscious. Millions of people are drinking poison for the simple reason to avoid those whom they had thought they loved.

A man was drinking whiskey…

His wife was tired of teaching him. Wives are great teachers! No wonder that in schools slowly, slowly men are being replaced by women. They are great teachers. They don't smoke, they don't drink, they don't go hunting. They don't do anything out of the way. They have manners and etiquette, they don't use dirty words.

When George Bernard Shaw published his dictionary – a valuable contribution to literature – three old women approached him, very angry, "You seem to be a sex maniac!"

He said, "My God, what have I done?"

They said, "Look at this book you have published."

In that twelve-hundred-page book, there were three words which people think are dirty.

George Bernard Shaw said, "You are great scholars. You must have read twelve hundred pages of a dictionary to find out three words. Are you the sex maniacs or am I the sex maniac?"

The wife was tired of teaching the husband. Finally she tried another way. She said, "Now I am going to drink if you don't stop."

The husband was a little shocked thinking that it would be very difficult – two drunkards in the home both teaching each other not to drink. It is a very rare experience. He tried saying, "No. It does not look good in a woman."

A woman is a pious being, a religious being. Just look in the church; it is filled with women. Only a few men go there – just to find some woman if they can. Their interest is not in the crucified Jesus. Who is interested in criminals and who is interested in a boring sermon?

The man said, "It does not look good."

The woman said, "I am determined. Either you stop or I am going to start."

The man said, "My stopping is impossible. If you are stubborn, just take a little taste."

He gave her a little cup full of whiskey. These things don't taste good. The woman took one sip and threw the cup and said, "My God! It is almost poison."

And the man laughed and said, "And you always thought that I was enjoying! It is not a joy. You do your work… It takes long practice and great guts. It is not for you."

But why do people drink? – to avoid those whom they love or at least think they love.

Every day, two men sit in a bar. Late at night when the bar is due to close, the barman has to almost push them out. They go on drinking and drinking. One day, just before they started drinking one man asked the other, "We are the only two real drinkers; the others are just learners, immature. Can I ask why you drink so much?"

He said, "I have to, otherwise I cannot face my wife. When I am utterly drunk I have so much courage I could face a lion! And when I am absolutely drunk I go home, I kick the door open with my boot, throw things here and there, make a great noise, enter my wife's room, give her a good hit on the hips and say to her, 'Darling, how about it?' And she pretends to be deeply asleep!

"It is because of her I have to drink. Since I got married, I have not married my wife, I have married this alcohol. But what is your reason? Are you also in the same position?"

The other said, "No. I am not married. I am a bachelor."

The other man said, "Bachelor? It is unbelievable. Being a bachelor, what are you doing here? Drinking late in the night and you are just a bachelor?"

The bachelor said, "What else to do? There is nothing but darkness in the house. Sitting alone one becomes bored. Here it is very colorful and so many strange things happen every day. I started as what you call an amateur, but slowly, slowly… Now I am a perfect drunkard."

There are people who are drinking because they have wives and there are people who are drinking because they don't have any wives. It is a strange world. One does not know on what logical basis it is being run, whether there is any logic at all in life or it is absolutely absurd.

You have to take your love out from the emotional grip where it has been since your birth, and you have to find a route to your being. Unless your love becomes part of your being, it is not much different from pain, suffering, sadness. Emotions are not going to help you become an integrated individual. They are not going to give you a granite soul. You will remain just like dead wood moving in the stream here and there, not knowing why.

Emotions blind man exactly as alcohol does. They may have good names like love, they may have bad names like anger, but once in a while, if you have been observant, you will have seen that you need to be angry at someone; it relieves you. You will see dogs making love on the roads and people hitting them with stones. Now, those poor fellows are not doing any harm to anyone and they are performing a biological ritual that you perform – they just don't have to hide in houses – and they do so well. A crowd will move around them throwing stones, beating them. Strange behavior!

People need to be angry once in a while, just as once in a while they need to be in love, and once in a while to hate someone. It doesn't matter. That's why people like Adolf Hitler can manage to find followers, on the grounds that it is because of the Jews that the world is in misery, so we have to erase the Jews from the earth and there will be no problem.

All the problems are created by a Jewish conspiracy. He killed six million Jews and not a single problem of the world is solved. Now the world has more problems than it had before, but he convinced people like Martin Heidegger, the greatest philosopher of the contemporary world. Martin Heidegger was a follower of Adolf Hitler and also believed that it was the Jews...

Just now I have received information from Japan, although in Japan there are not many Jews. There may be more Jews here in this place than in the whole of Japan! Here you can suspect that you are surrounded by Jews; still, they don't have any conspiracy or anything. Two books have appeared – again the same logic or illogic – claiming that because of the Jews the world is in trouble, that there is a global Jewish conspiracy. And unless Jews are eradicated completely, the world will never be at ease. And those two books have become best-sellers in Japan!

Man gathers anger, rage, hate, and then it is only a question of finding some opportunity so that he can express his destructiveness. Any excuse will do. Religions give a good cause. One worries that if there is only one God, then the Jews are killing the Mohammedans, the Mohammedans are killing the Christians, the Christians are killing others – and it goes round and round everywhere in the name of God!

In fact, Mohammed had written on his sword: My Religion Is Peace. That is the meaning of Islam, that is the name Mohammedans give to themselves. And these peaceful Mohammedans have killed so many people, not only people, but have destroyed so many temples and so many beautiful statues because they don't believe in statues. It is perfectly okay, who is saying that you should believe? The statue is not following you insisting, "Believe me." If you go to ancient Indian temples, you will see the destruction that Mohammedans have caused.

They have destroyed much beautiful sculpture which would take hundreds of years to make. They have done this in the name of God, that there is only one God and he has no statue. That may be your idea, so *you* should not have any statue, but who are you to interfere with someone else whose idea is that there is a God who has as many statues as you can conceive?

Hindus believe in hundreds of gods – but what is the harm? That is their business, their problem. If they are doing something stupid, you can enjoy, but it is not right to destroy their statues. But the reality is that the labels of "God" and "religion" are all superficial. In reality people are angry and they don't have objects to show their anger to, so they go on collecting anger, hate, rage. And then there is a limit. It explodes like bombs – anything will do!

In India, Mohammedans and Hindus were fighting. Now Sikhs and Hindus are fighting because the Constitution of India has accepted Hindi as the national language. Although forty years have passed, they have not been able to impose Hindi as a national language because every other group which speaks a different language starts fighting.

In the south there are different languages, in the north there are different languages – and in the name of languages, riots go on happening.

I used to live in a city… They destroyed all the boards on the shops – anything on which English was written, and forced people to write the boards on their shops in Hindi. Now it is a very, very difficult problem because trains pass from one province to another province. In one province they will paint the name in one language and then the train will enter another province and they will paint it in their language. It was a constant trouble and fight, and trains were delayed for days because unless their writing is complete… In each compartment the passengers have to write down the name in the language of that province, and whoever resists them – immediately there is going to be killing!

Trains were set on fire because people were resisting. Buses were set on fire because the board was not in the language which the people spoke. But buses have to travel all over the country. India has thirty states, and if entering every state, the buses and trains have to change, then it will become a tremendous and hilarious job – but any excuse is enough! Emotions are dangerous in the sense that they overwhelm you and they are almost alcoholic.

Paddy gets an invitation to his rich cousin's wedding in Dublin. At the reception he feels a bit conspicuous in his country clothes, so he spends most of his time in the corner drinking whiskey. Finally, he decides to join the party, and asks the most important looking lady guest to dance a Viennese waltz with him. Paddy is angrily refused.

"There are four reasons why I won't dance with you," says the guest. "First, you have had too much to drink. Second, the band is not playing a waltz. Third, I am not a woman. Fourth, I am the archbishop of Dublin!"

But when they are drunk, people start seeing things…

The hostess at a kid's birthday party goes up to little Ernie, "How come," she asks, "your little brother is so shy? He has not moved from that corner all afternoon."

"He is not shy at all," insists Ernie. "It is just that he has never had to wear a necktie before and he thinks he is tied to something."

Just a little more awareness is needed and all your overwhelming things will start disappearing. A man is really clean and clear when he never gets overwhelmed by anything; when he is always alert, aware, himself, and is not lost in any emotion, whether it is love or anger or anything else.

Young Herbie, on vacation in Florida, is getting frustrated because he cannot attract any girls. Every day on the beach he watches as

Bernie Bernstein, an older man, is surrounded by young, beautiful women.

One evening Herbie approaches him at the bar and asks Bernie for some advice.

"Well," says Bernie, "the first thing is to get a smart haircut, then buy yourself a skimpy swimsuit instead of those baggy shorts. And for a finishing touch, put a rolled up pair of socks in your swimsuit. It works every time!"

Herbie follows the advice, but has no luck. The next evening in the bar he complains to Bernie, "Ah," says Bernie, "I saw you on the beach. The haircut looks great and you bought a fantastic looking swimsuit, but the next time, try putting the socks in front!"

Just a little awareness about what you are doing…

Ruthie Finkelstein goes to buy shoes, wearing a miniskirt with no underwear underneath. The shoe salesman is overcome by the sight and says to her, "I would like to fill your pussy with ice cream and eat it all out!"

"That is the most disgusting thing anyone has ever said to me," she cried. "I am going to tell my husband and he is going to beat you up!"

Ruthie stomps home and tells her husband Moishe, who happened to be reading his newspaper.

"Honey," he says, "I am not going to fight with that man for three reasons. First, you have a whole closet full of shoes and we really can't afford any more. Second, you were provoking the man by not wearing any underwear. And third, I don't want to mess with anyone who can eat that much ice cream!"

18

The World Is Absolutely Simple

Osho,

As far back as I can remember, from my early childhood until I took sannyas, I was suffering from the strong feeling that everything was too complicated. Since I met you eight years ago, things have started to be become slowly, slowly more and more simple. For me, this is a miracle for which I can say thanks forever.

To be simple is very significant for me. Please can you speak about simplicity?

The world is as you are. It is complicated if you are complicated. It is very simple if you are simple. In other words, you are the world. The mind makes everything complicated. Even the simplest thing becomes complicated for the simple reason that the mind's function is to fight against complexities and win over lands which it itself has projected.

But for the heart, everything is simple. It simply takes the world as it is. If you go a little deeper, even the word *simplicity* is too complicated for the being. Things are as they are. And in this experience, existence becomes your home – not a struggle to solve problems, not a turmoil of emotions, but a place to rest and relax and let things be as they are.

So you have a three-layer system in your being. The uppermost is the mind, which is only interested in complexities. If it meets God it will not be interested at all because there is no God and no possibility to meet him. For centuries, the mind has gone on complicating, fabricating, theorizing philosophies about one who in the first place does not exist.

The mind creates the idea of God and then starts inquiring what God is. And naturally, you cannot find God so it becomes more and more complex; you have to develop belief systems. God has been the center of all theologies, all religions, and thousands of scholars are worrying about God.

The second layer, of the heart, does not project anything, it simply accepts things as they are. But a man of the heart is not acceptable to society. He is too simple, almost a simpleton. At the fundamental roots of your being, the world's complexity, simplicity and the problems they create, have never arisen. There it is utter silence; there are no problems at all. Things are so beautiful and the world is so full of music, songs, playfulness. But it opens itself only to the person who has centered himself in his being.

You say, "Since I met you eight years ago, things have started to become slowly, slowly more and more simple. For me, this is a miracle for which I can say thanks forever. To be simple is very significant for me." Being with me is in fact being with yourself. Being sincerely with me, you are yourself. You have touched the world of being – and just the word *being* is enough. These birds singing all around – and just see how joyous the trees look basking in the early morning sun. That seems to be no problem at all. But the mind cannot live without problems and it cannot easily allow retirement; it gives a fight. That's why what can happen in an instant is happening slowly, slowly.

Either you are simple or you are not. There are not categories, that one is a little more simple and the other a little more… Simplicity does not belong to the world of categories, measurements. It is a quality, and you have not to do anything to be simple.

That is one of the most important things to remember. Millions of religious people have tried to be simple, but when you try to be simple, your simplicity itself becomes tremendously complex. Simplicity which is created by effort is not authentic. Simplicity has to be spontaneous, by understanding and not by effort; by meditation, not by action. You have simply to understand that the mind has a certain sickness of making things complex.

A German philosopher, Immanuel Kant, was approached by a beautiful young woman. She waited long, but he must have been a man like Niskriya. He never looked this way or that way. He simply went from his home directly to the university. He functioned almost like a robot. People used to fix their watches on seeing Immanuel Kant going to the university. And when he returned, it again showed the time.

The girl gathered courage and told him that she loved him. He was very shocked that someone loved him; it is becoming a dangerous situation. He said, "I will think about it."

She said, "No, I really love you."

He said, "*You* may love; that is your problem."

She replied, "And I want to get married to you."

He said, "It is a very complicated problem. First, I have to find out all the pros and cons about marriage – what will be the benefit and what will be the trouble – and weigh them. Unless I come to a point where I see that to be married is better, you will have to forgive me."

And he worked hard, looking into encyclopedias, poetry, love stories. Then he said, "My God, what trouble I'm getting into. I am not married and already my whole time is wasted by investigation." In three years he accumulated three hundred points against marriage and two hundred and ninety-nine points in favor of marriage.

A friend said to him, "You should understand one thing: this intellectual agony that you are going through, even without getting married, you have got a real taste of it in three years. And I suggest one more thing: whenever it is a question of whether to experience a thing or not to experience a thing, it is better to experience. That will make you more mature."

So the list was now equal. And the friend said, "Don't be afraid. All over the world everyone is married."

So he said, "Okay, if you all say it – and now the points are the same. I will go." And he knocked on the door of the girl's house.

Her father came out and said, "You have come a little late. My girl got married three years ago. Now she has two children. You will have to find someone else."

He said, "No, I don't want to find someone else. I am relieved of such a burden. In these three years I have been in such a torture. It is enough experience."

The mind only thinks about things: "What will happen after death?" Why can't you wait? One thing is certain: you will die. I guarantee it! How you prefer to die, that is another matter, but there are books and books about death and what will happen after death. In India twenty-five centuries ago, people were more philosophically minded, but not now.

In the golden days of Gautam Buddha, they even started to think about what was happening before birth. Ordinarily, no one bothers. Have you ever been concerned where you were and what was happening to you before birth? The problem simply does not arise. Once they have created a belief system that something was happening before birth, then the whole philosophy of reincarnation comes. And there are complexities in the philosophy, different interpretations.

The day Gautam Buddha died, his followers became divided over small points, and became thirty-two schools: How many hells are there? Now these are purely mind games. You have not been in a hell, nor have you met anyone who has been in a hell.

Jainas believe there are three hells – just a mind calculation because there are small-time sinners who drink tea and eat in the night, and smoke once in a while. Just small sins! Some place has to be made for them. So the first layer is of small sinners. Then there are bigger sinners who steal, murder, commit suicide and so on and so forth. The third is specially for the greatest sinners: Adolf Hitler, Benito Mussolini, Ronald Reagan. The categories are absolutely necessary for the mind to figure things out. And no one bothers whether there is any hell or not. Similarly, there are three heavens, just to equalize and balance.

Buddhists believe that there are seven hells because there are so many sins that they cannot be divided into only three categories. And the followers of Buddha thought, "Our approach is far more scientific; you have only three hells."

There was a man who must have had a great sense of humor; his name was Makkhali Gosal. He too was a competitor theologian. He said, "All these people who are talking know nothing. There are seventy-seven hells." Sins have to be categorized in a more mathematical, accurate way, and this is just an example. The mind has been creating all kinds of problems which don't exist, but once the mind has created them, then they become very complicated – and all answers bring more new questions.

In the Middle Ages, all the Christian theologians were concerned with a special discussion – you will think they were all idiots – how many angels can stand on the point of a pin? What business is it…? That is their problem, how many can stand on the point of a pin. In the first place, why should they stand? Is there not something else to do? But the problem was to prove the weightlessness of the angel, and different theologies were giving different answers; they were all conflicting.

The whole world has lived in controversies which have to be understood as mind-created. The mind enjoys it very much. If there are no problems and life is simple, there is no work for the mind. The mind goes out of employment.

The heart does not project problems, but gets caught into a small net of things, jealousy, anger, love, and makes too much of it. They are not theological problems, they are not very philosophical.

They are simple but there is a shadow of the mind in them. Only your being has no emotions and no thought. It simply *is*. In that isness a tremendous world opens all its mysteries.

It is good that you are going slowly, slowly, but it will be better to take an instantaneous jump because you can go on and on for lives slowly, slowly. And if you see the point that as the mind becomes simple, a beauty, a grace arises in your being, a childlike wonder about everything, a peace and a silence and a blissfulness, why should you go slowly? You go everywhere with speed. Slowly means that you are going reluctantly, trying to postpone it as long as you can and meanwhile solve a few problems. This will not take you to it. This is the experience of the mystics: that if you see the point, in that very point all problems, all questions, all philosophies, everything disappears.

Miss Goodbody has been teaching for twenty years, so all the kids bring her presents. They line up in front of her holding the gifts and she tries to guess what they are.

Little Ernie's father owns a liquor store and she notices that little Ernie's package is leaking, so she tastes it.

"Did you bring me Scotch whiskey?" she asks.

"No," replies little Ernie.

So Miss Goodbody turns to little Ronnie. Little Ronnie's father is a florist.

"Did you bring me some love roses?" asks Miss Goodbody.

"Yes, teacher," replies Ronny, passing her the flowers.

Then Miss Goodbody goes back to Ernie's leaking package and tastes it again.

"Did you bring me gin?" she says.

"No," replies little Ernie.

Little Ruthy's father has a candy store.

"Have you brought me candy?" asks Miss Goodbody.

"Yes, teacher," replies Ruthy and gives her the package.

Then Miss Goodbody goes back to Ernie and tastes the leaking packet again.

"Did you bring me rum?" she asks.

"No," replies little Ernie, "I brought you a puppy."

This world is so hilarious. What complications? The poor puppy is just doing his thing.

Little Ernie gives a loud wolf whistle in the middle of Father Murphy's sermon, and his grandfather picks him up and carries him out of the church.

Once they are outside, he starts to scold. "How could you?" he cries, "Making such a noise in the church!"

"Well," replies little Ernie looking quite excited, "I have been praying for a long time that God would teach me to whistle, and this morning he did."

Just look at life with more playful eyes. Don't be serious. Seriousness becomes like a blindness. Don't pretend to be a thinker, a philosopher. Just simply be a human being. The whole world is showering its joy on you in so many ways, but you are too serious, you cannot open your heart.

Mendel Kravitz, an American from New York, goes to Japan on a business trip and meets a lovely young Japanese woman. She cannot speak much English and he does not know Japanese.

After dinner together they go back to her apartment and Mendel starts to make passionate love to her. All the time the beautiful Japanese girl is yelling, "*Titti gochi*, *titti gochi*, ah *titti gochi*."

Mendel thinks that she must never have had such a great lover as himself.

The next day Mendel and a Japanese businessman are playing golf. Halfway through the game, the Japanese man hits a hole in one. Not knowing any Japanese, but delighted for his friend, Mendel wants to show his excitement and cries out, "Ah, *titti gochi*!"

The Japanese businessman spins around and looking amazed asks, "What do you mean by wrong hole?"

Young Fergin Finkelstein has just graduated from law school and is applying for a job at a large corporation. The personnel manager looks him in the eye and says, "Mr. Finkelstein, are you an honest attorney?"

"Honest?" says young Fink. "Let me tell you something. My father lent me ten thousand dollars for my college education and I paid him back in full after my very first case."

"I am impressed," says the manager. "And what was the case?"

Young Fink turns red and says, "My father sued me for the money."

As far as I am concerned, I don't see any complexity anywhere. All complexities are man-made. Simplicity is divine. It is not manufactured; it is simply here. You just have to open your eyes, your sensitivity, receptivity, and allow it to touch your heart, to enter your being.

A beautiful world is possible if people are just simple, but to be simple is the exact meaning of religious. To be simple can be reduced to the first part of the statement on the temple of Delphi: "Be." And you will be surprised that everything is so juicy. But you never enter the world of being and everything becomes a trouble, a puzzle, a complication, a complexity – and you have to solve it without knowing that the problem is false, it cannot have a right solution.

Mulla Nasruddin was given an interview with a shipping company. The manager asked, "Nasruddin, it is a dangerous job. Sometimes the ocean behaves so roughly. If you are caught in tidal waves, what are you going to do with your ship?"

He said, "No problem at all. I will simply lower down the defense mechanism that every ship has, just weights, huge weights which keep the ship stable even when there is so much turmoil all around."

The manager said, "Another tidal wave is arising?"

He said, "No problem. I will again lower down a huge weight." – In the shipping world these weights are called anchors.

The manager said, "But if a third wave comes, what will you do?"

He said, "No problem, a bigger anchor."

The manager is in a difficulty what to do with this man. He says, "Where are you getting all these anchors from?"

Mulla Nasruddin said, "And from where are you getting these tidal waves?"

The source is the same: you go on bringing tidal waves and I will go on lowering bigger and bigger anchors. The mind creates problems, raises tidal waves and then searches for anchors and creates those anchors also. But more tidal waves are coming, and things become very difficult.

Paddy and Sean are sitting in the pub one day talking about their wives when Paddy looks into the distance, sighs and says, "Do you know what it means to come home at night to a woman who will give you a little love, a little affection, a little tenderness?"

"No," says Sean, "I am afraid I don't."

"I will tell you what it means," replies Paddy sipping his beer, "it means you are in the wrong bloody house."

It is not going to happen in your own house. Wherever I have lived I have always loved to be friends with drunkards because they are such juicy people and they say such great things – and no newspaper takes any note!

In my village, just in front of my house was a barber's shop. And that barber was a miracle man. He was so opium addicted that it was a miracle that he managed to find where his shop was and where his house was.

But every day I used to sit in his shop and something was bound to happen. He would cut half someone's mustache and then he would say, "Wait. I have urgent work to do in the market."

And the man would say, "But this is stupid, sitting here in the barber's chair with half a mustache! You are not reliable. When will you return? And will you return or not? I have other things to do."

And the barber would say, "Don't be worried. I will come."

Sometimes it would happen that someone had come to be shaved, and he would shave his head. And once he had started, half of the hair gone – now there is no way. He was a great philosopher. He would say, "Don't worry. The hair will grow like grass. It will grow. And as far as I am concerned, you need not pay until it grows. Then you can pay me if you feel like it. But you had such beautiful hair that I felt to shave it completely. So what do you say? Should I complete the process or leave it as it is?"

Naturally, the man would say, "Complete the process, you idiot! Everyone warned me, 'Never go to this barber. He is not in his senses.'"

He would shave him completely and he would say, "Don't be worried. I will not charge you anything."

The man said, "It is not a question of charging anything. The whole village is going to laugh."

And in India particularly, you shave your head completely only when your father is dead. So everyone is going to ask, "My God, what happened to your father?"

He would advise, "No, it is just a question of a few days – it will grow."

I would spread the rumor that his father is dead and then say, "Mistakenly he thought he was dead, so he shaved his hair. Don't torture him."

One day he said to me, "What do you think…? Because you are my greatest friend."

I said, "That's true."

He asked, "If all the opium addicts make a political party, can they create a revolution in the country?"

I said, "If they can manage to make a party, the revolution has already happened."

He said, "You are right, because opium addicts don't agree with anyone else. Even among themselves they are continuously disagreeing about everything. These are the most difficult people, but it is the absolute necessity of the times if you want this country to be liberated from the politicians. You should do something."

I said, "But what can I do?"

He said, "You can at least start a party for opium addicts."

I said, "The idea is good, but I am not an opium addict myself."

He said, "That I will teach you, but promise me that after that you will take great care. These opium addicts are very dangerous people."

A man was pissing behind his shop – in India it is common – and the barber caught hold of him and the man was trying... "What are you doing?"

And he said, "You idiot. In my absence you are milking my cow? I heard the noise!"

You have just to look and you will find a very simple world, and it will give your being such a shower of blessings. You don't have to go to any church; those churches are created by very complicated people. You don't have to go to a temple; those gods are mind-manufactured. You don't have to go anywhere. Just go within yourself and relax, and go on relaxing till you touch the very center of your being. Suddenly, the whole scene of the world changes: everything becomes totally new and fresh.

Just these owls... Just this silence... What is complicated? These trees trying to reach the stars. What is complicated? You are complicated. The world is absolutely simple. And you are complicated because you are not rooted in your being. So please, don't go slowly and don't go with speed; just don't go anywhere. Remain within you. That sentence on the Delphi center: "Be." But if you cannot do that, then "Know Thyself" – then find out some meditative method, some awareness technique and "Keep the Measure." In everything remain balanced, and life itself is a teaching in simplicity.

19

It Is Human to Err and More Human to Realize It

Osho,
Why can I not just fall in love with any woman and be blind like every man?

Niskriya, your question is very special. You are asking, "Why can I not just fall in love with any woman and be blind like every man?" It is simple, Niskriya – because you are not a blind man. And as far as women are concerned, they like blind men! They don't fall in love with buddhas. You are so alert and aware and meditative – women don't like these things at all. Just seeing you once, they will never come close to you.

Falling in love is possible only when the woman understands that the other is also going to fall. Looking at you, it does not seem possible. You may stand in love, but you cannot fall. Nothing can be done about it. This is your type, and I don't think it is good to make any effort to change your type. You are a unique person in this unique community.

Everyone is falling in love and falling out of love [*there is laughter all around the auditorium, especially from one woman in particular, who laughs from time to time as Osho continues to speak*] and Niskriya is standing, watching the whole scene and wondering, "Why am I not falling?" You are not just another man; you are yourself. And it is a great quality not to fall, particularly in love, because then you have to fall out. It is an unnecessary exercise. A few people like doing exercise, a few people don't like. You are a silent man – beyond all these exercises. Only this woman seems to be interested in you! So find out later on – she will come to you by herself. But it will last only one night. In the morning you will find you are standing alone again. This is your destiny.

Moishe Finkelstein pays his bill and starts to get up from the table.

"By the way, sir," says the anxious-looking waiter, "do you believe that history repeats itself?"

"I certainly do," exclaims Moishe, "I know of a number of cases."

"Well, sir," replies the waiter, rubbing his hands together, "one gentleman who was in here yesterday left me a five dollar tip."

"Amazing," says Moishe, reaching for his hat, "perhaps he will be here again tomorrow."

Everyone understands things in his own way and everyone has to be himself. History may be repeating, but no individual repeats.

Paddy has been suffering from chest pains, and although the tests have been inconclusive, the doctor tells him that if he wants to live much longer, he will have to lead a quiet life – no late nights, no exercise, and no sex.

"Okay," says Maureen when she hears the news. "From now on I will sleep downstairs on the sofa, then we won't be tempted."

They live like this for three weeks. Then one night they bump into each other on the stairs.

"What are you doing out of bed?" asks Maureen.

"I can't stay upstairs on my own anymore," replies Paddy. "I'm coming downstairs to die."

"Thank God for that," says Maureen, "because I was just coming upstairs to kill you!"

Big Chief Running Bear walks into the drugstore and starts complaining to the druggist.

"Rubbers you give me no good!" he says, "Chief go, 'Ugh!' Squaw go, 'Ugh!' Rubbers go boom!"

The druggist is very sorry and gives the Indian a new package.

"These are the strongest rubbers made," he says.

The next day, the chief is back.

"Rubber no good!" He explains, "Chief go, 'Ugh!' Squaw go, 'Ugh!' Rubbers go boom!"

The frustrated druggist goes into the back of his shop, cuts a piece from a bicycle tire, and glues one end shut. He then goes back into the shop and hands it to the chief.

Next morning, the squaw comes into the drugstore.

"Rubber you sell chief too good," she says, "Chief go, 'Ugh!' Squaw go, 'Ugh!' Chief's ball go boom!"

This is a world where a variety of people exist. You are a special case. But this woman, just wait, she is going to torture you! Beware of this woman, otherwise tomorrow will come the question of how to get rid of a woman – and everything has gone boom!

Niskriya, it is better to be silent. You are here to meditate. But that woman is too much for you, absolutely determined, unafraid, not knowing you. A few others are also becoming interested. Have you asked the question or is it a kind of advertisement?

Osho,
The more I meditate, the more empty I get inside. I had an idea that when one meditates, one is slowly transformed into being more laughing and loving, but I just get hollow and empty and start withdrawing myself from others. I prefer now to be alone, but I do

not feel happy; the hollowness in me makes me feel deep sorrow. What is happening to me?

Dolma, I know what is missing in you and that is trust, and you have not been able to get rid of your guilt that you are carrying within you. I have been asked if Dolma should be allowed in the commune or not – because you were part of that company who destroyed the commune in America. But I could not say that you should be stopped from entering the commune.

It would have been tremendously helpful if you had revealed in what ways you participated in the destructive things because you were very intimately part of the gang, but you are hiding all that. That is making you hollow; otherwise, no one is hollow in this place. And everyone who goes in does not find emptiness, but finds nothingness which is totally different from emptiness.

Emptiness is something sad. Nothingness is another name of fullness; it is overflowing. You don't find love arising because the guilt is heavy. There is still time: if you confess everything that you have done, you will be relieved of it.

Just a few days ago, Patipada was here and she wrote asking to be in the commune. I asked her first for an apology because she was also like you, although not that deep in the destructiveness. She replied, "I don't feel that I have done anything wrong and I don't feel like apologizing."

I said, "Then it is up to you, but you cannot be part; it is better you leave."

After two months she came again and with tears wrote a letter saying, "I am very sorry. I know I have done wrong things and I know I have been part of many things which culminated in helping the government to destroy the commune. I was wrong to say that I have nothing to be sorry for. I am sorry and I ask for forgiveness."

I said, "If it is coming from your deepest heart – not just a political, diplomatic strategy – then you will find your home again among my people. I will not prevent you. I will give you another chance."

I was hoping Dolma would express her guilt and her apology by herself, but she has not done that. She is here but she cannot be part because of that guilty feeling: "I have misbehaved, I have misused the trust and love and compassion." She will find herself alone in the thousands of people who are here, surrounded by a wall of her own guilt.

If she wants to be free, she has to confess it and the confession has not to be diplomatic. If it is diplomatic, it is not going to help. If it is authentic, it will immediately transform your sadness into laughter, your aloneness into a meaningful meeting and merging in the commune. You have not even asked the real thing in your question. It is very strange: people have problems, but they ask something else; they don't expose themselves. You are asking about meditation as if you are a meditator. And you are saying, "…the more empty I get inside," and I know you have never been inside.

If even once you have been inside, your first realization would have been that you owe something to the commune – an apology at least. You are saying, "I had an idea that when one meditates, one slowly is transformed into being more laughing and loving…" Do you understand what you are writing in your question: "I had an idea that when one meditates…" Certainly it is not your experience, it is just "…an idea, that when one meditates one slowly is transformed into being more laughing and loving, but I just get hollow and empty and start withdrawing myself from others." But this is not because you are meditating.

Just face the reality, look in the mirror and remove your masks. And what is only your idea will be found, just phony. Meditate, but right now, the condition in which you are, you cannot meditate. And because you cannot meditate, the guilt does not allow you to mix with people because these are the same people you have betrayed.

It is so easy to accept because it is very human to err. It is more human to realize that one has erred, that one has committed a mistake. It is not something that one has to be afraid of. I am not sending you into hell, but if you don't accept and realize what has been done by you or by the company in which you were an intrinsic part, you will remain empty and you will start withdrawing from people. And finally you will create hell.

Hell is not somewhere else. It is not geographical. It is your psychology: a psychology which is messed up, confused and has become ugly and is afraid to expose itself to the sun, to the wind. Dolma, just do that. Search within yourself, because no one knows more than you what has been happening in the group you were part of: what kind of power trip, and in that power trip what kind of blindness, the things that you did in that blindness or supported or you did not object to.

Unless you unburden your heart it is very difficult for me to help you. And you will feel deep sorrow. I feel compassion for you because I don't have any condemnation for anyone. People are unconscious, they go on doing things and they don't know where it will lead them, what the consequences will be.

So it is not just you; everyone is in the same boat. And one should always be alert that whenever he finds that he has done something wrong – although there was a certain feeling that this is not the thing to do – still one went on doing it because it was giving power, prestige, respectability.

The group to which you belonged in the commune in America – none of that group were meditators. They had no time to meditate, but they were conspiring to do all kinds of things, even trying to murder people. You may not have done anything, but if you were part of the group and you remained silent, you are as much responsible as the person who did it.

There is no problem: simply confess everything. Just write a letter in *The Osho Times* confessing everything that you did, that you knew was being done by other people and that you never objected to but on the contrary, you supported. You will be free of this guilt, this hollowness. Happiness is not very far away, and meditation is your birthright. One who goes into meditation, always goes into fullness, into nothingness. But nothingness is not emptiness.

Nothingness is simply no-thing-ness, a space, pure, unobstructed. The whole sky becomes available to you within your own being.

Kowalski's son has been acting strangely, so Kowalski takes him to the psychiatrist.

"Tell me, son," asks the psychiatrist, "how many wheels are there on a car?"

"Four," replies the boy.

"Very good," says the shrink. "And what is it that a cow has four of that a woman has two of?"

"Legs," answers the kid.

"Good," says the shrink. "And what does your father have that your mother likes the most?"

"Money," replies the boy.

The psychiatrist turns to Kowalski and says,

"You don't have to worry about your son, he is smart."

"He sure is!" says Kowalski. "I missed the last two questions myself!"

Just accept what you have missed and you will feel unburdened, happy, and you will be accepted back; no one is going to reject you. But in the commune in America, you had become part of a group which separated itself from the whole commune of five thousand people. Just twenty women and the desire was to dominate? It is very human.

Because I was silent, in isolation, and I was not talking to anyone, not meeting with anyone, this power group became superior to others, starting the egoist trip.

The simple thing for you is to accept that you have been wrong; that you feel deeply sorry for it and no one is going to be angry about it. I don't teach people to be judgmental. They will all feel sympathetic toward you, loving toward you. What happened, happened, but we can change the future. The past is already gone, but if you go on carrying the past inside yourself, then it is not gone. It is present and it will remain your future also. This will be like a cancer which will kill you.

Paddy is driving along a winding mountain road in his old Ford car.

Suddenly a sleek sports car going in the opposite direction almost runs him off the road. And to make things worse, a young woman driving the sports car sticks her head out of the window and yells at him, "Pig!"

Paddy immediately reacts angrily by sticking his head out of his car and yelling back at her, "Bitch!"

He then rounds the next bend in the road and smashes straight into a huge pig!

You cannot avoid what you are. You will meet yourself again and again. On some other bend of the road, you will meet yourself.

Old man Finkelstein comes to the doctor's office.

"Doc," he says, "you have got to give me something to pep me up. I have got a date tonight with my twenty-five-year-old secretary and I want to be sure that I am able to perform."

The physician smiles and gives him some pills. Later that night, out of curiosity, he telephones Finkelstein.

"Did the medicine help any?" asks the doctor.

"It was great!" replies Finkelstein, "I have managed three times already."

"And how about the girl?" chuckles the doctor.

"Ah," replies Finkelstein, "She has not got here yet."

Osho,

Sometimes, sitting with you in discourse, everything inside me becomes so relaxed, so silent, that my mind seems to stop thinking thoughts. And although I hear the sound of your voice, the words cease to carry any meaning. However, this state lacks a certain alertness, as if when the mind becomes silent I fall unconscious. Have you an alarm clock for my witness?

What do you think my jokes are for? I know that you will fall asleep. If I talk great theology, you will enjoy a good evening, but I don't let you enjoy. My jokes are the alarm clock. So many people laughing, how can you relax and fall asleep? Impossible! I have to tell these jokes; otherwise I may fall asleep also. Because you are so many and I am alone! Just think.

Now before I fall asleep…

After Fagin and Rosa Finkelstein get married, they soon establish a household routine that includes having sex every evening at 9:15. [Osho pauses, looks at his watch and declares…] There is still time!

After several weeks of this, Rosa catches flu and gets an injection that kills all but three of the germs in her body. The trio of surviving germs holds an emergency meeting to discuss how they might escape.

"I am moving up to the tip of her ear," says the first germ. "That flu shot will never get me up there!"

The second germ says, "I am going to the tip of her toe!"

"You guys can go and do what you want," says the third, "but when that old '9:15' pulls out tonight, I am going to be on top of it!"

20

The Art of Love

Osho,

I have never been loved by a man. Either there is a very strong sexual connection, but without lovingness or caring, or there is caring and understanding, but sex doesn't happen. I want so much to connect with a man in totality that I am always looking. My feeling is that there is a lesson for me here in receptivity, but perhaps also in humbleness.

Osho, please comment.

Mayoori, it is one of the oldest problems human beings have faced. Their fancy is about pure love, care, concern, but their biology has a different program. It has no concern with your pure love or caring. Its concern is to reproduce the species. Biology is purely sexual.

The effort is going to fail if you want a love which is nonbiological. And the problem becomes more complicated. The woman can perhaps wait because her sexuality is a passive sexuality, it is spread all over her body. It feels immensely joyful to her just to be cuddled, loved, cared. Sex seems to her to be something lower, animalistic.

But one has to consider the man also. His sexuality is localized. The first thing is that it is not all over his body. And the second thing is that it has to be aggressive. The woman's egg waits inside – it can wait for infinity – but the man's sperm cannot wait that long.

He wants to have the marathon race as quickly as possible. That's why he pretends romance and all goody-goody things, but his real intention is when it is 9:15! He is constantly looking at his watch. Everything else is good, but the real goal is 9:15.

And the situation is determined very quickly. Those one million sperms that will be released in one sexual act will never have such a marathon race again; it is a question of life and death. Only one out of one million will reach the woman's egg which is just sitting there.

Once a sperm has reached the egg, the egg is closed. Sometimes it happens that a few friends reach together; then you have twins. But that is very rare and anyway one million people cannot reach – they will kill the woman if they reach at the same time. 9:15! There are wiser ones who stand by the side and see the whole scene, and there are idiots who don't look here and there and go direct like an arrow because there is not much time. The life of a sperm out of a man's body is only two hours.

Once a man's sperms are released, he wants to sleep. He's tired and it is enough. Now he doesn't think about romance, he does not have any inbuilt program for a little afterplay – before, he has to. So within two or three minutes – that is 9:17 – he is already thinking, "When will this nonsense stop?" Certainly it is tiring for him; it is his energy that is going out.

The woman is not losing energy, she is gaining energy. And she could not even get an orgasm because the orgasm takes some time. The man should play with her body, provoke every cell and fiber of her body so she becomes afire. But no man is concerned and it looks stupid also, "What are you doing? Just do the real thing and go to sleep."

It is very difficult to find a man who will love you and not just as an object of sexual release. It does not mean there will not be any sex. It may be just a small part in a big, romantic, loving, caring atmosphere. It will be very difficult for you to find such a man, and meanwhile you will be becoming older. So my suggestion is, if that man ever comes into your life – very good; meanwhile, Niskriya is perfectly okay. And I am not making a story! Niskriya has been interested in Mayoori for at least three years, but Mayoori never gave him any chance to come close. But when she saw that one witch had already got him, the next night she reached Niskriya!

Niskriya could not believe it – this is the woman he has been fancying. But Niskriya is a very scientific, mathematical person – a technologist, and that too a German technologist. So Mayoori was coming to him; he was happy, but it did not last. The next day he asked the question, "Every girl has a boyfriend, every boy has a girlfriend. There are even boys who have boyfriends and girls who have girlfriends. Why is nature so hard on me? I only have my camera!"

You can do everything with the camera, but doing romance is a little too much. You can talk to the camera, say, "Sweetheart." But for more than that the poor camera cannot help much. And particularly Niskriya's camera; he won't even allow anyone to touch it. He is such a perfectionist!

So Mayoori, as far as I know, right now Niskriya is free. You can give him a try. And don't ask the impossible. Try! The impossible also can happen, but it needs tremendous intelligence, understanding, playfulness. You can create the atmosphere in which even a man like Niskriya may start feeling love for you. I am risking my own cameraman because he cannot have two romances. His romance is filming and everything has to be perfect.

The most you can do is have your sexual relationship with people who are not romantic in any sense, and have your friendship with people who have gone beyond sex. You will either have to make a certain arrangement or you will have to change the man. It is not only the man's responsibility to love you, to give you care and understanding and sex, it is also your responsibility. It is a question of a very subtle dialogue.

If you are loving, caring, you will create a kind of synchronicity in the man also. That is the whole art of love. Nature has missed it or did not bother about it because its concern was different. But your poetic heart, your individuality, is far bigger than your biology.

It cannot be satisfied only by biology. But remember, don't go on looking for that man. Create the situation from your side too.

I have heard…

A man was saying that he has toured around the world looking for a perfect woman. A listener asked him, "Did you find her?"

He said, "Yes, but she was looking for a perfect man."

Love has to be a sort of creativity. Only then does sex remain as a small part in it. My understanding is that the woman has more capacity to create the atmosphere of caring because she is by nature programmed to be a mother. Every woman should also be a mother to her lover.

So take care of him, his clothes, his food, his cleanliness and slowly, slowly the man and his hardness – which is natural to him – will start melting. He will also start thinking, "Poor Mayoori is doing so much for me; I should also do something." Then he is certain to bring ice cream. And without ice cream, no love is complete. I don't know why it is so, but it is so!

Niskriya was very happy when he saw Mayoori approaching him. For three years he has been dreaming about her – a beautiful woman – but I don't think they could manage to be together long. They both need a certain art and a certain understanding.

Unfortunately the world has taken it for granted that everyone knows how to love, so no educational system, no university has courses for the art of love. It is very strange that the most important thing is neglected.

One day when I was sitting with the vice-chancellor in his room, a girl came in with tears in her eyes, but I could see that behind her tears there was a subtle joy. She said that a certain boy was harassing her. He takes out the air of her bicycle tires, he throws small stones at her, he continually writes letters.

"Even my family has become concerned because he never signs the letters. They also harass me: 'Who is this man and why does he go on writing love letters to you?' I know who he is, but I cannot tell them because then there will unnecessarily be a quarrel and fight. I have come to ask you to do something and prevent this harassment."

The vice-chancellor said, "Don't be worried, I will call this boy right now and it will not happen again."

I said, "Wait."

He said, "Why?"

I said, "Wait. Before you call the boy I have to ask a few questions of you in front of this girl."

He looked a little shocked – I was a professor in his university. He said, "You always behave strangely. It is none of your concern."

I said, "It is my concern, it is everyone's concern. Answer me honestly. When you were a student in the university, at this age, have you not done the same things to a girl?"

He said, "My God!"

And I said, "Remember, you cannot deceive me and you will lose all your honor in my eyes if you deceive. Tell the truth."

He said, "Yes, I used to do such things."

I said, "One part of it is clear."

The girl was amazed. Tears disappeared, she was almost smiling and I said to her, "Now you ask yourself, are you really interested that no one should harass you, no one should throw stones at you, no one should take the air out of your bicycle tires, no one should write you love letters? Be honest the way the vice-chancellor has been honest. Will you be happy then?"

For a moment she hesitated and she said, "No, in fact I enjoy whatever he is doing."

"Then why have you come here to complain?"

She said, "Talking about him makes me very happy. He writes such beautiful letters."

And the vice-chancellor said, "This is a strange situation. Now what am I supposed to do?"

I said, "Simply don't do anything. If you do anything, I am going to your house and will inform your wife what you have been doing in your college days."

He said, "No, don't do that. That will make my life hell. It is already a hell. Have mercy on me! I'm an old man and those are very faraway echoes of when I was a postgraduate in a university. Yes, once in a while I remember those beautiful faces which have all faded. And I have ended up with a bitch."

I said to the girl, "From tomorrow – at least in my class – you should sit with the boy."

She said, "With the boy?"

I said, "Yes, with the boy. Nag him. Start what is going to happen in the end. It is better to be finished beforehand. Pinch him and I assure you he will enjoy."

She said, "This is a strange solution, I have never heard… And what will the others say?"

I said, "Don't be worried about others. If anyone says anything, send that person to me and I will put him right."

This is the situation because no one is taught a simple art of love. Because the boy cannot touch the girl, he throws a stone. At least the stone he has touched will touch the girl. It does not appear clearly to people who don't understand the human mind that he is touching the girl from a distance because closeness is not allowed, or he is letting the air out of her bicycle. In fact, he wants her to be on his bicycle, but neither does he understand nor does she understand.

"Send your boy to me and I will teach him how he should behave."

She said, "I have come here so that he should be punished. It seems you have punished me and you have punished the vice-chancellor too. And that boy who is harassing me is being rewarded."

I said, "He has to be rewarded, he is courageous for writing love letters. Where are all those love letters?"

She said, "I have collected them."

I said, "If you hate that boy, why have you collected those love letters? You should have burned them, but you enjoy them. Do you read them again and again?"

She said, "You know so much! Yes, it is true. Every night when everyone is asleep I read them again and again. He writes such beautiful things, so nice – and he looks beautiful."

I said, "Then what is the problem?"

The problem is that society is not providing the proper guidance for what you should do, and man's sexuality, his love, is one of the most fundamental problems of man's life. Somehow he has to learn how to rise above biology. So biology remains a part. I am not against biology, but biology is very mediocre and ordinary. Some poetry, some music, some dance – and finally, some ice cream. They are absolutely needed.

Mayoori, give poor Niskriya a try. He was immensely happy when he saw you approaching him.

The world has been teaching girls: "You should run away and allow the boys to chase you." But don't run away so fast that they lose hope. Run away and then wait. Let them come closer and then run away and wait, and finally be caught. It is just to give the boy a sense that he is responsible for whatever happens afterward. Because the girl was running away, the boy chased her, he caught her. And in fact the truth is that she is arranging it so that the boy can chase her. She is arranging it so that the boy can catch her. So she remains higher than the boy and she will remind him again and again, "I was not after you, you were after me."

But there is no need for chasing and being caught. People should be more understanding and approach each other saying, "I have something in my heart that starts dancing when I come close to you. If you also have something of the same perhaps we can have a few days…" And life is not so long!

One famous Urdu poem is…

> Life consists of four days.
> Two are for preparation and two for waiting.

Waiting for what? Preparing for what? In a small life, don't waste time in unnecessary moralities, puritan ideologies, preachers and their teachings. They are all hypocrites. Be authentic and say to a man or a woman, "I love you. I like your eyes, I like your face. That does not mean that I will like everything about you, but I will try to avoid those things. If you have any sensitivity for me, I am available. I don't ask for your totality nor should you ask for my totality."

That's what you are asking: totality. Poor human beings cannot be total, and things go on changing. What seems to be great love today, tomorrow will not seem to be so great. And the day after tomorrow, it will be an ordinary repetition and you will start looking here and there for how to have that great totality again.

There is no totality, there is only an illusion of totality in life. The man of intelligence understands that life is not perfect and is not meant to be perfect. It is imperfect. We are all imperfect beings. So although there may be nooks and corners which you don't like about a person, there may be things that you do like. Don't wait for a dream girl. Be more realistic and try to understand that everyone has faults, and to love someone does not mean that you have to change that person. To love that person does not mean that you have to destroy his freedom.

To love simply means that you feel that something clicks within the two of you. As long as that dance within your heart remains, good. I have always considered that every couple should have a weekend apart, just a change. I don't see that there is any immorality in it but simply intelligence. Why force people to live in boredom? Such a small life. Four days and they too are wasted in boredom. And after the weekend your own wife will again look... "My God, she looks beautiful!"

Every woman is almost the same and every man is almost the same. The nonessentials are different: someone has a beard and someone has not. The whole humanity should live in a kind of loving atmosphere which allows freedom so that boredom does not set in.

Mayoori, you have a great chance. A man who has been thinking of you in his dreams is here just in front of me. No one dreams about the poor fellow because he is so statue-like that one feels afraid.

I have heard people ask for photographs of Niskriya just to make their children afraid, but a woman like Mayoori may change his stone-like… Just last night he was standing almost the way the soldiers of Adolf Hitler used to stand: straight. And the day before he was wearing the Chinaman's cap with a small note: Excuse Me. You will have to think of the whole joke, then you will understand what "Excuse Me" means. He is trying his best. Just see what he does today!

Paddy picks up a girl in the pub and then takes her for a drive in his old Ford car. He stops on a deserted section of country road, turns to the girl and begins to make some rather predictable advances.

"Just a minute," the girl declares, pushing him away. "I'm really a prostitute and I have to charge you fifty dollars."

Paddy reluctantly pays her and they make love. Later Paddy sits silently at the wheel.

"What is the matter?" asks the girl. "Are we not leaving?"

"Not quite yet," says Paddy, "I am really a taxi driver and the fare back is fifty dollars."

But people manage…

A young fireman is becoming bored with his sex life and feels he needs to make it more juicy.

He gets the idea of using codes, like he does when he is fighting fires and explains the idea to his wife. "When I say Code One," says the fireman, "that is your signal to run upstairs to the bedroom. Code Two means get undressed and jump into bed and Code Three means we make mad passionate love."

All goes well for a week and their love life reaches new heights. But one night after going through all three codes, the wife suddenly yells out, "Code Four!"

The fireman looks at her and says, "What is that?"
"Code Four!" she cries. "More hose!"

Gorgeous Gloria is very fond of her parrot, but is always embarrassed by its bad habits. Whenever Gloria brings home a boyfriend, the parrot cries, "Someone is going to get it tonight!" So she takes the parrot to the vet for treatment, but the vet tells her that her bird must be lonely and in need of female companionship.

At the pet shop Gloria explains her story and asks about a female parrot.

"I'm afraid we are out of female parrots at the moment," says the storekeeper, "but in the meantime, why don't you take home this nice lady owl and see how they get on together?"

A few nights later, Gloria comes home with a new boyfriend.

The parrot takes one look and screeches, "Someone's going to get it tonight!"

"Whooo?" hoots the owl.

The parrot glares at the owl and squawks, "Not *you*, you big-eyed bitch!"

Father Murphy is explaining the meaning of faith to his congregation.

"In the front row," he says, "we have Paddy and Maureen and their five children. Maureen knows they are her children – that is knowledge. Paddy believes they are his children – that is faith."

Old man Finkelstein is having lunch with his young grandson, Fagin Finkelstein, the lawyer. Over brandy and cigars, the old man explains how he has succeeded in business.

"When I arrived in this town, my boy," he begins, "I had nothing but the suit I was wearing and a small brown parcel which represented my entire worldly possessions. And now I own three factories, employ two thousand people, live in a large mansion and drive a Rolls Royce."

"Amazing," says Fagin. "That is some achievement. But, tell me, what did you have in your brown paper parcel?"

Old man Fink puffs on his cigar and says, "Two million in cash!"

Mayoori, Niskriya may not look like a romantic lover, but he has good cash.

21

What Autobiography?

Osho,
The other night I heard you give an answer to the American sannyasin, Dolma, in response to a question asked by another Dolma.

It seems as if it was the question Dolma needed to ask, but hadn't, so you helped her to. Your compassion is simply stunning. Interestingly, several sannyasins were quite concerned that you seemed to have got the Dolmas mixed up and that you were "wrong." Would you please comment?

I knowingly have not used the whole name, Deva Dolma, because I wanted to answer another Dolma who was here two months ago. She just remained two days and said to people, "This is not the place for me anymore and these are not the people with whom I would like to live" – and left.

I certainly knew that this question cannot be from that Dolma. But just as she needed the answer, you also needed the answer. The Dolmas may have been different, their questions deep down were the same. And moreover, I answered not the question but the person.

Both of the Dolmas have a similar problem of personality. You are more courageous because you have remained, the other one was a coward. Rather than accepting that she has betrayed the commune, she thought it better to leave the place. She could not see herself in the mirror of the thousands of eyes all around. Every eye would have reflected her guilt. And how was she going to face me? She had not even written a question or a letter.

There is nothing wrong – I have my own ways. This is not a teaching school; this is a world of a master who is concerned with your potential being. And as far as your potential being is concerned, most of the questions are exactly about you. You may not have stumbled upon it today, perhaps tomorrow. Or perhaps you may have raised the question within yourself yesterday, but were not courageous enough to expose yourself.

Every question has to be understood as the question of the whole commune. Only then can you learn as much as is possible to learn. If you think, "It is a question of Deva Dolma, it has nothing to do with us," you are missing something. Something in it must be a part in you too, expressed, unexpressed. Perhaps a few have betrayed, a few are waiting to betray. I am not addressing questions, I am addressing the whole commune, the whole atmosphere in which I want you to live and grow. It is just a strategy that I answer someone's question. There is no need at all even to mention the name because the question as such belongs to almost every human being more or less.

Mick Jagger orders an extremely expensive, custom-made suit, but is very dissatisfied with the finished garment.

"I told you to make the pants tight!" he remarks angrily to the tailor. "I want them tight enough to show my sex."

"I am sorry, sir," the tailor protests, "but if they were any tighter they would show your religion!"

I have been told by my bodyworker, Anubuddha, to keep looking around. He says that because I go on looking in one direction, people want their seats in that direction. And according to him my neck gets disturbed. So from now onward, once in a while I'm going to look all around, just as an exercise.

Where is Avirbhava? She must be holding the wall, because twice the wall has moved toward me!

Osho,
I don't usually ask personal questions about your private life, because I feel it is private and none of our business.

However, one question intrigues me deeply, and I can't resist asking it: What is your relationship with little Ernie?

Maneesha, it would have been right if you had not asked this. Little Ernie is your brother, but he is not my son. But he is really cute, intelligent and anyone can be really proud of him.

Little Ernie's father invites his boss to dinner, in the hope of getting a promotion at work.

Days are spent planning the menu and getting the house just right, but the effect is ruined when little Ernie appears on the stairs just as the boss arrives.

"I wanted to see you," says Ernie, "because Mum said you were a self-made man."

"I am," smiles the boss, "and proud of it!"

"In that case," says Ernie, "why did you make yourself look so ugly?"

The elevator on a New York skyscraper is packed with people.

Suddenly a tall man screams out in agony.

Little Ernie looks up at his mother, "I don't care, Mom," he says, "it was in my face, so I bit it."

Maneesha, he is everyone's brother, not only yours. There are a few universal characters. Ernie is one of those universal characters. And you know I talk about all of those universal characters.

But it is good not to ask me personal questions because they are not going to help you in any way. You are here for your own personal growth, you are not to be worried about my personal life; in fact, I don't have much personal life. At least eighteen hours a day is for sleeping.

I have been asked many times that I should write my autobiography. What autobiography? No love affair… Even Niskriya is smiling. He must be thinking, "Now look at what trouble I have been up to now."

I am not in trouble. Just to avoid trouble I am not in any love relationship. And without love relationships, without a wife and children, what autobiography? I am not a man of actions.

Today after I finished lunch, my Coke was just sitting in front of me on the table, but I waited and waited for Shunyo. Finally she showed up. She said, "You have finished?"

I said, "I have finished long ago, I am just waiting for my Coke."

She said, "But the Coke is here."

I said, "It is there, that's what I am thinking. The Coke is here; I am here – nothing is happening. I am simply waiting for someone."

You don't know these people. Anando opens the door and forces me into my bathroom: "It is time to take a bath."

I said, "This is strange, I could have walked myself."

They don't even allow me to open the door of the car!

I have looked many times – at the most, half a page will do for my autobiography, and the rest of my life I have been sleeping. Seeing the fact that one has to sleep for eternity, I thought, why bother? Just start right now.

My physician, Dr. Amrito, goes on trying to cure my troubles. My hand hurts – he has been injecting it as many times as he wants. I am so lazy that I will not even stop… So let them do what they want to do. Finally, this morning I said, "Just wait a few days. When I am gone, keep my skeleton and study it well, and wherever things are incorrect correct them. Why torture me unnecessarily now?"

I don't have any personal life. Just today I told Hasya not to answer any letter from someone who addresses me as "friend," because I don't have any friends. I don't take any responsibility.

Once you accept someone as a friend, you have accepted someone to be an enemy in the future. It is better from the very beginning to be on the safe side. Already I have so many enemies, why go on increasing them?

A person who is asking questions but is not ready to be a disciple does not deserve to be answered either, because *disciple* simply means one who is capable of learning. And a person who himself is accepting: "I am not going to be a disciple, but I want these questions answered" – why should I bother? He has not even the respect.

You don't ask your friends spiritual questions; you don't ask your friends questions about meditation and the inner life. Friends are in the same boat; I am not your friend. I may call you friends just out of my love, but that does not mean that you can call me your friend. The moment you call me your friend, I am not going to answer because you are in the same state of consciousness as I am. What is the point of answering? You must know!

If you want to learn, you have to be a learner, a disciple. If, because of my love, I call you my friend that does not give you the permission to start calling me your friend. The distance between our consciousnesses is infinite. I am calling you from a sunlit peak. And you are in a dark valley. And anyway Maneesha, neither do I have any personality nor any personal life.

Reduced simply: I talk to you twice a day if my body allows. Once in a while it freaks out. Then twice a day a bath – just a quick shower, as quick as one can do. Fifteen hundred calories of food, which even small babies will find insufficient, because if I take more I will have to become a member of the Couch Potato Club. I don't have any antagonism as far as potatoes are concerned. They are very good people; they have never done any harm to anyone. But still I don't want to enter that company.

So for your information, this is my autobiography. And then twice sleeping; in total that is eighteen hours. I don't have any ambition for tomorrow. If by chance I am still here, I will talk to you about things which may help you on the path. If I am not here, perhaps that may also help you because then you cannot take me for granted. Perhaps my remembrance may give you much more light than I can give you.

Never take me for granted because I have nothing to hang around for: no desire, no ambition, nowhere to go. I have not even visited the M.G. Road market. I hope that some time, by chance... Just a few days ago I had to go to Jehangir Hospital to see one of my old lovers, Manik Bafna because he had a second heart attack. If it was the first I would not have gone. A second is too much. The third is the last, and after the third, I will also not go because there is no point. The right point was the second.

And I heard from sannyasins that there is a rumor in the hospital that I had had a heart attack, and that I had come to be checked. But I did not like the place so I did not go because within two minutes I was out. Naturally the hospital servants and doctors must have thought that I did not like the place. Who likes places like hospitals?

So Maneesha, there is not much. I think I could have given you more information. Maneesha is writing books about me; she would have been helped, but I am helpless. You can invent anything you like. I will agree, so you need not be worried. Even if you say that I have a wife and five children, I am not going to contradict it. What is wrong in it? Everyone has a wife, everyone has many children. And there is no harm; one really feels proud. But it is better not to ask such questions.

Adolf Hitler is inspecting his Panzer division. Every boot and button is shining bright and there is a deathly silence over the parade ground.

All of a sudden someone sneezes.

"Who sneezed?" Hitler shrieks at the men.

No one dares answer. Hitler raises his arm and the first row of soldiers is shot dead.

"Who sneezed?" Hitler shrieks again.

There is no reply, so Hitler raises his arm and the next row of soldiers is shot dead.

"I will ask you one more time," says Hitler. "Who sneezed?"

A man in the back row timidly raises his hand.

"It was me," says the soldier.

"A-ha!" says Hitler, "Gesundheit!"

Can I have a little exercise? Because I don't have any other time to do the exercise. [*Osho slowly moves his head around the semicircle of meditators sitting in front of him.*]

Luigi comes home after eighteen months abroad and is amazed to find his wife, Carlotta, has a three-week-old baby.

Carlotta explains that she dreamed she had sex with him and she got pregnant.

Luigi files for a divorce, and in court the judge is astounded by Carlotta's story. The judge stands up and asks the audience if they ever had intercourse with a ghost.

In the back of the courtroom, Luigi's grandfather raises his hand, and the judge calls him up to testify.

"Now-a," says the judge, "you say-a you had-a intercourse with a ghost?"

"Ah, scusa," says the old Italian, "I thought-a you say-a goat!"

Before another exercise… No one is willing for a small exercise – Anubuddha, this is not good!

One bright Sunday in the morning after church, Mother Superior takes the nuns out for a bicycle ride.

But before long, most of the nuns are squealing and giggling and fooling around.

"All right, girls," shouts Mother Superior, "if you don't calm down and behave yourselves, I am going to make you put the bicycles seats back on!"

Just the last...

Gertie Kowalski goes to visit Dr. Bones with cuts and scratches on her knees.

"How did this happen?" asks Bones.

Gertie blushes a deep red, but then she finally tells him.

"The truth is, Doctor," she says, "that I have been doing it doggie style."

"Well, that is no problem to cure," says Bones. "Just roll over and do it in the missionary position."

"I have tried it," says Gertie, "but each time I do, I get knocked out by the smell of my dog's breath!"

22

A Man of Understanding Cannot Commit a Crime

Osho,

An old Spanish mystic, San Juan de la Cruz, symbolically described the spiritual journey like a mountain, which he named Monte Carmelo. In his mystic representation, the trail before the summit suddenly disappears and he specifies: "Here there is no trail because for the right man there is no law."

Who is the "right man"? And what does it mean, "there is no law"?

In the first place a spiritual journey is only symbolic. You don't go anywhere. You simply reveal yourself, wherever you are and whatever you are. It is not a journey from one point to another point, not horizontal. It is a journey…if you can be deep down within yourself right now, the journey will be complete without ever being begun. But the mystic has a problem: language is not made to express the inner truths of life. It is mundane and of the marketplace. The problem of the mystic is that he has to use the same language. But don't take it seriously.

A spiritual journey is no journey. There is no spiritual goal. In fact, you are already there but simply not aware. If you can become just a little alert, you will be surprised that you were seeking unnecessarily, searching here and there – and the seeker was the search. I have told you that I don't agree with Jesus Christ on the point when he says, "Seek and ye shall find."

I say unto you, "Seek not – because you are already there. Seek, and you shall miss."

Jesus says, "Ask and the answer will be given to you." You are the answer. The asking has to be dropped – not asked. When there is no question in you, that silence, that tranquility, that peace, that music of the eternal is the answer. No one gives it to you, it is your inheritance.

And Jesus finally says, "Knock and the doors shall be opened unto you." The doors are always open and there is no need for knocking. In fact, a person who is knocking is certainly blind because he cannot see that the door is open.

My approach is totally different. There is no need to postpone in seeking, searching, questioning. All postponement is unspiritual. A man of integrity does not postpone the most important thing of his life: knowing himself. Hence I say unto you, "Enter, the doors are open." If you are so much in love with knocking, you can knock later on.

A few people have strange kinds of fixations…

The great English linguist, Johnson, had a very strange and weird habit. He could not go for a walk without knocking on every lamp post.

His friends were tired of it saying, "This is absolutely meaningless."

He said, "I know, but what I can do? If I don't knock, that lamp post haunts me. I'll go on thinking that something is missing. Sometimes I have tried with great courage to go straight on without knocking, but then I have to come back and knock it. Unless I knock all the lamp posts on the morning walk, I am not satisfied. But it takes unnecessary time and people think I am mad."

He was not mad, just a little eccentric. So if you are in love with knocking, you cannot accept the open door. You can knock from the other side, but first enter.

You are quoting an old Spanish mystic, San Juan, describing the spiritual journey as a mountain which he named Monte Carmelo. Man's mind is very interested in things which are very far away. It becomes a little fidgety if things can be done right now. If there is some mountain far away, Carmelo, then you are at ease that there is no hurry. And what can you do? It will take time, preparation, discipline. And who knows where that mountain is? We will need guides and maps and the whole theology, Christian, Hindu, Mohammedan and all kinds of nonsense just because San Juan could not find – and no one can find – expressions about the ultimate, without using ordinary words. The words are like stones lying on the ground and the experiences are like birds flying high in the sky. It is very difficult to tell the birds about the stones, but it is even more difficult to tell the stones about the birds because the stones cannot believe that you can fly into the sky: "What nonsense are you saying?"

Then you have to give some symbols and those symbols have become a hindrance rather than a help, because people have got caught in those symbols as if they are reality. There is no mountain and there is no journey. In your intrinsic being you are all that you need to be. But you never look inward; your eyes are always searching far away. The mind is extrovert, but there is nothing wrong in it.

There are many things in the outside world that only the mind can explore: science, technology, the faraway stars. All that is the contribution of the extrovert mind. But the difficulty is that behind the mind there is another possibility – meditation.

Meditation is introvert; hence in the East, we could not create technology, we could not create great science, we could not create riches, comforts, luxuries. The East has remained poor because we have never bothered about the extrovert mind, knowing that whatever it accumulates, inside you remain empty. And finally, frustration sets in.

Just as the mind is the extroversion, meditation is an arrow entering within yourself. There is no mountain and there is no journey, just an understanding. Never be caught in symbols. They can be helpful if you understand. If you do not understand then you start looking and searching for symbols, which are just words. They were used to provoke you, to challenge you. But on the contrary, rather than being challenged by them and entering your own being, you go even further away from yourself.

It is very difficult for the mind, almost impossible, to go inside. Outside, the whole sky is available, but the mind has no roots going inside. That's why meditation first silences the mind, puts it aside as if it does not exist. Only then, a new consciousness arises in you which moves inward. It is not a journey because it happens on its own accord. It is spontaneous – not something that you are doing, but something that you are being.

Your question goes on "…the trail before the summit suddenly disappears and he specifies: 'Here there is no trail because for the right man there is no law.'" Now, if you start thinking about it, you are bound to go crazy. First, the search for the mountain, then the mountain disappears; even the trail to the mountain disappears. Now you are hanging in a very precarious condition.

The old is lost, the new has not arrived and you are standing in the middle. Neither can you go back nor can you go forward. But that is very significant because that's where the whole world of mysticism wants you to be: in a place where you cannot go back and you cannot go forward; where you cannot go anywhere but within yourself.

All trails and all mountains disappear; this is the point when you need "the right man." That right man is not someone else. You are that right man for whom all desires, all ambitions, all goals, all greed, in fact all time, has disappeared. Just a single point of existence, of utter purity and blissfulness. You are the right man and for the right man there is no law.

That has puzzled many people and many mystics have been condemned for this – not only condemned, Socrates was poisoned.

The reason was the same, that he was teaching people to attain a situation where you are no longer under any law. But the society thinks that a man who is above the law is dangerous. You cannot dictate to him what is right and what is wrong. Your courts and your constitutions and your legalities are all futile. The right man knows exactly what is right.

The law exists for the wrong man, not for the right man. And because this whole world lives in a wrong psychology, whenever a right man appears, he seems to be such a stranger, an outsider that people start thinking he is going to corrupt us. The charge against Socrates was, "He is going to corrupt people because he teaches a lawlessness, a freedom." The same was the crime of Jesus – that he was a right man. The same was the case about al-Hillaj Mansoor – that he was a right man.

Al-Hillaj Mansoor was the disciple of a great master, Junnaid. He realized his own spirituality and divinity, his own luminosity – which has been realized in the East as *aham brahmasmi* – even to the point of declaring: "I am the ultimate, I am God." It is not out of any ego. These people who were saying these things were very humble. When Mansoor realized the point, the right point where you *are*, he said, "*Ana'l haq*" which means, "I am the right, I am the law; in other words, I am God and there is nothing above me."

Junnaid said, "Be quiet. I know it is true, but you are too young and you don't know that the whole world is full of wrong people. They will not understand you. They will kill you because you are corrupting their youth, their minds. They are continually afraid that no one should touch their beliefs."

Junnaid continued, "I also experienced the same, but being an older man, much more experienced of the world, I don't want to create unnecessary trouble for myself."

But Mansoor was young, he could not resist. In the marketplaces he would shout, "*Ana'l haq!* – I am the truth."

And the same charge was made against him, that he was corrupting people: "If everyone starts saying, 'I am God, I am the truth,

I am the law,' then the whole society will collapse." Yes, if people start saying such things without experiencing the innermost being, the society will collapse. But if people assert their understanding of being, this society will rise in consciousness to heights only known by a very few mystics, and which have rarely been known by man.

I was in Greece and the archbishop of Greece started creating a protest against me. I was just a tourist for four weeks. He would send telegrams to the prime minister, the president, the home ministry. And he would give interviews to television and to the newspapers saying, "This man staying in Greece is dangerous. His influence is going to be corruptive. He will corrupt our tradition, our morality."

And I wondered how a morality that has been established for twenty centuries can be corrupted by a man who is only a tourist for four weeks. In fact, that morality is trembling inside and afraid because it is based on the wrong man and the wrong man's perception.

The right man is not worried. I have been around the world; twenty-one countries have stopped me from entering their lands because my influence is going to corrupt their younger generation. Not a single one, any archbishop, any *shankaracharya*, any imam or any pope has been able to say exactly what it is that I am going to corrupt. But this is enough; the very word *corruption* is enough.

To help people to enter their own being seems to be the greatest sin in the world. They have behaved more brutally with Socrates and Jesus and al-Hillaj and others than they have ever behaved with criminals.

For the right man, the man who is centered in himself, a man who is conscious of his being, that very consciousness is enough. Whatever he will do will be right. He does not need any law imposed upon him from outside, and imposed by people who are utterly rotten. Gutter politicians making laws – and they themselves are absolutely corrupt according to their own laws.

But whenever they are in power, you cannot say that you are against the law. They will change the law, they will manipulate the law, they will find loopholes in the law, and they will manage to do whatever they want to do. These are the people who should be crucified, but on the contrary, simple people like Mansoor and Socrates are crucified. Up to now, truth has been crucified and untruth has ruled over the world. But the mystics are absolutely right that for the right man there is no law.

Now you are asking, "Who is 'the right man'?" I am sitting before you. I don't have any law; there is no need. Glasses are needed if your eyes cannot see. Blind men need a staff to find their way. But if your eyes are right, you don't need any glasses. You don't go on tapping with your staff finding your way. The right man is certainly beyond the law.

And you are asking, "Who is 'the right man'?" Have you not recognized me? And have you not seen that the same behavior has been done to me on a vast scale? Jesus was crucified in a very small part of the world, almost unknown to the other parts of the world – Judea. He was neither known all over the world nor condemned all over the world, just by the Jews. Socrates was condemned only by a city, Athens, because at that time Greece had only city-states; there was no nation as such.

But I sometimes wonder...

Just the other day I received the news that the second biggest party, the opposition party in Germany, has been fighting the ruling party so that they cannot make a law against me entering their country. A few days ago they had their party convention. In the party convention they said, "We are going to fight because of something absolutely absurd and ridiculous." The German law passed by the parliament is that not only can I not enter their land, but my airplane cannot land on any airport in Germany even for refueling.

I don't think that in fifteen minutes I will be able to destroy their long tradition, great religion, all the morality – and from the airport! I would not be leaving the airplane because I cannot land on their land according to their parliamentary law.

This Green Party, which is the second major party, has a future. Soon it might be the ruling party, and because this is becoming a possibility in the next general election, now they themselves have become afraid. It was good to fight the ruling party – any excuse is enough to fight with the ruling party. Now they have become aware of what they are doing. When they become the ruling party, what are they going to do? "This man is certainly dangerous!"

So they have made an amendment in their fight: "We are against making laws against a single man who has never entered Germany and who has no intention either, but we want to make it clear that we don't agree with this man. It is a question of legal parliamentarianism. It doesn't look right so we will withdraw it, but that does not mean that we agree with this man."

This amendment was amazing. It means that the moment they come into power, they will do the same, perhaps in a different way. Twenty-one countries have made laws that I cannot enter their countries. And the Indian government has been pressured by American, British, German and other governments that I should not even be allowed to move out of Pune – they cannot deport me from this country – and that people who want to come to see me should be prevented and turned back from the airport. Hundreds of sannyasins have been deported. They have never entered the country. From the airport they have been forced to return on the next plane going back to their country. What crime have I committed?

To think, to be, to be authentic, perhaps is the worst crime. Down the centuries the right man has always been in the same trouble, stoned, killed. And these few right men. All the truth, beauty dignity that they have spread around into humanity. Even by their deaths they have raised human consciousness. Their lives could have raised human consciousness to unknown heights.

You are asking, "Who is 'the right man'?" If you cannot recognize me, you will not recognize the right man anywhere. I am the most corrupt man in the eyes of all those who are blind. My only crime is that I am trying to sell glasses to the blind. Naturally, they don't want that. I persuade them, but they don't want it.

And finally you ask, "And what does it mean 'there is no law'?" There is no law for the man of consciousness because the man of consciousness cannot do anything wrong. What law is needed for a Gautam Buddha? His own light is enough, more than enough to show him the right path. His consciousness is enough to create his actions as beautiful and graceful as possible. His understanding of himself is enough to be compassionate and to be loving.

One beautiful morning like this…

Gautam Buddha is passing by a town and the people of the town are all against him because they say he is corrupting people. He is telling them what is not right. He is telling them not to worship but to meditate, not to bow down to stone statues but to "Enter your own being, your own life source." He is destroying people's religion.

The people of the town had gathered to condemn him, to insult him. He silently listened. Their words were ugly. Even Gautam Buddha's nearest disciples became angry. But in Buddha's presence of course they had to be silent and not speak; otherwise they would have killed those people.

Buddha finally said, "I have to reach another town and the people there must be waiting. The sun is rising and becoming hotter. You will have to excuse me. I have heard whatever you wanted to say. If you are still in need of saying something more, on my return trip you can fulfill that desire too. But I just want to ask you one question."

They said, "But we are enemies – and it is not a conversation. We have not come here to ask questions or to talk to you, or to listen to you."

Buddha said, "No, that is not a problem. Just a small question: In the last town, people who love me came to offer me flowers and sweets. But we eat only one time a day so we told them, 'We are sorry, we are thankful to you, but you will have to take them back. It is too early for us to eat.'"

Buddhists eat only one time in the middle of the day. And the Buddhist cannot carry food or anything edible with him.

"I want to ask you," he said to the people, "what should they have done with the sweets and the flowers?"

One man from the crowd said, "They should have distributed them to the children, who would have eaten and enjoyed them."

Buddha said, "That's all. Just as I rejected what they brought, I reject what you have brought. Now go back home and enjoy. Distribute whatever you have brought to your children, your friends, your wife.

"If you had come ten years ago, none of you would have gone back alive. I am a warrior." And he was a prince, well trained in swordsmanship. He could have finished them all. He said, "But you came too late. Now I have only compassion for you and love for you and a prayer that existence may bring you some light so that you see that I am not the problem. The real problem is that you are not certain of your religion, not certain of your beliefs. You have repressed many doubts inside and my presence brings those doubts. It is not my problem. Now what can I do? I had not even entered your town. I was leaving from the outside, not to disturb you."

They were stunned. They could not believe that you can insult someone and he says that he doesn't accept it; it is not natural. You are insulting the man and he is silently saying, "You can keep it, I don't want it. It is your problem, it is not my problem. You are angry; burn into your anger, but why harass me?"

A man of truth behaves so totally differently from the common masses that it becomes very difficult for the crowd to accept him. Only very intelligent people, very alert people, can understand that there cannot be any law for a man of understanding.

Laws are made for criminals. A man of understanding cannot commit a crime. He cannot even dream of committing a crime. His meditation cleanses his whole being of any possibility of the poisons that can erupt any moment. His eyes become pure clarity, perceptivity. He can see far away to each action and its consequence.

There have been people like Prince Kropotkin who imagined that sometime in a future, perhaps millions of years after we are gone, there would be human beings who will not need governments, who will not need constitutions. Looking at the people all around, it looks dreamlike. Looking at the politicians of the world, it does not seem that even after millions of years the dream will be realized. Most probably that day will never come before humanity will be destroyed, life will be erased from the earth. But one feels a deep love for people like Prince Kropotkin who at least can conceive of a world... They give dignity to man: "Maybe you are not right now, but one day you will be." They trust you.

Others have called their ideas a utopia. *Utopia* by its roots means that which never comes. It would be very sad if a utopia never comes. If it can happen to one man that there is no law, if it can happen to thousands of mystics that there is no law; it shows our potential. We are also made of the same stuff, the same consciousness. We are just fast asleep. We can also rise up beyond the ugly world of laws and courts. They show our barbariousness, our animality.

It is very strange that we make our courts very big, very palatial. Our judges are almost superhuman beings. Millions of people are in jail. And millions of people are trying to make their whole living from them. Millions of people are judging, millions of people are fighting with each other. This is really a lawless world because people don't have an inner insight.

Don't just go on thinking about it, become the right man. It is not a journey. You don't have to go to the Kaaba, or to Carmelo or to Kashi. You have to go to your own being. You are the only temple. All other temples are man-made. The way humanity is – just watch it and witness it – is hilarious.

Mendel Kravitz meets a gorgeous young woman at a cocktail party and soon they strike up a friendly conversation about human nature.

"Would you sleep with a complete stranger for a million dollars?" asks Mendel.

"Yes," the girl declares, "I think I would."

"I see," says Mendel. "Would you sleep with me for twenty-five dollars?"

"My God," cries the girl, "what do you think I am?"

"We have already established that," replies Mendel. "Now we are just haggling over the price."

Abraham Grossman meets his old friend, Moishe Finkelstein, in the street one day.

"Abe, old pal!" begins Moishe, "How are things going? I hear you married an Italian girl. What is the matter – a Jewish girl won't do for you?"

"Well," says Abe, "it is like this. You marry a Jewish girl and the next thing you know she has to get her teeth fixed – dentist bills like you would not believe. Then she has got women's trouble – more doctor's bills. Then there is the psychiatrist – she needs to see him three times a week."

"I understand," says Moishe. "But this can all happen to an Italian girl too."

"I know," says Abe, "but with an Italian girl, who cares?"

Two Jews arrive at the pearly gates of heaven and ask Saint Peter if they can come in.

"Certainly not!" says Saint Peter, "We don't allow your sort in here. Get lost!"

He then goes to tell Jesus proudly what he has done. Jesus becomes furious.

"Peter!" he shouts, "You can't do that! Quick, go and get them back." Saint Peter runs off and comes back a few minutes later, puffing.

"They have gone!" he says.

"Who? The Jews?" asks Jesus.

"No," gasps Saint Peter, "the pearly gates."

A nervous young man walks into the drugstore and is very embarrassed when a prim, middle-aged woman comes to serve him.

"Can I see the druggist?" he stammers.

"I am the druggist," she replies cheerfully. "What can I do for you?"

"Well, it is nothing important," says the man, and turns to leave.

"Young man," says the woman, "my sister and I have been running this drugstore for thirty years. There is nothing you can tell us that will embarrass us."

"Well, all right," says the man. "I have this awful sexual hunger that nothing will satisfy. No matter how many times I make love, I still want to make love again. Is there anything you can give me for it?"

"Just a moment," says the little lady, "I will have to discuss this with my sister."

A few moments later she returns.

"The best we can offer," she says, "is five hundred dollars a week."

And the last…

Bernie Bernstein is in the urinal standing next to a very large black man. Looking over, Bernie is astonished and very jealous to notice the huge size of his neighbor's equipment.

"Excuse me, mister," he says, "but could you tell me how you managed to get such a magnificent member?"

"Simple, man," says the black guy. "When I was a boy, my mamma tied a brick to it and for a whole month I walked around like that."

Bernie runs home and tells Sara, his wife. "Sara," he shouts, "cancel all visits and engagements. I'm not even going to work. I'm going to get myself a wonderful big prick!"

So Bernie ties a brick to his prick and does not go out of the house for a month.

Eventually, Sara says, "So, let us take a look and see how it is growing."

So Bernie opens his pants, takes a good look and says,

"Well, we are halfway there, it has turned black already!"

23

When You Meet Me, Just Say Good-bye

Osho,

To meet the buddha on the way and kill him also implies the death of the disciple.

Can you say something about the master-disciple experience and being in the presence of the master?

Gautama the Buddha is the only master in the whole history of mankind who could assert this tremendously important statement. It is not for ordinarily so-called religious people. It is for those who are authentically devoted, committed to reach themselves. The statement is very strange in a way because what it says is exactly what it hides. The statement is: "If you meet me on the way, kill me immediately."

And the question which has been asked is that to kill the master certainly means the death of the disciple. You have exactly understood the meaning of Gautam Buddha's statement. He is saying, "If you meet me on the way, even I don't matter – the master is the ultimate; even the master does not matter – kill me immediately because I don't want to become a hindrance on your path. I want to become a stepping stone."

But naturally you can kill the master only if you have killed the disciple first. In fact the master and the disciple are not two words, but two sides of the same coin. Instead of thinking of the master and disciple relationship, look at it as if the master and the disciple are two sides of the same coin. And if you drop the coin, both sides are dropped. The moment the master is killed, how can the disciple survive?

But Gautam Buddha could have said, "If you meet me on the way, kill the disciple." That would not have served the purpose, nor would the statement have been meaningful. That is exactly what he wants, but the only way to kill the disciple is to kill the master. The only way is to disappear together and just leave the energy searching and seeking the paradise lost, as one whole.

Ordinarily people have always understood that the master and disciple relationship is just like other relationships: the wife and the husband, the teacher and the taught. It is not of the same category; it is a very strange relationship. It is as if one heart starts throbbing in two bodies. You cannot call it a relationship, because a relationship needs out of necessity the existence of the two, and this phenomenon of master and disciple intrinsically needs the disappearance of duality.

Gautam Buddha is immensely compassionate. Rather than telling you to disappear, rather than telling you to drop your ego and no longer be a separate entity, he has found a very subtle way of saying the same thing, but in a far more sophisticated way: "If you meet me on the way, kill me."

In meditation, when you are moving inward, you will meet many things. You will meet your repressed desires, you will meet your incomplete experiences, you will meet your ambitions, but it is easy to destroy them, it is easy to go beyond them. Finally, you will meet your master because that is your last love. You have left everything for him, now only the master remains. But even that small clinging is enough to prevent your eyes from seeing the truth.

In another statement Gautam Buddha has said – and you may wonder how such a small clinging can prevent the immense truth from being seen – "Just a small particle of sand in your eyes is enough to prevent you from seeing the whole sky." It is not a question of a small piece of sand, it is a question of your vision. Your vision is closed, your vision is very small. The world, the truth, the universe is immense, but your eyes… And the master is certainly the biggest experience of your life. He overwhelms you, he throbs in your nerves, he dances in your heart, he thrills every cell of your being. If you don't drop him, you will not be able to know the infinite and the eternal.

But the moment you drop the master, certainly you are no longer a disciple; they disappear together. What remains is utter silence, a nondual state of tranquility.

No other master in the world has been able to pinpoint it so clearly and in such a sophisticated way that you never think he is asking *you* to dissolve. You start thinking he is asking you to kill him. He will certainly meet you on the path. He will meet you only at the last, when all other attachments and relationships are gone. He will meet you and it is going to be hard. It is going to be very hard to kill your own master. But it is only a metaphor; it only indicates to say good-bye to Gautam Buddha: "You have been enough for me, now leave me alone. Just move out of the way."

I will not tell you to kill me. Gautam Buddha was a warrior, trained as a prince in swordsmanship. He talks the same language: "If you meet me on the way, kill me immediately." I don't even know how to hold a sword so I cannot say that. What to say of a sword? I have never even touched a razor blade with my hands. I don't think you will find anyone else in the world who has an original beard. I have never cut it, but everyone in my family was continually telling me to. I said, "I love originality so much that even if nothing is original in me, at least it can be noncontroversially said that my beard is original."

So I cannot say to you, "When I meet you, kill me." That very word *kill* was perfectly good for a prince but I will simply say, "When you meet me, just say good-bye." More than that is not needed. Unnecessary killing and bloodshed – I have so many disciples, if everyone starts killing me, how many times will I be killed?

No, that is too much; good-bye is perfectly mannerly. No one can object about its beauty and grace.

Remember, to say good-bye is more difficult than to kill because when you say good-bye, your eyes will be full of tears, your heart will be weeping. As far as killing is concerned that is very simple, not complicated. A single blow and the poor master is dead. And then you will be surprised that it is not only the poor master who is dead, but with the poor master dead you are also dead. He was your life – you have committed suicide!

But these words *killing* and *suicide* are not very poetic. I say, "When you meet me on the path, say gracefully, without tears in your eyes, 'Good-bye.' And don't look back." Naturally you will also disappear. What remains is the pure existence. We are simply waves in the pure existence and its ocean. When the wave disappears nothing disappears. A curve is simply no more. A curve has become a straight line. No one dies and no one disappears. Existence remains the same through all the changes, climates, forms, seasons, and through life, birth, death. You should not take it very seriously.

A Christian monk said to me, "This seems to be very strange that a man who taught nonviolence for his whole life says, 'If I meet you on the way, kill me.'" In a way, the Christian monk was right because the word *killing* does not give you the sense of compassion and love. But he did not understand that as far as Gautam Buddha or people like Krishna are concerned, nothing is killed. Only the form is dissolved into a new form. You cannot destroy anything in this world, you can only change, and change is continuously happening.

It is good that you accept this change as the very nature of existence, and with it drop all resistance and change with a deep surrender, let-go. Don't even swim downstream, just flow. Wherever the stream is going is home.

And you are also asking what it means "...being in the presence of the master?" It means to be absent as yourself and let the master's presence surround you, penetrate you, burn you, change you, transform you. You drop all defense, all distance, all fear; you simply melt and merge in the energy that surrounds the master. That is what is meant to be in the presence of the master. Everyone who is present is not present in the sense that I am telling you to be present. You can be present as yourself for years and nothing will happen. And you can be present the way I am telling you, just for a single moment, and you will be reborn.

The presence of the master is a fire in which you have to be burned, but whatever is gold will remain and whatever is not gold will be burned. To be twenty-four carat gold is a sheer joy. Utter purity like a flower that will start surrounding you. A new energy that you had not known, although it is your own but has been asleep, dormant, becomes radiant. You start to glow in a new style of life and love, you dance and sing and celebrate in a new way. If the master's presence does not become a dance in you, you have not been present, you must have been somewhere else.

I have told you the story…

Two friends were talking. One friend said, "You will not be able to believe that last night in my dream I went fishing. And my God, what a great fish, so huge. The whole night I was fishing and fishing and there was no end: greater and greater fish!"

The other man said, "This is nothing. You will certainly not believe what I saw last night: On one side I saw that Marilyn Monroe is lying naked and on the other side another beauty."

As he asserted this the first man said, "You idiot. You pretend to be my best friend. Why did you not call me?"

The man said, "I did. I went running to your house and your wife told me that you had gone fishing!"

No one is where he thinks he is. You think you are here? Really, you think… If you look within yourself you may not believe it. It is strange, you are here and your mind is wandering somewhere else, is thinking about something else. To be in the presence of a master is not to be just physically present. It has to be a presence of consciousness, of awareness, as if the whole world has disappeared. Only this moment, and you are gripped by a great silence. Out of this silence will arise the dance, the celebration.

Mahakashyapa was one of the most important disciples of Gautam Buddha. It is strange that he is rarely mentioned in Buddhist scriptures. As far as I know he is mentioned only once. There were other great disciples, Sariputta, Moggalayan, Ananda and many more, and they are mentioned thousands of times. There are so many incidents in which they are involved.

Mahakashyapa is mentioned only once because his first encounter with Gautam Buddha was his last. He looked into Buddha's eyes, he touched his feet and he sat by his side. And for forty years he was simply rejoicing, celebrating.

People used to think that he was somewhat crazy: "Why does he go on smiling? No one has said anything, nothing has happened and he is smiling as if someone has cracked a joke?"

He was asked and he said, "What more? I have seen the greatest height of consciousness. I have seen the purest love. I have seen silence that is eternal, and I am utterly satisfied. Out of that satisfaction comes my smile. I am not smiling at someone else. My smile is just like a flower. It is not flowering for you. It is just the juice of the bush that is blossoming in the flower. Flowers go on blossoming because I am so full of my master's presence."

To be in the presence of the master is to disappear as a separate entity. It is just like the dropping of a dewdrop from the lotus leaf into the ocean – not that the dewdrop disappears, it simply becomes the ocean.

Now something serious. I really mean *serious*. Niskriya, *awake*! He was falling asleep…

Farmer Rumple is getting on in years, but the pretty young wench who milks his cows catches his eye. He decides to marry her and they settle down happily at the farmhouse.

Some time later, Farmer Rumple goes to visit his doctor. "I have this problem," he says. "I don't get the urge very often, but sometimes it happens when I'm out in the fields and by the time I run back to my wife at the farmhouse, it is gone!"

"Well," says the doctor, thoughtfully, "why don't you take your gun with you, so when you get the urge, you can fire off a shot and she can come running to you?"

"Great idea!" says Rumple and goes home.

All is well until one day the doctor sees the farmer looking a bit miserable.

"How is your love life?" asks the doctor.

"It was wonderful since you gave me that advice," says Rumple.

"And how is your lovely wife?" asks the doctor.

"Well," replies Rumple, "that is just it. I have hardly seen her at all since the hunting season started!"

A psychology professor is teaching a class and tells his students that he is going to conduct a sex survey. He says to the class, "If you have sex once a day, raise your hand."

About fifteen percent of the students raise their hands. "Okay," he continues, "if you have sex three times a week, raise your hand."

About forty percent do so.

"Interesting," he says. "If you have sex once a week, raise your hand."

About twenty percent do so.

The professor then asks, "If you have sex once a month, raise your hand."

A few hands go up. Then as an afterthought he says, "If you have sex once a year, raise your hand."

A little guy at the back of the class waves wildly, grinning from ear to ear.

"Why are you so happy?" asks the professor.

The little guy jumps up and starts to dance with joy, singing, "Tonight's the night!"

Jack and Ida Blinkoff, an old retired couple, are taking their yearly winter vacation, driving from New York City to Florida.

Jack is driving with Ida sitting beside him giving instructions. As they are passing through Virginia, they are pulled over by a traffic cop.

The officer says to Jack, "You realize that you were exceeding the speed limit, don't you?"

Ida nudges Jack and asks, "What did he say?"

"He is telling me that I was speeding," replies Jack.

Then the cop asks Jack to present his driver's license and registration.

"What did he say?" asks Ida.

"He wants to see my license, dear," replies Jack.

Seeing that they are from New York, the officer remarks, "I have been to New York. That is where I had the worst screw of my life!"

"What did he say?" asks Ida.

Coolly, Jack replies, "He says, dear, that he thinks he knows you!"

Niskriya, are you awake now? Just to be on the safe side...

There is great excitement in the cannibal tribe when a white hunter and his beautiful girlfriend are brought into the village and tied up to a tree. The cannibals boil up a huge pot of water and the man is thrown in, cooked, and served up for a great feast.

By dawn the next morning, another pot is boiling and the cannibals untie the girl and lead her toward it. She is just about to be thrown in when a man comes running from the chief's hut.

"Wait!" cries the man, "Wait! The chief wants his breakfast in bed!"

23

Life Is a Game and So Is Death

Osho,
The other night you spoke about how our emotions get drunk with love.

Can you speak about that delicious intoxication that we feel when we drink your wine?

Prem Madir, my wine is not of this world. In fact, my wine is not even mine. It belongs to the very life source. I sing the song of existence. So when you get intoxicated with me, I am just an excuse; you are intoxicated with existence itself, with all its beautitude, with all its glory, with all its tremendous splendor. The infinity, the eternity, the immortality – in a single moment all are yours, and when you are intoxicated you are no more. Only in these moments has truth been found, God has been found, liberation has been found. These are all different names of something which cannot be named.

That's why, when I say God is dead, don't think that I am an atheist; I am simply saying that the symbol of God is no longer significant. The priests have exploited that symbol in thousands of ways, in all the religions around the earth. Now that word simply denotes our slavery, not our freedom. It symbolizes the organized religions, but not the individual bird on the wing in the sky of freedom. That bird which used to have the whole sky is encaged.

All the religions have been preparing chains, handcuffs, imprisonment for your soul. I offer you nothing but intoxication with existence itself, with the trees, with the wind, with the clouds. I offer you to be in love, dance with the wind, dance with the rain, laugh with the river. Unless you are so free that you become almost a part of the cosmos, you have not known the taste of religion, you have not known the taste of your own dignity, of your own great potential.

Listening to me, this immense silence descends on you, envelops you – a great waiting, a great longing for the unknown, a complete forgetfulness of the ego and a remembrance of your innocence, your individuality. They all happen simultaneously in a single split second.

I have given you the name Prem Madir; it means the wine of love. It is strange, all the religions are against life, love, joy, and still we have tolerated them. It is time that all these gods and all these temples should be erased. And all these priests who have been parasites of humanity should be forced to work in the farms, in the vineyards. They should be taught how to be in contact with the immensity that surrounds you. It does not need any mediator.

All that you need is a silent heart which can listen, clean eyes which can see, a childlike innocence which gives you grace and which gives you a great feeling of wonder. You don't know anything, but your very not knowing becomes such a purity, such an unburdening. Suddenly you see that with your knowledge, your chains, are disappearing. With your knowledge, your Christianity, your Hinduism, your communism is disappearing and leaving behind two innocent eyes and a heart ready to dance with the whole without any barriers.

Up to now we have been supporting our own enemies, we have been supporting the people who crucified Jesus. We have been supporting the people who poisoned Socrates without knowing that the people who poisoned Socrates are the people who have poisoned our very consciousness. No man is an island: in the crucifixion of Jesus I am also crucified, you are also crucified. We have tolerated these people not knowing that what they are doing to al-Hillaj

Mansoor and to Sarmad, they are doing to the whole of humanity. These were our greatest flowers, the most precious heights which man's consciousness has ever reached.

But the blindness of humanity is such that rather than destroying the whole priesthood; the priests, according to me, are the greatest criminals in the world. Whether they are Hindu brahmins, Christian priests, Jewish rabbis does not matter, they are all doing the same thing: exploiting man's potential and growth, obstructing any possibility of laughter and celebration. Their whole contribution is seriousness, sadness, misery and a hope which will be fulfilled after you are dead. We have been living with this hope for millions of years. How many people have died? No one returns, no one even gives a call saying, "Don't worry, on this side everything is great."

One of India's famous singers always tells a story about his friend...

He meets his friend who lives in London and has come back to the Punjab. Naturally the singer asks him, "How are you?"

He says, "All right."

The singer asks, "And how is your wife?"

The friend says, "She is also all right."

The singer asks him, "How are your children?"

And the man says, "They are also all right."

Finally the singer asks him, "What about your Daddy?"

The man says, "About my Daddy – he has been all right for almost four years!"

After death certainly there is no question, everyone is all right, but no one has authentic information. It is just an assumption that they must be all right. Here, you have to be miserable; there, all is delight. Here, you have to be sad and your sadness will make you a saint, and there, rivers of wine. No ordinary small pubs because God is compassionate, he is not miserly.

Here, to renounce your woman is a great religious and virtuous deed. There, thousands of naked film actresses are waiting for you. You are just going to be in difficulty whom to choose – Sophia Loren? But there are so many Sophia Lorens. No hunger, no thirst and everyone always remains young. What more can you expect? Saints do only one thing: sitting on white clouds playing on their harps, "Hallelujah!"

I have heard…

By mistake a poor porter from Munich was taken away by Death. He resisted hard. He said, "I am going to the pub; this is not the time to die. After the pub you can take me."

But Death never listens to anyone. He dragged the porter away. The whole way the porter was angry and said, "This is absolutely unmannerly. I am a poor porter. What is the need? What does God want of me? I am living a silent life. Every evening I go to my pub and every morning somehow I get back to the station. I am not a criminal, I don't do any harm."

But Death said, "What can I do? Your number has come."

The porter said, "Strange, I have been purchasing a lottery ticket every month and the number never came. And now the number has come; this is the number."

Death thought that this man was absolutely stupid and useless to talk to; he said, "Just wait, you will not be miserable once you enter paradise."

The porter said, "At least I must know what I am supposed to do there. Are there any pubs?"

Death said, "You don't understand. There are rivers of wine. What to say about a pub! And you will be given a harp and a white cloud. Sit on the white cloud, sing the song 'Hallelujah' in praise of God and drink as much wine as you want. There is no other work except playing on the harp."

He said, "This is a strange kind of world. I am a porter, I don't know how to play the harp."

Death said, "You will learn, because on every cloud you will find saints doing the same thing. You will learn. In the beginning everyone feels a little hesitant."

The porter was given a harp. He looked at himself and the harp and said, "It is so stupid. This is the time my pub will be closing and where are those rivers?"

Some kindly saint said, "There are no rivers; that is just a fiction. All that you have to do is sing the song of God, 'Hallelujah,' and play on the harp. No work because there is no need, no food…"

He said, "This is very strange – and I don't see any women here. I have been told that there are young girls available."

The young saint said, "That was all propaganda. Just sit on this cloud and learn to play the harp."

He said, "If this is all, how long am I going to sit on this cloud? When will I go to my station?"

The saint said, "It is very far away; you cannot go there."

Seeing that there was no possibility and every saint was singing "Hallelujah! Hallelujah!" he started singing "Hallelujah! Hallelujah!" with very great anger, asking, "Where *is* God?"

The saint said, "We have been here, but we have not seen him."

He said, "If I see him, I will hit him with this harp on his head – Hallelujah! It is the time, my pub will be closing. Is it a joke or something?"

God would not have heard, but between his "Hallelujah! Hallelujah!" he shouted upward, "Fuck you!"

God thought, "This is strange. No saint has ever done this. This man does not seem to be the right man."

Again, "Hallelujah! Hallelujah!" And in between he became angry because it was time to go to the station.

God called Death and said, "It seems you have brought a wrong man. This is a poor porter from Munich. Take him back – because he can corrupt all the saints – before everyone hears what he is singing. He is thinking it is praise. Take him away before anyone hears him. Just throw him back in his pub in Munich."

The porter opened his eyes, he looked all around. He said, "It seems to be my familiar pub. What happened?"

Someone said, "But you have not been here for many hours – your friends have been waiting for you."

He said, "Some mistake, either I was dreaming, but you say that I have not been here. My God, what a tragedy could have happened. If I had been able to find God, I would have killed him. I am not against God, I have never been against him, but the way he has behaved with me, a poor man. And he wants me to sing his praise, 'Hallelujah.'"

But a porter is a porter. He said, "I managed, I could not see where he was, but I thought if I shout loudly, 'Fuck you,' he is bound to hear. He is not going to hear 'Hallelujah,' everyone is doing that – and he heard it."

In my experience of reading my whole life, this is the only instance when God heard someone – he had to – and the only prayer which has been answered. I don't want to give you a hope and a dream beyond life. This life is so beautiful. Who cares of the beyond? And if we can live this life beautifully, we will be able to live in the beyond also more beautifully. Death cannot take away our consciousness, our joy, our celebration, our laughter.

Hamish MacTavish is visiting his married friends Sandy and Glenda MacDougal.

"Sandy, I can't help it," says Hamish, "but Glenda really turns me on. If I could pinch her bare backside just once, I would give you a thousand dollars."

"For that kind of money," says Sandy, "I don't think that Glenda would mind. Would you, Glenda? Go ahead and pinch her."

Glenda leans over a chair and exposes her behind. Hamish looks at it, and just keeps looking. Finally, after five minutes, he says, "I just can't do it."

"Why not?" asks Sandy, "haven't you got the nerve?"

"It is not that," says Hamish, "I haven't got the money."

Grandma Rosenbaum, aged seventy, is complaining of stomach pains to Dr. Bones.

Bones examines her thoroughly and announces his findings.

"The truth is, Mrs. Rosenbaum," he says, "you are pregnant."

"That is impossible!" cries Grandma. "I am seventy years old and my husband is eighty-two."

Bones insists that his tests are right, so Grandma Rosenbaum reaches for the telephone and dials the nursing home, where Grandpa Rosenbaum is rocking in his chair.

When he is on the phone, Grandma yells out, "You old goat, you have got me pregnant!"

"Please," says Grandpa, "who did you say is calling?"

This is such a hilarious world and religions have made it so sad. It should be full of songs, music, dance. But it seems we are so deeply contaminated, poisoned with misery and suffering that even when you laugh you don't laugh with your totality. You are even holding your laughter; you can watch that you are holding it – except one man. You all know who that one man is. Give a real good laugh so everyone knows. [*Everyone in Buddha Hall laughs, but the laughter of Sardar Gurudayal Singh is still the loudest.*]

Osho,

For the past two months I have been taking care of my sister while she was dying of cancer in hospital. I was able to give her love and physical care. Although, while she was in the last days of coma I was constantly playing your discourses to her, I felt I failed to introduce her to meditation; she refused to face death.

It's a puzzle to me that after all the torture and suffering she must have felt, at the last moment a big smile started to grow more and more on her face. Could you comment on her smile and on my trying to introduce her to meditation?

The question you have asked raises a very fundamental thing, and that is: if by chance – and I will explain to you what I mean by chance – someone dies in great suffering like cancer, the suffering from the cancer does not allow the person to fall into unconsciousness.

So just before death, when the body separates from the soul, a tremendous experience happens which happens only to the mystics, to the meditators. It does not happen to them by accident, they have been preparing for it. Their meditation is nothing but an effort to disidentify themselves with the body.

Meditation does prepare them for death, so they can die without being unconscious; otherwise in ordinary cases one dies in unconsciousness. So he does not know that he was separate from the body, that he has not died. Only the connection between himself and the body has disappeared, and his consciousness is so thin that the separation of the body from the soul breaks that small thread of consciousness.

But the meditator goes into the same position consciously many times, where he stands out, away from his own body. In other words, the meditator experiences death many times consciously, so that when death comes it is not a new experience. The meditator has always died with laughter.

You were trying to teach your sister meditation. But it is difficult because when one is in such suffering all your talk seems to be nonsense. But when she really died, just a moment before, as the separation happened, she must have realized, "My God, I was thinking I am the body and that was my suffering. My identification was my suffering." Now the separation, the thread, is cut – and she smiled.

Certainly you must have been puzzled about what happened because she was fighting with death, fighting with suffering, was not listening to you or making any effort to learn meditation. Still she died in a very meditative state. This happened accidentally.

The most important thing in life is to learn that you are not the body. That will give you such freedom from pain and suffering. Not that suffering will disappear, not that there will not be any pain or cancer; they will be there but you will not be identified with them. You will be just a watcher. And if you can watch your own body as if it is someone else's body, you have attained something of tremendous importance. Your life has not been in vain. You have learned the lesson, the greatest lesson that is possible for any human being.

My own approach is that meditation should be a compulsory thing for every student, for every retired person. There should be universities and colleges available to teach meditation. Every hospital should have a section specially for those who are going to die. Before they die they must be able to learn meditation. Then millions of people can die with laughter on their faces, with joy. Then death is simply freedom, freedom from the cage you have been calling your body. You are not the body.

That's what your sister understood at the last moment. She must have smiled at her own misunderstanding, and she must have smiled that she resisted death. She must have smiled that she was not willing to learn meditation. Her smile contains many strains, and I can understand that you have been puzzled. Do not forget it. Her smile may become a tremendously meaningful experience for you. She has given you a gift, an invaluable gift. She could not say a single word, there was not enough time, but her smile has said everything.

There are stories about mystics which may explain to you the difference between the accidental and the well cultivated. Your sister's smile was accidental; she was not prepared for it. But there is no need to wait for the accidental. You can be prepared for it.

A great Zen monk declared to his disciples, "I am going to die today. Don't prevent me."

They said, "Who is preventing you? But it is strange! No one declares his death like this out of nowhere. You were just talking about great things and suddenly, you say you are going to die!"

He said, "I am tired. Don't harass me. That's why I am saying don't prevent. You just have to do one thing: you have to suggest the way to me."

The disciples said, "But what way can we suggest? If you want to die, you die."

He said, "I don't want to die the ordinary way."

They said, "What is the ordinary way?"

He said, "The ordinary way is lying on your bed and you die. Ninety-nine point nine percent of people choose that way. That is their choice. I don't want to belong to that crowd. Just think a little and suggest some original idea because I will not be dying every day – only one time! It is absolutely appropriate to die in an original way. I lived originally, why should I die like everyone else?"

The disciples were in a difficulty. What original way? Someone suggested, "You can die sitting; people die lying."

He said, "This is not very original. In the first place there is not much difference between lying and sitting; moreover, there have been many saints who have died sitting in the lotus posture. I will not do that. Can't you suggest… And you pretend to be my disciples!"

They said, "We have never thought that you would ask such a question."

Someone said, "If you think sitting is not very original, die standing."

He said, "That looks a little better."

But one person objected. He said, "Once I heard that another saint died standing."

The old saint said, "This is very difficult; that man has destroyed that possibility too. Now think it over again. Now you suggest because you have destroyed… I had decided to die standing – now you say it is not original."

He said, "The original will be to stand on your head."

The saint said, "I am so glad that I have an original thinker as my disciple. I will try my best."

And he stood on his head and died. Now the disciples were at a loss what to do because every ritual takes it for granted that the person is lying down on the bed – there was no precedent. Now, first you have to put him on the bed. And he was very much against that; he would be very angry. He is such a man that even after death he may punish them, or he may start saying again, "This is not… You are again doing it the ordinary way."

Someone suggested, "The best way is to call his sister. She is in a nearby monastery and she is older than him; it is better to call her. Anyway we have to inform her that her brother has died. Let her suggest what to do."

The sister came and proved to be really a sister to the man. She said, "You idiot! Your whole life you have been a disturbance, never doing anything the right way. This is not the way. Get up and lie down on the bed!"

And the story is that the dead man got up, lay on the bed and the sister said, "Now close your eyes and die." And she did not stay, she went away.

To people of deep meditation, life is a game and so is death.

When the sister was gone the dead saint opened one eye and inquired, "Has that bitch gone? She has always been a torture to me, just because she is three years older than me. But now there is no point. I am going to die in the ordinary way."

He closed his eyes and died. Now it was even more difficult for the disciples to decide whether he was dead or not. So they tried pinching him, opening his eyes, "Are you still… Or gone?" But he was really dead. They waited so that there was no hurry, just to give him half an hour. Perhaps he may open his eyes again. But the old man was gone.

This is the way a meditator should die: with joy, playfulness, not taking things seriously. Life is a play and death has to be a greater play.

Ronald Reagan is driving in the countryside when he loses control and skids into a ditch.

He walks to the nearby farmhouse and introduces himself to the farmer and manages to persuade him to come and pull the car out of the ditch. The farmer gets his cart horse, hitches it to the car, and after a lot of effort, gets the car back on the road.

Ronald Reagan gets out his wallet and offers the farmer five dollars. The farmer looks at him hard and then leans over to his horse and whispers something. Immediately the horse pricks up its ears and drops its giant dong.

Reagan is amazed. "I will give you another five dollars," he says, "if you tell me what you said to make your horse get such an erection."

The farmer grabs the five dollars and says, "I told him that all politicians are cocksuckers!"

The last prayer…

Rabbi Nussbaum comes to visit Mendel Kravitz. "Mendel," says the Rabbi, "it may be none of my business, but after all, we have been friends for a long time and I am concerned about your reputation. You see, people in the neighborhood are beginning to talk about you. It just does not look right when a sixteen-year-old girl comes to visit you every night at such an hour."

"Ah," says Mendel, "don't you worry about that. It is a purely platonic relationship."

"Really?" asks Rabbi Nussbaum. "How can it be platonic?"

"Well," replies Mendel, "it is play for her and a tonic for me!"

25

From the Tribe to the Family to Individuality

Osho,
I have heard you say that the natural development of the human community is from the tribe to the family, to the commune – because of the unstoppable demand for individual freedom. Japan, which still functions with strong family and perhaps even tribal ties, is behind the United States in this progression.

Japan is now overtaking the United States as the world's leading economic power. The reason seems to be that the Japanese are able to work together better as a group. By contrast, in areas that require individual brilliance, the United States still excels.

When the United States destroyed Rajneeshpuram, the prototype of the commune, an environment which would provide the advantages of cooperative endeavor while satisfying the growth toward personal freedom, did they lose the chance of enjoying the best of both worlds? Has the United States lost the chance of moving ahead into the twenty-first century as the leading part of the world? Instead, do North Americans face a future of social and economic malaise based on cultural disintegration that could have been so easily and so successfully guided by your vision?

Dr. Amrito, the question of humanity's struggle for the freedom of the individual is very complicated. It does not start with the tribe. Thousands of years before tribes formed, there were small groups which cannot be called tribal. They had no commitment to each other nor were they families, because they were not born out of marriage or any kind of relationship.

Those groups really don't have any name. They had gathered together because of fear. I am talking of the times when there was even no fire. Humanity was really Gandhian – not even a spinning wheel. The fear of darkness, because the night was dangerous, still carries its imprint in our unconscious.

Why do you become afraid on a dark night? – this is your collective unconscious, still carrying the memory of days which have passed thousands of years before. Why do you become afraid when you are alone? Perhaps you have never thought about it in this perspective. Why do you want to be with someone?

Loneliness makes people sad. They do anything stupid just to avoid loneliness. They play chess knowing perfectly that everything is bogus. Neither the king is the king nor the queen is the queen. The queen is as valuable as the queen of England. But just look at chess players: so intent, pouring their whole consciousness... And it is not only chess, there are thousands of ways to avoid your loneliness. It comes from those days when to be lonely was really dangerous. Wild animals were all around, and every animal is stronger than man. The days I am talking about are the days of the mammoths – animals which were ten times bigger than our elephants.

There is no problem. Why should you not feel afraid being alone? During the nights, you had to hide yourself in caves or climb the trees – and it was very natural to make a kind of Lions Club or Rotary Club. Those were only out of fear. They joined together and whoever was powerful, naturally became the leader. And since that day the story continues. Even today, whoever is powerful is the leader. He himself is the law.

That's what Napoleon used to say: "I am the law. Whatever I say becomes the law. No law is above me." Certainly there are differences of physical strength, differences of intelligence. Since those days, women have been tortured by men, just because their bodies are more delicate and are not muscular; more soft, more warm, more loving – but not strong enough to become wrestlers or boxers.

So the person who was the leader sorted out the most beautiful women. They were his property. And the remaining members of the Rotary Club were left with the leftovers. Basically, that has not changed at all; still the poor man gets the leftovers. The kings and the prime ministers and the presidents choose whatever is the best.

Just fifty years ago one man alone, the Nizam of Hyderabad, had five hundred wives. He was the richest man in the world, just by chance because his state has the mine where all the great diamonds have been found, from the Kohinoor to many others. It still yields diamonds of tremendous value.

Naturally, the Nizam would take whatever he liked first and the leftovers were sold to the world. This went on for almost one thousand years. He had accumulated so many diamonds that it had become impossible to count them. So vast basements in the Nizam's palace were filled with diamonds, not counted but weighed, one kilo, two kilos. It had never happened in the world; diamonds are not weighed in kilos. Even he was not aware how much his wealth was.

Any beautiful woman born within his state was his first choice. If he rejected her then anyone else could have her. Then other members of the Rotary Club… This was not only the case with Nizam, it has been the case with many kings down the ages – and I am talking about those days. Those small groups used to clash with each other. The only treasure they had was the woman. There was no currency, no gold, no precious stones. There was only one thing: the woman. So those small groups were continuously fighting and snatching women from other groups.

This must have continued for thousands of years. Finally, it dawned on people's minds – the mind of man is very slow growing

– that this was not the right way: "We should create bigger tribes with power and strength." Small groups could not survive, either they had to die or they had to become part of the bigger tribe. Tribes had no families. The same rule continued. The women were allotted according to power. The woman has been a commodity for millions of years, and at one time, she was the only commodity.

But soon a new phenomenon started happening because all these tribes were living from hunting. A hunting tribe cannot live in one place for long, because sooner or later, it has hunted all the animals or the remaining ones have escaped. The tribe has to move. You will be surprised to know that the whole population of today's civilized world has arisen from Mongolia. Tribes had to move in different directions. The same tribe as reached Iran – a different section, a different faction – reached Germany, to India.

Linguists have found that all these sophisticated and cultured countries of the world have only one mother tongue and that is Sanskrit. The German language has thirty percent of its words originating from Sanskrit. So is the case with English and so is the case with Dutch. The whole of Europe are all brothers and sisters. Their forefathers one day were living in central Mongolia. But a hunting tribe has to move and has to move in different directions. A small portion of people moves in one direction, the other in another direction; wherever there is a possibility to find food.

But the day soon came – and that day came because of women. The credit of a stable society with cities, houses, stability in life, the whole credit goes to the woman because she was not going out hunting. She was mostly pregnant, taking care of small children. And one child after another child, her whole life was just like an assembly line producing all kinds of idiots. Taking care of them, she had neither time nor strength. Naturally, her insistence was, "We should live on fruits, not on meat. Trees are available." And soon man had to listen to her because animals were disappearing.

But you cannot depend on fruits unless you start cultivation. And the woman, watching the growth of the trees and the fruits and then the fruits ripening and falling back on the earth bringing new sprouts, started asking for cultivation. The nomads were continuously going from here to there, and in a certain sense man still remains a nomad. Deep in his mind, something is always hunting – hunting this woman, hunting that woman, going to see the Taj Mahal. For what?

The woman is more interested in the house, in decorating it, making it beautiful, making it warmer, making it welcoming to strangers. The whole credit of the cities goes to the woman. Man is not the creator of the cities. If man is allowed freedom, he would like to have a really good Arabian horse and just go hunting, just to go to places – a strange desire to always be somewhere else.

Look at the tourists; all kinds of cameras and the latest lenses hanging on their shoulders. They are running from Ajanta to Ellora, from Khajuraho to Kathmandu, and all that they do is photography. That is absolutely stupid because all those photographs are available in every city, and better, because they have been taken by professionals. These amateurs take so much trouble and finally find the film is blank. And they have been from Kabul to Kathmandu.

Their desire is that, "Back home we will be able to see all the beautiful places in the album." When they are looking at the beautiful places, they don't have time to really look. They are looking through their cameras: the right angle, a meter in the other hand, watching the light. And not one, but dozens of idiots doing the same kind of thing. Just one idiot could do it and distribute copies to other idiot fans. It seems strange, but the reality is that the nomad in man is still alive. It has gone deep into his unconscious, but it erupts in different ways.

In America, surveys show that every man changes his house every three years. The same is the average that every man changes his wife after three years. The same is the average that every man changes his job after three years. Three years seems to be the limit one can tolerate, the maximum limit one can remain bored. And then comes the ultimate quantum leap. He changes the car, he changes the house, he changes the wife, he changes his clothes!

People are even changing their faces by plastic surgery. With just a little longer nose, what will you get? People are getting facelifts so that they can look a little younger. But new, younger people *have* arrived on the scene. Who is going to take care? – secondhand young people.

But change! Don't sit silently, do something! The woman has been the cause of great cities developing. Because of the children the woman insisted on marriage, because without marriage who is going to take the burden of the children? It is under compulsion that man agreed to marry. That's why if you look at married people's faces, they really need a facelift. It is all under compulsion, otherwise the society, the government and the woman herself are not going to have any contact with you; hence virginity is so much praised. It is to force man: "First get married, then come close; otherwise, I am going to scream."

The tribe finally became the foundation of marriages because the tribe is a big thing and it became bigger every day. And it was certainly a move for individual freedom because in a tribe you don't have any individual freedom. In a tribe, you are simply a part. If you don't function according to the tribal orders, the tribe simply boycotts you.

In Indian villages, I have seen with my own eyes. In India you cannot marry a widow. It is really the same logic because if people start marrying widows then who cares about virginity? In a strange way, widows look more beautiful. Perhaps they have to look more beautiful, otherwise who is going to be interested in them? Virgins are inexperienced, look childish; widows are experienced, well-polished, more attractive. But in an Indian village, if you marry a widow, the whole village – which is still a tribe – boycotts you and the boycott is total. You cannot take water from the village well, you cannot purchase anything from any village shop; no one will welcome you into his home.

The village will simply forget about you as if you don't exist. You cannot live; it is impossible. If you cannot purchase anything and no one speaks to you, if you cannot even get water from the well, life has become impossible. What kind of freedom is this? In a tribal structure there is no freedom. It is the desire to create freedom that caused the tribe to slowly, slowly divide into individual units, small units called families.

The family has a certain freedom. And particularly as vehicles like cars have become available. One cannot conceive how this existence works. No one could have conceived that cars could bring some freedom into the world. Now you can go ten miles away from your wife with your girlfriend – and the wife will never know. Boys and girls who are not married can meet. Cars have created a revolution. But the search is for freedom. Still, the family tries to hinder in every way and not to go beyond the limits. It is a question of prestige.

I am teaching you something final: the world cannot be free unless families also disappear. With families disappearing, nations will disappear – the family is the unit, the bricks of the nation – churches and religions will disappear. We need a world of individuals. Certainly it means tremendous responsibility. But all that is needed is available. You need not be worried about what will happen if two unmarried people without the bondage of law and society, the tribe, the family, and the country produce children – what will happen to those poor children?

There is no need for those children. Their only function is to help Mother Teresa; otherwise, they are not needed at all. Now three kinds of birth pills are available. The first pill was a great revolution, but it was not one hundred percent foolproof. You have to take it continuously, and one day you don't take and, strange world, the boyfriend suddenly appears. The human mind always thinks in this way: "Don't be worried. Making love every time does not produce children. Just once in a while a child is produced. Take a chance!" And it does not look right to reject the boyfriend.

That pill was greatly helpful to reduce the number of children, but once in a while a virgin girl would become pregnant. That's what I think: Mary must have forgotten to take the pill. Christians and Jews should take great pride that they are the people who invented the pill. The proof is Jesus Christ.

The second pill is very significant. You can take it after. You can make love and then you can take the pill. There is no need to take it continuously. And the third pill makes men and women equal. There is no necessity for the woman to take a pill; the man takes it. But certainly the man has to take it before making love. After making love he may take the whole box of pills, it is not going to help. Children have continuously been a problem. How can people be freed from all the bondage of possessiveness? But now there is no need; people can live as individuals. There are no wild animals; you don't need a continuous togetherness. There are no wild animals; even in dark nights you can be alone without any fear. The function of the family is finished.

It freed you from the tribe; now, you have to be free from marriage and the family too. It does not mean that it is compulsory because that will again be a slavery. It does not mean that you have to, it simply means it is optional to live together with the woman you love – or not to live together; to love a woman for your whole life – or to go on changing in the American way. Nothing is wrong in it. Anything that makes you happy is perfectly good.

Amrito, you are worried; it is certainly something to be concerned about. In the Second World War, Germany, Japan, Italy were friends, allies, against America and the whole world. For five years continuously they went on winning. It was the foolishness of Adolf Hitler – which seems to be natural: if you go on winning for five years and great nations simply give way in one day. You become so arrogant that you start forgetting that a thousand and one things can change the situation. He could have won in the West – and Japan was winning. Even Kolkata was being vacated because Japanese forces had reached Yangon and their bombs were hitting Kolkata.

The combination of the Japanese and the Germans was a strange combination – I am also always wondering that most of my sannyasins are either from Japan or from Germany. But because Adolf Hitler attacked Soviet Russia… He had a treaty with them that they would never be enemies, they would be friends. But seeing that he was winning, he broke the treaty. He had almost won the whole of Europe. And Japan, his colleague, was all over the East. Hitler completely forgot that to defeat Russia is a very difficult task. He forgot that in history many attempts have been made to defeat Russia, but its geography and its climate are such that no one has ever been able to win it.

The same point arises: nine months a year, thick snow is falling all over Russia. And Russia is so vast that it is spread over two continents. One side ends in the East, another side in the West; it is two continents together. It has enough soldiers to prevent anyone from defeating it for three months. After three months it does not bother, then the climate takes care. In that thick snow, the armies of the enemy start losing their way, forgetting where they have come from and why they have come. Food does not reach, all communication with their original country is broken.

In the whole history of Russia, it has always remained invincible at the same point. Adolf Hitler thought perhaps he could manage. Certainly he did manage, but after those three months he had to surrender. Because he surrendered in the West, his colleague Japan had to surrender in the East. They were together either to be victorious or to be defeated.

But the miracle is that America was victorious over Germany and Japan and Italy – Italy I don't count because they are nice people. They never bothered whether they were defeated or victorious. They were so deep into their spaghetti that by the time they came out, they saw that the whole scene had changed. Back they went to their spaghetti.

Only Italy remained the same before the war as after the war – but they are very loving people. That is the only country which is fighting for me continuously for two years. And now the Radical Party has asked me for blessings, "Should we start a movement that the Vatican should be dissolved into mainland Italy, and that the pope should not be both the head of a religion and the head of a state?" I have sent them my blessings: "Fight! The very existence of the Vatican is very disrespectful. What has a religious head got to do with being a sovereign?"

In fact a religious person should not have anything to do with politics. But you know, Italians are Italians; they will fight, but their fight is going to be lousy. They will make much noise – radical noise, but if no one is listening why bother? Pasta is being prepared – the revolution can happen later on.

But Japan and Germany proved to be a miracle. They are both more powerful than they were before the world war. Their defeat has not destroyed them but strengthened them. Now Germany is more powerful than it was in the hands of Adolf Hitler, and Japan has proved even better.

Economically, Japan is now a far superior force to America. The greatest American rich man has only four billion dollars, and the greatest Japanese counterpart has twenty-two million dollars. For the first time the Japanese currency is at the top in the whole world. The dollar has fallen. It is going down the drain with Ronald Reagan.

Amrito's question is that Japan is a very tribal country, perhaps the most tribal country in the world, very traditional, very orthodox. Here, my group therapy leaders inquired of me what do we have to do with these Japanese. The group leaders are trained in the psychoanalysis of Sigmund Freud and other schools of therapy of the West where it is assumed as a scientific fact – and perhaps it is a scientific fact to those people whom Sigmund Freud studied – that every girl hates her mother, every boy falls in love with his mother. Every boy wants to kill the father because he is the obstacle and every girl somehow wants to destroy the mother because she is taking away her love affair with the father. These assumptions in the West have almost become scientific facts, and they have a truth in them.

But if you tell a Japanese, "In your unconscious you are thinking to kill your father." The father is so much respected that even the idea – and the Japanese will kill the therapist: "How do you dare to say such a thing to me?" Say to a Japanese, "You are in love with your mother," and he will give you such a karate chop that you will forget all your psychoanalysis that we don't even want to do.

For many years I had to prevent the Japanese from doing therapy groups saying, "These groups are not for you." Their whole tradition is too heavy and they have grown from a different branch. They do not come from Mongolia; Japanese, Chinese, Burmese, Negroes, have different origins. Their languages are different. They don't have any relationship with Sanskrit and they don't have the same type of culture, education, history. You will be surprised to know that they believe in proper behavior and mannerisms to such a point that it is almost something sacred and religious.

I am reminded of a man…

A great warrior who was also a great master of swordsmanship had gone to see the emperor. He forgot to bow down properly – just a small thing – but he felt so much guilt that he immediately committed hara-kiri then and there. That is the only way to get rid of the guilt. No apology that, "I am sorry, sir." This won't do. Only one thing shows that you are really sorry: "I am finished."

He pushed his sword into his center of life, his hara and died then and there. When his students heard – and he had three hundred disciples who were learning swordsmanship under him – they all committed suicide because their master misbehaved. Their master: "How could they live with this burden their whole life?" It is better to be finished. The whole school of the warrior was finished because of just a small gesture. Now, these are a different kind of people. Sigmund Freud won't do.

Amrito's question is that these tribal people have been so successful in teamwork, they don't ask for individuality, they ask for integrity. They want to lose themselves in the name of religion or in the name of nation.

There have been so many hilarious cases...

One man was found just thirteen years after the Second World War, alone in the jungles of Burma, fighting, killing people. Whoever would come he would kill: the Second World War was still on. He had not heard that thirteen years had passed.

It was so difficult to catch hold of him. He was caught, brought to Japan and saw with his own eyes that his country had been defeated. The people who caught him forgot that he was Japanese, and he immediately committed hara-kiri. Defeat of the country? How can you live with such a wound? Thirteen years he had been fighting alone, against the whole world. Anyone who happened to pass in the forest, he would kill. The war was on. This was not an isolated case. Three other cases were found also in other places. They wouldn't believe – and once they believed they committed hara-kiri.

Now, this is a different culture and a different society. Amrito's question is about...these people's integrity, even being defeated, Hiroshima and Nagasaki destroyed completely – cities as big as Mumbai.

Yesterday I was just asking one Japanese scientist who loves me... For twenty years he has been working on radiation in Hiroshima. I asked him, "What is the situation? Is the land still barren, unpopulated?"

He looked at me; he could not believe me. Finally, he understood. He said, "No, now Nagasaki is a far bigger city than New York. Hiroshima is a bigger city than Tokyo."

These are a different kind of people. They have produced everything and they are competitors in the world. And in that competition, America seems to be very much at a loss what to do, because the Japanese yen is rising higher in value and the American dollar is dropping.

It is true that if a community can be conditioned the way the Japanese are conditioned, and on a smaller scale the way the Germans are conditioned, that they are the superior race...

The Japanese believe that they are the direct sons of the sun, they are a divine race.

That's what Adolf Hitler was trying to convince Germans: "You are pure Nordic Aryans. Your very existence is to rule over the world." And he killed six million Jews because they were claiming that they are the chosen people of God. Adolf Hitler had to kill them to prove, "Look who is the chosen? Are you the chosen or are we the chosen?" By killing six million Jews he convinced the remaining Germans that, "Certainly, we are the chosen."

These people are conditioned and a conditioned mind can work better. The unconditioned, a meditative mind, a silent relaxed mind, is not a workaholic; he enjoys life, he loves life. Work is only secondary; it is needed so he does it. But he is not for the work, the work is for him. These values change.

Certainly in a country which has utterly independent individuals, the production rate will fall, but its blissfulness will increase. Its currency will not start reaching the stars, but its ecstasy will certainly reach the stars. There will be a totally different kind of atmosphere, not bothered about winning over anyone, noncompetitive. Victory will no longer be of any value; in fact, it will be ugly. To defeat someone is not a value which can be called human. Victory is part of our animal past.

So certainly it is true that if people become more and more independent from the family, traditions, moralities, many things which today seem to be significant will disappear. But many new things will appear which have not appeared even in your wildest dreams.

Just to be a silent and joyous being, healthy enough to produce food and clothes for yourself and for those you love; noncompetitive, nonpolitical, but immensely religious in the sense that you are grateful to existence for giving a life of so much splendor, so much joy, so much uncontainable blissfulness... If it happens in even one country, it is going to spread like a wildfire in which the Japanese or German conditionings, however old, will disappear.

It is not a surprise that the German politicians and the German parliament are so afraid of me. It may not be apparent ordinarily, but I know perfectly well I am dangerous, and their fear is true. But any act arising out of fear is not going to succeed. They will have to face the reality that my sannyasins are bound to create on returning to Germany: They are creating a stir: "Why are you afraid?"

Is it not strange that Germany allowed terrorists to have their international conference in Germany? At the same time they passed a law in the parliament that I could not enter or land at any of their airports. They are not worried about terrorists. And the conference was of world terrorists, terrorists from all over the world – they are not a danger!

I *am* a danger because what can the terrorists do? The German army can face *them*, but what I can do, no German politician is capable of facing. Even if Adolf Hitler somehow gets resurrected, I am going to put him right. He was a crackpot. My sannyasins will catch hold of him and immediately register him for therapy groups.

A Japanese scientist was here and he is a friend of the emperor of Japan. He said, "I would have liked to invite you to Japan. Even the emperor is my friend. He knows you, he reads you, but unfortunately he has no power at all, he is only a formal head. He has to sign everything that the parliament passes. And I am worried that if I mention your name, the parliament may not accept you even as a tourist."

These people's fears are understandable. Amrito's question is exactly right. I don't want a world producing more and more arms, producing more and more unnecessary things. For example, producing so much butter in Europe that mountains of butter have to be drowned in the ocean. And the same is being done in America: every six months, billions of dollars' worth of foodstuff has to be drowned in the ocean. But they will not tell people, "Relax, don't produce so much." We need not have buildings like New York skyscrapers, and we don't need a thousand and one things which have become almost necessary just because advertisements go on forcing you – and then your mind starts clicking.

Now in this whole world, there is only one thing that is international: Coca Cola. Even in Russia! Even I have to drink Coca Cola. That is the only international brotherhood: The Coca Cola Brotherhood. There are thousands of things which are not necessary, but they are being produced because people are greedy to earn more money, people are greedy and their greed knows no limit.

Just the other day I have told you about the movement in America, The Couch Potato Movement. Thousands of people have joined it. It is not a joke, because what else can you be? If seven and a half hours is the average that you sit in your seat and watch television, you are just a potato, you are not even a human being. This is your whole life. When you meet God he will say, "What have you been doing?" And you will say, "Nothing. We were members of the Television Coca Cola Movement. We are potatoes."

In a simpler society, whatever is needful should be provided, should be produced. But so much is unnecessarily wasted. Man has no time to be himself, to be with himself or to be just silent, playing on the flute. It is true that we don't need that conditioned mind which makes man almost a robot.

The Japanese conditioning, the German conditioning is that of a robot. My own proposition is that we can create robots which can do all kinds of work and man should be freed to enjoy life, to love, to dance, to sing, to find new pleasures, new adventures, new challenges.

There is so much beautiful literature – these potatoes will never know about it. There is such great music, such great poetry – these workaholics will never become aware, they don't have time. And what they are producing is junk.

Amrito, I am in favor of a simpler world where the individuals' basic needs are certainly fulfilled, and basic opportunities for his spiritual growth are given to him; where individuality becomes the most fundamental value. Nothing is higher than the individual and his freedom is sacred.

Now, after Dr. Amrito's very scholarly and difficult question something simple, something human…

Old Man Finkelstein is brought to court for alleged rape. He pleads guilty by reason of insanity.

"Insanity?" asks the judge. "You look perfectly sane to me."

"Oh, I am," says the old man. "It is sex I'm crazy about."

Zabriski arrives at work one morning with a big smile on his face.

"Why are you so happy?" asks a friend.

"Well," explains Zabriski, "last Thursday I found my wife in bed with the electricity meter reader. On Friday, she was taking samples from a salesman on the couch. Saturday morning I found her doing business with the milkman on the kitchen table. But I've fixed all of them. I just phoned the Salvation Army and told them to come and take away all that furniture from the house."

Mendel Kravitz is having a little chat with his new mistress. "Tell me, darling," he says, "what would you do if you found yourself pregnant and abandoned?"

"Ah, that would be awful," cries the pretty young girl. "I think I would kill myself."

Mendel replies, "Good girl."

And now this is Italia…

Late on Friday afternoon the foreman tells Enrico that he is going to have to work late. So Enrico asks his friend, Gondolfo, to stop at the house and tell his wife, Lucia.

Gondolfo knocks on the door and Lucia opens it. "Your old man is not coming home till late," says Gondolfo. "How about we go up-a the stairs and make-a screw?"

Lucia is shocked and tries to slam the door.

"I give-a you fifty bucks!" pleads Gondolfo.

"How dare you?" shrieks Lucia.

"A hundred then," says Gondolfo.

"Well," says Lucia, "it would not be right."

"Come on, two hundred dollars," says Gondolfo, "just for half an hour and Enrico will-a never know."

Lucia takes the money and Gondolfo has the time of his life.

When Enrico gets home late, he asks his wife, "Did my friend Gondolfo tell-a you I work-a late?"

"Yes," replies Lucia, "he stop-a here for a minute."

"And I hope-a," says Enrico, "that he give-a you my wages, two hundred dollars."

And the last…

Rajiv Gandhi, Mikhail Gorbachev, and Ronald Reagan are doing a fact-finding tour of India. They are driving through Kolkata when they see a little boy squatting by the side of the road and decide to talk to him. Gandhi walks over and asks him what he is doing.

"I'm mixing shit and sand," replies the boy.

"And what are you doing that for?" asks Gandhi.

"I'm going to make a statue of Gorbachev," replies the boy. Gandhi goes back to the car and reports what the boy has said. Gorbachev is very impressed, and seeing a potential communist, goes to speak to the boy himself.

"What are you doing, my boy?" he asks.

"I'm mixing shit and sand," replies the boy.

"And what will you do with it?" asks the Soviet premier.

"I'm going to make a statue of Mahatma Gandhi," says the boy. Gorbachev is confused and reports back to the car. So then Reagan walks over to the boy and asks,

"What are you doing, my son?"

"I'm mixing shit and sand," replies the boy.

"And I suppose," says Reagan, "that you are going to make a statue of me."

"No," says the boy. "I can't. I have not got enough shit."

26

Existence Believes In a Slow, Silent Growth

Osho,
The other day was my eighth sannyas birthday. Although it is such a long time I often have the feeling that I have just started to understand what it means to be a sannyasin, and I have just very short glimpses of that silence. On the other hand, it feels for me that sannyas has become slowly, almost unknowingly, the medium my whole life flows in, like a fish in the sea.

Osho, am I too sleepy and moving too slowly?

Not only are you moving slowly, your question is also moving slowly. Every day I think to answer it – it must have been with me almost two weeks, and still you say "The other day…" Finally I have decided to put it on top; otherwise you would have to write another year!

The experience of sannyas… Silence, beauty, gratitude all deepen slowly, so slowly that you don't know that you are moving at all. Have you seen the trees growing during the night when you are asleep? Do you know when the flowers open while you are looking the other way? Have you observed when childhood disappeared when you were young, or when you became old and youth was no longer there?

Existence does not believe in speed. Existence believes in a very slow, silent growth. You soon become one with your meditation, with your silence. You soon start feeling the beatitude, the blissfulness as part of your breathing. You are still growing, you are still going on the pilgrimage. It is an unending journey, but it is so slow.

Existence knows no hurry because it has no shortage of time. Eternity is its time – it has no beginning and no end. For example, in the East, people are not very speedy; in the West, speed is their God. And the reason is that all the religions which are born outside India – Judaism, Christianity, Mohammedanism – believe only in one life. They give you only seventy years. You will be asleep for one third of it, you will be working for your livelihood for another third, and the remaining one third you will be watching TV because you are a member of The Couch Potato Movement. In between you may smoke a cigarette, or you may kiss a woman, but in a hurry because the television is on.

It happened…

Thomas Alva Edison, one of the famous scientists of America, was such a speedy person; he was always on the go.

He was going to a university to deliver a lecture in another town. He rushed out of the house in a hurry, waved to his wife and kissed the maid servant. One can do anything in a hurry, and he was in such a hurry that there was no way to cancel the past. He simply said from the window of the car, "I am sorry."

The reason the whole Western world and education that has spread all over the world has caused you to do everything quickly is because death is not far away. Seventy years is not long. In the East it is totally different.

When the first railway lines were made in India, a British engineer was observing the work. He saw an old Indian coming every day, sitting under a shady tree and watching all the work.

The British engineer could not resist the temptation. He said, "You come here, the whole day you are here – why don't you join in the work?"

The man said, "For what?"

He said, "For what? You will earn money."

The man said, "But for what?"

The engineer said, "Then you can relax under a tree."

The man said, "This is stupid, I'm already resting under a tree. Why should I bother first to work, then to earn money, and then to rest under a tree, when I can relax in the very first place?"

All three Eastern religions – Buddhism, Jainism, Hinduism – were born in India and believe in reincarnation. That gives a tremendous expansion to your existence. Then you are not going to end in seventy years; there is no hurry. If not in this life, then we will see in the next. If I cannot meet you this life, I can say I will meet you next life. What is the problem? The centuries-old ideology that there are millions of lives has taken away the feverish speediness – one life, another life, another life. It has taken away the fear of death.

Your worry is that it seems your sannyas has just started. If the seed has started and has become a sprout, the spring will come and you will be full of the flowers of your being, of your truth. There is no hurry and there is no need to be in a hurry.

I have heard…

Two birds were sitting on a tree and they saw a jet airplane leaving behind it a line of smoke.

One bird said, "Do you see what happened to that poor bird, and what speed he is going at?"

The other said, "Don't bother! When someone's tail is on fire he has to be going at speed. There is nothing to be surprised at."

In the West, everyone's tail is on fire. They are going. Don't ask where and why because they don't have time to answer such philosophical questions and waste their lives.

A man was driving at one hundred and twenty miles per hour. His wife was trembling with fear and she said, "Just at least look at the map, to see whether we are on the right road or not."

The man said, "Forget the map. Just look at the speed! Who cares? The real thing is that we are going with great speed. We are bound to reach somewhere."

You have asked a beautiful question. The first implication of it is that the day you take the initiation into sannyas is not necessarily the beginning of sannyas. It is simply your indication that "I am willing to wait for sannyas to happen to me." Initiation is only your saying yes to existence; opening all your doors and windows for the fresh breeze and the sun to enter and cleanse you, and make you part of the whole.

Someday sannyas will begin. It can begin in the moment of initiation, if your intensity, integrity, your trust and your love are total, but it is rarely so. It is always sixty percent, forty percent; seventy percent, thirty percent. There are people who may have ninety-nine percent trust, but that one percent doubt is enough to prevent for years, even lives. Unless you are one hundred percent open, unless the very word *no* has dropped from your vocabulary, the great revolution of sannyas will not happen to you.

Just this morning I said to Shunyo that Anando has too much work – and I go on loading her with more and more work. I go on calling her morning, evening, and night. And if I don't call her she waits; if I don't call her I feel guilty that she must be waiting. And the strangest thing is she has never said no to anything. Howsoever burdened, she is immediately ready to take on a new project, knowing that it is almost impossible for her to do all these things. But if I am saying that is enough for her, she is thinking that "There must be the potential in me which I am not aware of – but my master has to be aware. If he is saying, 'Do it,' I will do it." I have never heard even a hesitation.

Sannyas needs a total yes and then it can happen this very moment. But your small doubt – it may be just very small – is just like a small piece of sand in your eyes, and you cannot open your eyes. Just a small piece of sand can deprive you of seeing this whole beautiful world. Doubt is just like a small piece of sand in your inner eye. It can prevent you from seeing the splendor and the glory of life, your own potential and your own flowers which have been waiting for lives to grow and blossom, but you have not given a chance.

And your feeling that slowly it seems, "...sannyas has become almost unknowingly, the medium my whole life flows in, like a fish in the sea. Am I too sleepy and moving too slowly?" – both are good. To be sleepy is not against spirituality. I cannot conceive of any way that to be sleepy is against spirituality. If to be sleepy is against spirituality then I am the most unspiritual person who has ever existed. Someone thinks I am meditating, someone thinks I have gone on some esoteric trip; someone thinks I am working upon my disciples, but the reality is, to be frank with you – I am simply sleeping.

I have not found that sleep has ever committed any sin against anyone. Sleep is the purest and the most virtuous state you can conceive. If you are awake, you are bound to do some nonsense – you cannot avoid. Just look at Niskriya! Mostly he is asleep. He fixes his camera and he knows I am not going to move my chair. So why waste time? But because of your laughter his sleep is disturbed again and again. And do you think I tell jokes for your joy? You are wrong. It is simply to disturb Niskriya.

It is perfectly good that you are sleepy and moving slowly. Fish also sleep and even in their sleep they go on moving. Just watch any fish. Even a fish cannot be awake twenty-four hours. She has times to wake up to have breakfast, to look at the newspaper, and there is not much work, political, social, philosophical. Then the fish sleeps, but even in sleep she is moving slowly. Movement is bound to be there because the river is moving. How can the fish remain unmoving in a moving river, even asleep?

Existence is moving. In this whole existence, except change, nothing is permanent. Only change does not change. Everything else changes. You are growing old, even without feeling it. And it is an absolute certainty that you are growing old. Do you think people suddenly jump and become old? They were going home and on the way suddenly they jump and they have become old? They have been becoming old when they were going to the office, when they were coming home. When they were sleeping they were becoming old. Whatever they were doing, change was continuous.

If your silence has become almost like breathing, a part of your being, just as with the circulation of the blood, then there is no need to be worried that you are too slow. In the inner world there is no question of speed. In the inner world everything is growing naturally according to its own pace. You cannot make someone enlightened, forcibly, on the point of a gun: "Become enlightened!" There is no way, even if the person says, "Okay, I am enlightened." He knows and you know that enlightenment does not happen on the point of a gun.

You are in a perfectly good state. But being a woman you are naturally worried about old age. It is very difficult for a woman to get rid of the idea that whatever she is doing, one thing is going on continuously by the side: she is growing old and that hurts. She tries hard. Most women stop growing old at the age of thirty-five. Then suddenly five years later they become thirty-six. When everyone starts looking worried, puzzled, they think, "Now is the time to become thirty-six."

A woman never tells the truth about her age. I have told you that even on the point of a loaded gun you may perhaps become enlightened, but a woman will not reveal her age.

It is an old understanding that there are seven ages of man…

Sixteen to twenty-five – twice daily.
Twenty-five to thirty-five – thrice weekly.
Thirty-five to forty-five – try weekly.
Forty-five to fifty-five – try weakly.
Fifty-five to sixty-five – try oysters.

Sixty-five to seventy-five – try anything.
Seventy-five and beyond – try to remember.

And just like the man, there are seven ages of woman…

Sixteen to twenty-five, like Africa – partly virgin, partly explored.
Twenty-five to thirty-five, like India – hot and mysterious.
Thirty-five to forty-five, like Europe – devastated but interesting in parts.
Forty-five to fifty-five, like America – efficient but unconscious.
Fifty-five to sixty-five, like Russia – everyone knows where it is but no one really wants to go there.
Sixty-five to seventy-five, like the UN – it functions, but no one is interested.
Seventy-five and beyond, like Atlantis – lost and forgotten.

You are doing perfectly well. Sleepily and slowly the light will come to you; the truth will awaken in your being. It is in fact already there. It will just make its presence silently without any whisper and without any notice. Spontaneously and suddenly, one suddenly feels, "My God, what I have been seeking is sitting within me; in fact, what I am seeking is what I am: I am seeking myself. There is no need for seeking. I cannot be otherwise; I am myself." Just be silent, utterly silent. Let peace descend over you and the revelation of the mysterious truth of existence is yours.

I hope you will not misunderstand me because this is my destiny to be misunderstood. I am not saying for you to be happily asleep, and not to worry that whenever the spring will come it will bring flowers. I am saying to you to respect your slow growth and even in your sleepiness, don't lose track of awareness. Sleepiness is not sleep. Just within the circle of sleepiness a small flame of awareness is burning. Who is aware of sleepiness and who is aware of slowness?

This awareness has to be sharpened more and more, like a sword. The day your awareness is total and complete is the day your enlightenment has come. So I am not supporting your sleepiness, I am supporting you to be aware of your sleepiness. I am supporting your awareness. I am supporting your awareness of slow growth. That awareness is your real treasure.

Little Ernie trots into the bathroom just as his pregnant mother is getting out of the bath.

"What is that?" he asks, pointing at her bulging belly.

Feeling a bit embarrassed, and not wanting to explain all about the birds and the bees, his mother tells him, "It is a present Daddy gave me."

A bit puzzled by this reply, little Ernie goes into the kitchen, where his father is reading the newspaper over breakfast.

"Dad?" says Ernie.

"Yes, Ernie," replies his father.

"You know that present you gave Mummy?" asks Ernie.

"Yes, son," replies his father.

"Well," says Ernie, "she has gone and eaten it!"

Don't misunderstand me. Whatever I say is always possible to be misunderstood because I am not talking about the ordinary world of things and objects. I am talking about the inner world of consciousness and being.

Just today a letter has arrived from Germany. Our sannyasins here are doing a meditation called The Four Dimensions. The letter says, "In your commune, people are doing a meditation called The Four Dimensions and we have the copyright over it."

I have told Neelam, my secretary, to write to them saying, "*Things* can be copyrighted, *thoughts* cannot be copyrighted, and certainly meditations cannot be copyrighted. They are not things of the marketplace."

No one can monopolize anything. But perhaps the West cannot understand the difference between an objective commodity and an inner experience.

Maharishi Mahesh Yogi has copyrighted Transcendental Meditation and just underneath in a small circle you will find written *TM* – that means trademark! The East has been meditating for ten thousand years and no one has put trademarks upon meditations. And above all, that transcendental meditation is neither transcendental nor meditation – just a trademark.

I have told Neelam to reply to these people saying, "You don't understand what meditation is. It is no one's belonging, possession. You cannot have any copyright. Perhaps if your country gives you trademarks and copyrights on things like meditation, then it will be good to have a copyright on stupidity. That will help the whole world to be relieved. Only you will be stupid and no one else can be stupid; it will be illegal."

I am going to direct my people here that they do the meditation called The Four Dimensions. But there are eight directions not four! Start doing the meditation Eight Dimensions – and certainly under eight dimensions, their four dimensions also come in.

But apart from their stupid letters and their stupid government which gives copyrights for such inner experiences, the truth is that consciousness cannot be either four dimensions or eight dimensions. Consciousness is a circle: no dimensions. It is neither directing to the north nor directing to the south. It simply is a circle. So my suggestion to you is that the best will be to call it "No-Dimensions."

We are going to sue those idiots in the courts in Germany, those who think they have a copyright over consciousness, Then we can get a copyright over enlightenment. Then no one can become enlightened unless we license him.

Osho,
Recently, after your talks – particularly after the answer to Maneesha's personal question – I felt sadness in my heart for no reason. Then I realized the reason was the discourse. You know I love you very much, and it's difficult for me to make a clear question. Something is happening in the air that is touching me very, very

deeply. I am not a well-educated woman. I can understand things only through vibration, touch and looking deep. It feels to me like a breath of death.

What is happening, beloved master?

I can understand your sadness, but your sadness is out of misunderstanding me. When I said, "No one is my friend," I was simply saying that if you start thinking of me as your friend you will be destroying the very possibility of your being a disciple. One is never a disciple of a friend. And I don't want to destroy your tremendous opportunity that exists in my presence to learn and to be.

I know you love me, and you know perfectly well that I love you far more than you can ever conceive. But still I want to remind you: let me call you my friend, but don't start thinking that you are my friend. It looks like a puzzle, but it is not. From my side, my love and compassion is showering over you. In my love you are all my beloveds, but remember, this is from my side.

If you start thinking of me as your friend from your side, it is not going to be a loss to me; it will be a loss to you because in calling me your friend you will have missed a master. When I call you a friend, I don't miss a disciple. Life is very subtle and very complicated. Your sadness is out of misunderstanding. You must have felt that your love is rejected because I am saying, "I am not your friend."

No, your love is not rejected. I am trying to prevent the great calamity that can happen if I accept your calling me a friend. I will not lose anything. If enemies cannot harm me, how can friends harm me? I have nothing to lose. You can call me a friend, you can call me anything you want to call me. The question is, "Is it going to help your spiritual growth?"

I have to be hard sometimes. That's why I was hard to Maneesha when she asked her question. Your love has to be purified, your love has to be raised higher, has to be made more conscious, and that I can do only by being very, very clear; otherwise I am alone and you are so many. In the whole dark night a single candle is trying to dispel the darkness. I have to be hard because I love you. And I will destroy everything that can prevent your growth.

You say, and you are right, "I am a woman… I can understand things only through vibration…" Can't you feel the vibration of love from me toward you? Can't you see the love in my eyes when I look at you? You cannot deceive me because I have seen my love reflected in your eyes, my joy reflected in your tears; I have almost seen a dance in your very being, and that is your true understanding.

Don't get lost in words. Listen to your own feeling. You are right that being a woman you can feel vibrations more than words. And words are not of much value; vibrations carry something of truth. You became afraid, just as when ordinary love is rejected one feels like dying. But I am rejecting your ordinary love to bring something *extra*ordinary in you. It is not just a death, but a resurrection. But as I said, it is always possible that in your unconsciousness you can misunderstand me.

But whatever you do, I have caught hold of your heart. However you misunderstand me, I am not going to leave. I have already entered you. Wherever you will be, I will be within you. Your intellectual understanding or misunderstanding doesn't matter.

The fire-and-brimstone preacher storms into a saloon in the Wild West and shouts, "Repent, you vile sinners! Drinking that disgusting liquid will send you all to hell. Join with me. All of you who want to go to heaven, stand on this side."

Everyone staggers to his side of the room, except for one old drunk.

The preacher shouts at him, "Don't you want to go to heaven?"

"No, I don't," replies the drunk.

"You mean to tell me that you don't want to go to heaven when you die?" asks the astonished preacher.

"Aha!" replies the drunk, "When I die! I thought you meant right now."

Just a special treat for you…

Paddy gets a job at an Antarctic weather station. He lives alone in a little hut and has to go out once a day to read the temperature. The rest of the days he spends reading through hundreds of old copies of the *Reader's Digest* magazine which have been left there.

After a while, Paddy writes a story and sends it to the magazine for them to publish. He receives a reply: "Dear Mr. Murphy, thank you for your article entitled, 'I Screwed a Polar Bear.' We are a family magazine and your article is not exactly our type of story, but please try again."

Paddy reads a few more *Reader's Digests* and writes another article. He sends it to the magazine and gets this reply: "Dear Mr. Murphy, we like your article, 'I Screwed a Polar Bear for Ronald Reagan's Government,' but we must remind you that we are a family magazine and we cannot publish it. However we like your style, so please try again."

After another hundred *Reader's Digests*, Paddy sends off another story. This time he gets a large check and the letter reads: "Dear Mr. Murphy, congratulations on your story entitled, 'I Screwed a Polar Bear for Ronald Reagan's Government and Found God.' We shall publish it in next month's issue."

27

A World Academy of Creative Science, Art, and Consciousness

Osho,
The other day I heard you mention our academy for meditation and our academy for bringing the body into one organic whole. Could you say more about this and how you see these two academies complementing each other?

It is one of the most complicated questions. It does not appear to be so because you are not aware that for centuries man has been told all kinds of life-negative things. Even to torture your body has been a spiritual discipline. My idea of having an academy is for science to become for the first time intentional and not accidental.

Up to now, science has been accidental. People have stumbled upon some discoveries, inventions. Even discoveries were made which they were not looking for, but just groping in the dark with no sense of direction. And obviously the politicians of the world – who like more and more destructive power in their hands – immediately got the idea to enslave scientists.

Now every scientist is a slave to some nation, to some government and he functions only for purposes which are antilife, destructive. The more destructive things he can find, the more he is praised, the more he is awarded by the governments. My idea of an academy is of creative science which will consciously avoid anything that destroys life and will seek and search only for that which enhances life.

This academy cannot be only of science because science is only a part of human reality. The academy has to be comprehensive, it has to be for creativity, for art, for consciousness; hence it will have three divisions, major divisions; not separated, but just for arbitrary purposes to be denominated as separate.

The most fundamental thing will be creating methods, techniques, ways of raising human consciousness, and certainly this consciousness cannot be against the body; this consciousness is residing in the body. They cannot be seen as inimical to each other; in every way, they are supportive. I say something to you and my hand makes a gesture without my telling the hand. There is a deep synchronicity between me and my hand.

You walk, eat, drink, and all these things indicate that you are both the body and consciousness as an organic whole. You cannot torture the body and raise your consciousness. The body has to be loved; you have to be a great friend to it. It is your home, you have to clean it of all junk and you have to remember that it is in your service continuously, day in, day out. Even when you are asleep, your body is continuously working for you, digesting, changing your food into blood, taking out the dead cells from the body and bringing new oxygen, fresh oxygen into the body – and you are fast asleep!

It is doing everything for your survival, for your life, although you are so ungrateful that you have never even thanked your body. On the contrary, your religions have been teaching you to torture it: the body is your enemy and you have to get free from the body, its attachments. I also know that you are more than the body and there is no need to have any attachment. But love is not an attachment, compassion is not an attachment. Love and compassion are absolutely needed for your body and its nourishment. And the better body you have, the more is the possibility for growing consciousness. It is an organic unity.

A totally new kind of education is needed in the world, where fundamentally everyone is introduced to the silences of the heart – in other words into meditation – where everyone has to be prepared to be compassionate to one's own body. Because unless you are compassionate to your own body, you cannot be compassionate to any other body. It is a living organism and it has done no harm to you. It has been continuously in service since you were conceived and will be till your death. It will do everything that you would like to do, even the impossible, and it will not be disobedient to you.

It is inconceivable to create such a mechanism which is so obedient and so wise. If you become aware of all the functions of your body, you will be surprised. You have never thought what your body has been doing. It is so miraculous, so mysterious. But you have never looked into it. You have never bothered to be acquainted with your own body and you pretend to love other people. You cannot because those other people also appear to you as bodies.

The body is the greatest mystery in the whole of existence. This mystery needs to be loved – its mysteries, its functioning, to be intimately inquired into. Unfortunately, the religions have been absolutely against the body. But it gives a clue, a definite indication that if a man learns the wisdom of the body and the mystery of the body, he will never bother about the priest or about God. He will have found the most mysterious within himself, and within the mystery of the body is the very shrine of your consciousness.

Once you have become aware of your consciousness, of your being, there is no God above you. Only such a person can be respectful of other human beings, other living beings. Because they all are as mysterious as he himself is, with different expressions, varieties which make life richer. And once a man has found consciousness in himself, he has found the key to the ultimate. Any education that does not teach you to love your body, to be compassionate to your body, how to enter its mysteries, will not be able to teach you how to enter your own consciousness.

The body is the door, the body is the stepping stone. And any education that does not touch the subject of your body and consciousness is not only absolutely incomplete, it is utterly harmful because it will go on being destructive. It is only the flowering of consciousness within you that prevents you from destruction. And that gives you a tremendous urge to create – to create more beauty in the world, to create more comfort in the world. That's why I include art as the second part of the academy. Art is a conscious effort to create beauty, to discover beauty, to make your life more joyful, to teach you to dance, to celebrate.

The third part is a creative science. Art can create beauty, science can discover objective truth, and consciousness can discover subjective reality. These three together can make any system of education complete. All else is secondary – may be useful for mundane purposes, but it is not useful for spiritual growth, it is not useful to bring you to the sources of joy, love, peace, silence. And a man who has not experienced the inner ecstasy has lived in vain unnecessarily. He vegetated, he dragged himself from the womb to the grave, but he could not dance, could not sing, could not contribute anything to the world.

According to me a religious person is one who contributes some beauty, some joy, some happiness, some celebration to the world which was not there – something new, something fresh, some more flowers. But religion has never been defined the way I am defining it.

All the ways religion has been defined have been proved absolutely ugly and wrong because they have not helped humanity to rise to the heights of joy, beauty, love. They have drowned the whole humanity in misery and suffering, they have not taught you freedom. On the contrary, they have enforced on you all kinds of slavery in the name of obedience. Obedience to whom? Obedience to the priests, obedience to those who have money, obedience to those who have power – in short, obedience to all the vested interests. A small minority has been enslaving the whole humanity for centuries. Only a right education can transform this ugly and sick situation. My idea of a

World Academy of Creative Science, Art, and Consciousness is really in other words my vision of a real religion.

Man needs a better body, a healthier body. Man needs a more conscious, alert being. Man needs all kinds of comforts and luxuries that existence is ready to deliver. Existence is ready to give you paradise herenow, but you go on postponing it – it is always after death.

In Sri Lanka a great mystic was dying…

He was worshipped by thousands of people. They gathered around him. He opened his eyes: he would take just a few more breaths on the shore and he would be gone, and gone forever. Everyone was eager to listen to his last words. The old man said, "I have been teaching you for my whole life about blissfulness, ecstasy, meditativeness. Now I am going to the other shore. I will not be available anymore. You have listened to me, but you have never practiced what I have been telling you. You have always been postponing. But now there is no point in postponing, I am going. Is anyone ready to go with me?"

There was a great pin-drop silence. People looked at each other thinking that perhaps this man who had been a disciple for forty years – he may be ready? But he was looking at the others – no one was standing up. Just from the very back a man raised his hand. The great mystic thought, "At least, one person is courageous enough."

But that man said, "Please let me make it clear to you why I am not standing up. I have only raised my hand. I want to know how to reach the other shore because today of course I am not ready. There are many things which are incomplete: a guest has come, my young son is getting married, and this day I cannot go. And you say you cannot come back from the other shore.

"Someday, one day certainly, I will come and meet you. If you can just explain to us once more – although you have been explaining to us for your whole life – how to reach the other shore? But please keep in mind that I am not ready to go right now. I just want to refresh my memory so that when the right time comes…"

That right time never comes. This is not a story only about that poor man, it is the story of millions of people, of almost all. They are all waiting for the right moment, the right constellation of stars. They are consulting astrologers, going to the palmist, inquiring in different ways what is going to happen tomorrow. Tomorrow does not happen; it never has happened. It is simply a stupid strategy of postponement. What happens is always today. A right kind of education will teach people to live herenow, to create a paradise of this earth; not to wait for death to come, not to be miserable till death stops your misery. Let death find you dancing, joyous, loving. It is a strange experience that if a man can live his life as if he is already in paradise, death cannot take away anything from that man's experience.

My approach is to teach you that this is paradise, there is no paradise anywhere else and no preparation is needed to be happy. No discipline is needed to be loving; just a little alertness, just a little wakefulness, just a little understanding. And if education cannot give you this little understanding, it is not education.

My conception of a world academy means that the whole world should have the same education of meditation, of art, of creative science. If we can create the same educational system around the world, then the divisions of religion and the discrimination between white and black and nations, the ugly politics that exists because of them, and the stupid behavior of men preparing continuously for war… Whenever I see a soldier I cannot believe that this man has a mind at all. Even animals don't become soldiers. But man seems to have only one interest: how to kill, how to kill more efficiently, how to go on refining instruments for killing.

A right education will teach you how to find your own song again, how to learn the dance and not be shy; how to celebrate the small things of life and make this whole planet alive. It is the only one, as far as we know, where people can love, where people can meditate, where people can become buddhas, where people like Socrates and Lao Tzu can exist.

We are most fortunate to be on this small planet. It is one of the smallest planets in the universe, but even the greatest stars, millions of times bigger than this earth, cannot claim a single Albert Einstein or a Jesus or a Yehudi Menuhin. It is strange that in this vast universe only on this small planet has existence been successful to create a little consciousness, a little life. Now it is in our hands to grow from this small beginning into the infinite heights which are our potential and which are our birthright.

Up to now, education has not been in the right direction. It has been torturing people unnecessarily with history, with geography. If someone is interested, these subjects should be available. If someone is interested to know about Istanbul, then let him know. And if someone is interested to know about Genghis Khan, Tamerlane, let him know. But there is no need to compulsorily teach people all the nonsense and garbage that has happened in the past. That is so stupid and so unbelievable.

To teach people that there have been people like Genghis Khan, Nadirshah, Tamerlane, Alexander the Great is to teach people about the wrong side of their being. I have been fighting in the universities, "Why don't you teach about Socrates? Why don't you teach about Chuang Tzu? Why don't you teach about Bodhidharma?" These are the right side of consciousness. And teaching about the wrong kind of people gives you an idea that it is perfectly good if you are wrong. If you are going slowly to be a Genghis Khan it is perfectly right. You are not doing something new, man has always been doing this.

We have to sort out history, cut out all those wrong people and protect our children from being conditioned that man has been involved in nothing but war, fighting, competition, greed. We should teach our children not what has been but what can be – not the past, but the future. Why waste so much time on teaching subjects which are of no significance in actual existential life? And not give them a single direction about the art of love, the art of life, the meaning of existence, preparation for death with joy, silence and meditativeness. All that is essential is missing; that which is nonessential and absolutely stupid is being forced.

They say history repeats. History does not repeat. It is our stupidity that we go on and on teaching the same thing to each generation. The poor children are conditioned to imitate the same great heroes who were really criminals, not heroes. Just a single man, Genghis Khan, killed forty million people. It is better to drop from education all information about these people. Educate them about the dance of a Shiva, the flute of Krishna. Teach them all that has been beautiful and good so that they become accustomed to all that is good is natural, and the bad is accidental; that the bad does not happen, has never happened, and the good is absolutely normal. To be a buddha is not something abnormal. It should be taught to every child that to be a buddha is a normal phenomenon. Anyone who is wise enough is going to become a buddha.

You are going to become a buddha. The greatest revolution has to happen in education and its systems; otherwise, man will go on repeating history.

Now time for silence and time for laughter…

Hymie Goldberg comes home from work one evening and Becky says, "Did you go to the store and pick up the snapshots, like I asked you? You probably did not! You never listen to me! You never remember anything! Oh! You *did* get them. Well, thank goodness for miracles. Let me see them! This shot is terrible and this one is even worse. My God! This one is horrible and this one is a disaster. In fact, this is the worst lot of photographs I have ever seen in my life.

"You can't do anything right! You can't drive a car properly! You can't even change a fuse. You can't sing in tune, and as a photographer, you are the worst!

"Just take a look at these pictures: in every one you took of me, I have my mouth open!"

A reformed prostitute is giving testimony on a street corner with the Salvation Army. She punctuates her talk by beating on a big drum.

"I used to be a sinner!" she shouts.

Boom! goes the drum.

"I used to be a bad woman!" she cries.

Boom!

"I used to drink!"

Boom!

"Gamble!"

Boom!

"Chase men!"

Boom! Boom!

"I used to go wild on Saturday nights and raise hell!"

Boom! Boom! Boom!

"And now what do I do on Saturday nights?" she cries. "I stand on the street corner beating this fucking drum!"

Mother Superior is returning from the bank one evening having deposited all the charity collections of the week when she is held up at gunpoint.

"You are wasting your time, young man," she tells the robber. "I have no money. I have just deposited it all in the bank."

"We will see about that," says the robber, and he begins fumbling under her black gown to search for the money.

"Oh! What are you doing?" cries the Mother Superior. "Oh! Oh!" she gasps as he looks disappointed. "Don't stop now. I'll write you a check!"

The plumber comes to fix some things in the house, and little Ernie follows him everywhere.

When the plumber pulls out a screwdriver, little Ernie says, "My Dad has two of those."

The plumber smiles and pulls out a wrench.

"My Dad has two of those," says Ernie.

The plumber smiles again and carries on working.

When he goes to the bathroom for a pee, little Ernie goes along. Taking out his prick, the plumber asks, "Has your dad got two of these too?"

"Yes, he has!" replies little Ernie. "He has got one small one like you to pee with, and a big one which he chases Mum around the kitchen table with!"

A Chinaman walks into a bar in a black neighborhood in San Francisco and says to the black bartender, "How about a jigger, nigger?"

The bartender gets mad and starts to lecture the Chinaman about racism and how he, being a Chinaman in America, should know better.

Finally, the bartender suggests that they change places to see how the Chinaman feels.

So they change places and the black bartender leaves the bar and comes back after a couple of minutes.

He walks up to the bar exactly as the Chinaman did.

"How about a drink, Chink?" says the black barman.

"So solly!" replies the Chinaman. "We don't serve niggers."

About Osho

Osho defies categorization. Mystic and scientist, a rebellious spirit whose sole interest is to alert humanity to the urgent need to discover a new way of living. To continue as before is to invite threats to our very survival on this unique and beautiful planet.

His thousands of talks cover everything from the individual quest for meaning to the most urgent social, political and environmental issues facing society today. Osho's books are not written but transcribed from audio and video recordings of his extemporaneous talks to international audiences. And he tells them, "Remember: whatever I am saying is not just for you...I am talking also for the future generations."

Osho has been described by *The Sunday Times* in London as one of the "1000 Makers of the 20th Century" and by American author Tom Robbins as "the most dangerous man since Jesus Christ." *Sunday Mid-Day* (Mumbai) has selected Osho as one of ten people – along with Gandhi, Nehru and Buddha – who have changed the destiny of India.

About his own work, Osho has said that he is helping to create the conditions for the birth of a new kind of human being. He often characterizes this new human being as "Zorba the Buddha" – capable both of enjoying the earthy pleasures of a Zorba the Greek and the silent serenity of a Gautama the Buddha.

Running like a thread through all aspects of Osho's talks and meditations is a vision that encompasses both the timeless wisdom of all ages past and the highest potential of today's (and tomorrow's) science and technology.

Osho is known for his revolutionary contribution to the science of inner transformation, with an approach to meditation that acknowledges the accelerated pace of contemporary life. His unique OSHO Active Meditations® are designed to first release the accumulated stresses of body and mind, so that it then becomes easier to experience a stillness and thought-free relaxation which can be taken into daily life.

Two autobiographical works by the author are available:

Autobiography of a Spiritually Incorrect Mystic, St. Martin's Press, New York (book and eBook)

Glimpses of a Golden Childhood, OSHO Media International, Pune, India (book and eBook)

OSHO International Meditation Resort

Each year the Meditation Resort welcomes thousands of people from more than 100 countries. The unique campus provides an opportunity for a direct personal experience of a new way of living – with more awareness, relaxation, celebration and creativity. A great variety of around-the-clock and around-the-year program options are available. Doing nothing and just relaxing is one of them!

All of the programs are based on Osho's vision of "Zorba the Buddha" – a qualitatively new kind of human being who is able *both* to participate creatively in everyday life *and* to relax into silence and meditation.

Location

Located 100 miles southeast of Mumbai in the thriving modern city of Pune, India, the OSHO International Meditation Resort is a holiday destination with a difference. The Meditation Resort is spread over 28 acres of spectacular gardens in a beautiful tree-lined residential area.

OSHO Meditations

A full daily schedule of meditations for every type of person includes both traditional and revolutionary methods, and particularly the OSHO Active Meditations®. The daily meditation program takes place in what must be the world's largest meditation hall, the OSHO Auditorium.

OSHO Multiversity

Individual sessions, courses and workshops cover everything from creative arts to holistic health, personal transformation, relationship and life transitions, transforming meditation into a lifestyle for life and work, esoteric sciences, and the Zen approach to sports and recreation. The secret of the OSHO Multiversity's success lies in the fact that all its programs are combined with meditation, supporting the understanding that as human beings we are far more than the sum of our parts.

Cuisine

A variety of different eating areas serve delicious Western, Asian and Indian vegetarian food – most of it organically grown especially for the Meditation Resort. Breads and cakes are baked in the resort's bakery.

Night life

There are many evening events to choose from – dancing being at the top of the list! Other activities include full-moon meditations beneath the stars, variety shows, music performances and "meditations for daily life."

Facilities

At the Meditation Resort you can buy all of your basic necessities and toiletries in the Galleria. In addition, the Multimedia Gallery sells a large range of OSHO media products. For those who enjoy shopping, Pune provides all the options, ranging from traditional and ethnic Indian products to all of the global brand-name stores.

Accommodation

You can choose to stay in the elegant rooms of the OSHO Guesthouse, or for longer stays on campus you can select one of the OSHO Living-In programs. Additionally there is a variety of nearby hotels and serviced apartments.

www.osho.com/meditationresort
www.osho.com/guesthouse
www.osho.com/livingin
Facebook: osho.international.meditation.resort

OSHO Books (English)

(OSHO books are available in Printed book and eBook formats, and most of them in audio format too. If a book is not available in one format, you can look up and buy it in another format.)

Early Talks

The Art of Living
Astrology
Breaking All Boundaries
Compassion and Revolution
Dimensions beyond the Known
The Eternal Quest
From Sex to Superconsciousness
The Great Challenge
Hidden Mysteries
I Am the Gate
The Independent Mind
Into the Void
Keys to a New Life
New Dimensions of Yoga
The Psychology of the Esoteric
Religion's Expiration Date
The Search for Peace
Woman and Rebellion
Work Is Love Made Visible

Meditation

And Now and Here
Body/Mind Balancing (Book & Audio)
Falling In Love with Darkness
In Search of the Miraculous
The Inner Journey
Just a Small Step
Meditation: The Art of Ecstasy
Meditation: The First and Last Freedom
The Path of Meditation
The Perfect Way
Silence: The Message of Your Being
Three Steps to Awakening

Buddha and Buddhist Masters

The Book of Wisdom
The Dhammapada: The Way of the Buddha (Vols 1-12)

The Diamond Sutra
The Discipline of Transcendence (Vols 1-4)
The Heart Sutra
The Great Secret
The Guest
The Path of Love
The Revolution

Indian Mystics

As if a Tree Starts Running (Yari))
The Beloved, Vols 1 & 2 (Baul Mystics)
Bliss:Living beyond Happiness and Misery (Shiva)
Die O Yogi Die (Gorakh)
Enlightenment: The Only Revolution (Ashtavakra)
Geeta Darshan Vol. 1 (Adhyaya 1-2)
Geeta Darshan, Vol.2 (Adhyaya 3)
Krishna: The Man and His Philosophy
The Last Morning Star (Daya)
Showering without Clouds (Sahajo)
The Song of Ecstasy (Adi Shankara)
The True Name (Vols 1&2) (Nanak)

Kabir

The Divine Melody
Ecstasy: The Forgotten Language
The Fabric of Life
The Fish in the Sea Is Not Thirsty

Western Mystics

The Art of Dying *(Hasidism)*
Come Follow to You, Vols 1-4 *(Jesus)*
Guida Spirituale (*Desiderata*)
The Hidden Harmony *(Heraclitus)*
I Say Unto You, Vols 1 & 2 *(Jesus)*
The Mustard Seed *(Jesus)*
The New Alchemy: To Turn You On (Mabel Collins)
Philosophia Perennis, Vols 1 & 2 (*Pythagoras*)
Reflections on Kahlil Gibran's *The Prophet*
Theologia Mystica *(Dionysius)*
The True Sage *(Hasidism)*
The Voice of Silence (Mabel Collins)
Zarathustra: A God That Can Dance (Nietzsche's *Thus Spake Zarathustra*)
Zarathustra: The Laughing Prophet (Nietzsche's *Thus Spake Zarathustra*)

Sufism

Just Like That

The Perfect Master, Vols 1 & 2
The Secret
Sufis: The People of the Path, Vols 1 & 2
Unio Mystica, Vols 1 & 2
Until You Die
The Wisdom of the Sands, Vols 1 & 2

Tantra

The Book of Secrets (Vigyan Bhairav Tantra)
The Tantra Experience (Saraha)
Tantra: The Supreme Understanding (Tilopa)
Tantric Transformation (Saraha)

The Upanishads

Behind a Thousand Names (Nirvana Upanishad)
Finger Pointing to the Moon (Adhyatma Upanishad)
Flight of the Alone to the Alone (Kaivalya Upanishad)
The Heartbeat of the Absolute (Ishavasya Upanishad)
I Am That (Isa Upanishad)
The Message beyond Words (Kathopanishad)
Philosophia Ultima (Mandukya Upanishad)
The Supreme Doctrine (Kenopanishad)
That Art Thou (Sarvasar Upanishad, Kaivalya Upanishad, Adhyatma Upanishad)
The Ultimate Alchemy, Vols 1 & 2 (Atma Pooja Upanishad)
Vedanta: Seven Steps to Samadhi (Akshaya Upanishad)
The Way beyond Any Way (Sarvasar Upanishad)

Tao

The Empty Boat (Chuang Tzu)
The Secret of Secrets (The Secret of Golden Flower)
Tao: The Golden Gate, Vols 1 & 2 (Ko Hsuan)
Tao: The Pathless Path, Vols 1 & 2 (Lieh Tzu)
Tao: The Three Treasures, Vols 1-4 (Lao Tzu)
When the Shoe Fits (Chuang Tzu)

Yoga (Patanjali)

Yoga: The Science of the Soul, Vols 1-10
- The Path of Yoga (Vol.1)
- The Heart of Yoga (Vol.2)
- Yoga: The Mystery beyond Mind (Vol.3)
- The Alchemy of Yoga (Vol.4)

- Yoga: A New Direction (Vol.5)
- Essence of Yoga (Vol.6)
- Yoga: The Science of Living (Vol.7)
- Secrets of Yoga (Vol.8)
- Yoga: The Path to Liberation (Vol.9)
- Yoga: The Supreme Science (Vol.10)

Zen and Zen Masters

Ah, This!
Ancient Music in the Pines
And the Flowers Showered…
And the Grass Grows By Itself…
A Bird on the Wing
Bodhidharma: The Greatest Zen Master
The Buddha: The Emptiness of the Heart
Christianity, the Deadliest Poison and Zen, the Antidote to All Poisons
Communism and Zen Fire, Zen Wind
Dang Dang Doko Dang
The First Principle
God Is Dead: Now Zen Is the Only Living Truth
The Great Zen Master Ta Hui
Hsin Hsin Ming: The Book of Nothing
I Celebrate Myself: God Is No Where, Life Is Now Here
Kyozan: A True Man of Zen
The Language of Existence
Live Zen
The Miracle
Nirvana: The Last Nightmare
No Mind: The Flowers of Eternity
No Water, No Moon
One Seed Makes the Whole Earth Green
The Original Man
Returning to the Source
The Search: Talks on the 10 Bulls of Zen
A Sudden Clash of Thunder
The Sun Rises in the Evening
Take it Easy
This. This. A Thousand Times This
This Very Body the Buddha
Turning In
The White Lotus
Yakusan: Straight to the Point of Enlightenment
The Zen Manifesto: Freedom from Oneself
Zen: The Diamond Thunderbolt
Zen: The Mystery and the Poetry of the Beyond
Zen: The Path of Paradox, Vols 1-3

Zen: The Quantum Leap from Mind to No-Mind
Zen: The Solitary Bird, Cuckoo of the Forest
Zen: The Special Transmission

Osho: On the Ancient Masters of Zen

Dogen: The Zen Master
Hyakujo: The Everest of Zen – With Basho's haikus
Isan: No Footprints in the Blue Sky
Joshu: The Lion's Roar
Ma Tzu: The Empty Mirror
Nansen: The Point of Departure
Rinzai: Master of the Irrational

Responses to Questions

Be Still and Know
Beyond Enlightenment (Talks in Bombay)
Beyond Psychology (Talks in Uruguay)
Come, Come, Yet Again Come
The Diamond Sword
From Bondage to Freedom
From Darkness to Light
From Death to Deathlessness
From Ignorance to Innocence
From Misery to Enlightenment
From Personality to Individuality
From the False to the Truth
From Unconsciousness to Consciousness
The Goose Is Out
The Great Pilgrimage: From Here to Here
The Invitation
Light on the Path (Talks in the Himalayas)
My Way: The Way of the White Clouds
Nowhere to Go but In
The Osho Upanishad (Talks in Bombay)
The Path of the Mystic (Talks in Uruguay)
The Razor's Edge
Sermons in Stones (Talks in Bombay)
Socrates Poisoned Again After 25 Centuries (Talks in Greece)
The Sword and the Lotus (Talks in the Himalayas)
Transmission of the Lamp (Talks in Uruguay)
Walk without Feet, Fly without Wings and Think without Mind
The Wild Geese and the Water
Yaa-Hoo! The Mystic Rose
Walking in Zen, Sitting in Zen
Zen: Zest, Zip, Zap and Zing

Osho's Vision for the World
The Golden Future
The Hidden Splendor
The New Dawn
The Rebel
The Rebellious Spirit

The Mantra Series
Hari Om Tat Sat
Om Mani Padme Hum
Om Shantih Shantih Shantih
Sat Chit Anand
Satyam Shivam Sundaram

Personal Glimpses
Books I Have Loved
Glimpses of a Golden Childhood
Notes of a Madman

Interviews with the World Press
The Man of Truth: A Majority of One

Meetings with Individuals
Above All Don't Wobble
Hammer on the Rock

Quotation Books
Gold Nuggets
More Gold Nuggets
Words From A Man of No Words

Letters and Writings
A Cup of Tea
Earthen Lamps
Flowers of Love
Life Is a Soap Bubble
Love Letters to Life
Seeds of Wisdom

For any information about OSHO Books, please contact:

OSHO Media International
17 Koregaon Park, Pune – 411001, MS, India
Phone: +91-20-66019999 Fax: +91-20-66019990
E-mail: distribution@osho.net
Website: http://www.osho.com

For More Information

The official website of OSHO International is www.OSHO.com

www.OSHO.com/AllAboutOSHO is a comprehensive portal to all things OSHO.

www.OSHO.com/AllAboutOSHO
www.OshoTimes.com
shop.OSHO.com
iOSHO.OSHO.com
YouTube: OSHO/OSHOinternational
Twitter: OSHO
Instagram: OSHOinternational
Facebook: OSHO.international
Facebook: OSHO.international.meditation.resort

ALSO IN THE MANTRA SERIES